For Dad
who taught me how to love buildings

Much love

Liz xx

How To Read a
VILLAGE

How To Read a
VILLAGE

Richard Muir

EBURY
PRESS

1 3 5 7 9 10 8 6 4 2

Published in 2007 by Ebury Press, an imprint of Ebury Publishing

Ebury Publishing is a division of the Random House Group

The Random House Group Limited Reg. No. 954009

Addresses for companies within the Random House Group can be
found at www.randomhouse.co.uk

A CIP catalogue record for this book is available from the British Library

The Random House Group makes every effort to ensure that the papers
used in our books are made from trees that have been legally sourced
from well-managed and credibly certified forests. Our paper procurement
policy can be found on www.randomhouse.co.uk

Editor: Anna Carroll
Series editor: Richard Taylor
Design: David Fordham

Printed and bound in Singapore by Tien Wah Press

ISBN: 9780091920111

To buy books by your favourite authors and register for offers
visit www.rbooks.co.uk

CONTENTS

ABOVE: *Stokesay Castle in Shropshire*
PAGE 1: *A scene at Earl Stonham, Suffolk*
PAGE 2: *Cottages at Lower Slaughter in the Cotswolds*

INTRODUCTION

READING A VILLAGE

*L*ANDSCAPES are like pages printed in a special code. If you learn to read the codes then you can decipher the history of a wood, a field pattern, a network of lanes or … *a village*. In the 1920s and 1930s, when outdoor interests and curiosity about geology, topography and Nature were considered wholesome pursuits for the 'educated classes', a great deal was published concerning landscape and its meaning. Since then, such pursuits do not seem to have taken off in the way that might have been hoped. Interest in the outdoors has taken on a passive character: we sit in front of the television set while some presenter delivers the text that the programme's consultants have written. Sometimes, the presenter concerned upstages or completely obscures the subject matter. Also, 'the heritage' has been commandeered by various quangos and so our encounters with historic countryside tends to become a progress around information boards, turnstiles and visitor centres. What was once a free and joyful celebration of the homeland becomes structured and organized – a thing of programmes, websites and fee-paying.

An understanding of the origins and evolution of landscape components, like villages, can be amazingly liberating. You can discover interest and challenges everywhere and anywhere. The turnstiles can be left behind and you can relish an independence of organizations and authorities. Then you progress around the countryside, drawn hither and thither by questions, clues and possibilities on a trail of discovery that has no ending. Each and every village can become your familiar friend and your entertainment: a puzzle packed with clues that are spread across many acres.

LEFT: *A row of large timber-framed houses at Kersey in Suffolk, reflecting the late-medieval affluence of East Anglia's textiles industry.*

It is a place of fascinating buildings, nooks and crannies, but it is also a human story, written by dozens of generations of largely forgotten villagers. The challenges are inexhaustible and the entertainment and stimulation are free.

Stimulation of the mind and curiosity can lead in valuable directions. Many of today's villagers are strangers, outsiders who have come to the countryside in search of solace in a world that is ever more stressed and who are seeking stability in a society that is increasingly demanding and footloose. For a new villager, a project of village discovery can become a process of bonding with a hitherto unfamiliar place – a means of sinking strong roots down into the new setting of life. It can also be a means of lowering barriers with an indigenous community. A huge cultural barrier separates the old and the new communities in thousands of villages. Old villagers sometimes feel marginalized by incomers, who may have high levels of education, mobility, affluence and influence, but generally very low levels of comprehension where rural matters are concerned. A project of discovery that demonstrates the importance of village traditions can bridge the cultural divide.

Knowledge is power. An exploration of a village will reveal an intensely fascinating story and the discoverer is very likely to become a leading and effective campaigner for village interests and village preservation. The project that may have been born of idle curiosity could bring forth the evidence that would help the salvation of a village threatened, as so many are, by forces of perhaps ill-judged change. On just the first day of researching a village, it is possible to surpass the knowledge of the place that is vested in the relevant planning office, so that everything newly learned can be used to further village conservation projects.

Through most of my working life I have switched between roles, sometimes writing for amateur enthusiasts and sometimes for academics (the former audience is much more demanding, for nobody has to read a non-specialist book if it ceases to interest them). Much of my academic writing has been concerned with landscapes and one of the first important lessons that I have learned is that nobody, however academically aloof and 'detached', can really stand *outside* the scene. We are the observers of life's human and environmental dramas but we are also members of the cast and we are parts of the action. While I can offer a view on the evolution of a village layout, I know that as soon as I talk about the village as a living community my personal experiences of village life will colour my thoughts. Community and contentiousness live side by side. The last time that I 'got involved' (though only slightly), it was to side with the old'uns who recalled the blackness of former nights and the hooting and screeching of owls coming from several quarters – and who did not want to have the village church illuminated. Where community and landscape are concerned, different people see things in quite different ways. Living in the East Anglian countryside in the 1970s I remember the farmers who had drained ponds, felled ancient trees and grubbed up hedgerows and yet took genuine pride in having, they believed, 'tidied up' their farms, which subsequently resembled the Canadian prairies.

Each of us has some sort of personal engagement with the village. For the writers of TV news scripts, the village is always the 'little village', leaving us to wonder why momentous events never seem to occur in villages that are large or medium in size? For the developer, the village can be a

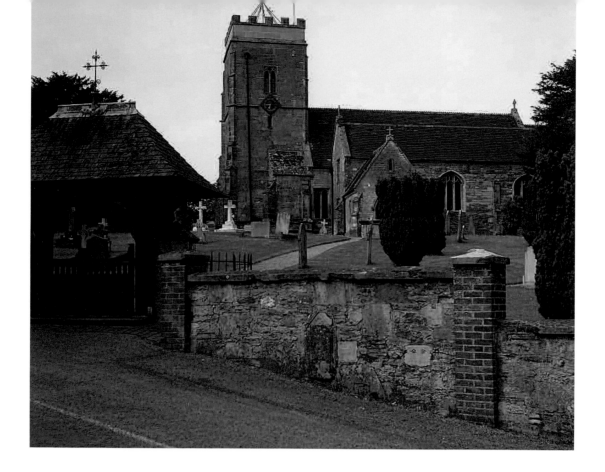

ABOVE: *Okeford Fitzpaine church, Dorset, stands in the site of the original Anglo-Saxon village. The village gained a short-lived green in Norman times.*

OVERLEAF: *The village as an icon: Kersey, Suffolk*

source of income, for the innkeeper, a source of regulars and for the planner, a source of trouble. For ordinary members of our nations, it is a symbol of the past and of the more wholesome and stalwart virtues that we imagine were current in the countrysides of old. For villagers, it is home – but a home that comes in many shapes and social textures. In our individual minds, the village takes many different forms and my own thoughts are strongly coloured by childhood memories of a wonderful if almost destitute community of Dales people, of a breed that is all but vanished. Whatever our feelings, we have to remember that the village was primarily a community. The hollows and stones at a deserted village site are scarcely worth a glance if one cannot see them as bridges to a community that perished centuries ago. We can revel in church architecture or some rustic examples of vernacular building, but to my mind the point is missed if we cannot see them as portholes on the worlds of the medieval housewright, mason or householder. In other words, villages are many things, but mainly, they are about people.

The message of this book is that the village can be a very fulfilling source of interest. It has many facets, encouraging us to acquire new forms of expertise as one or more facets are explored.

It is not only an interest — really, several interests — in its own right, but it also complements other very popular areas of study. The recent mushrooming of involvement in genealogy, facilitated by the mass of documentation now available online, will lead many tracers of ancestry to want to discover the sort of places that their village ancestors occupied. Similarly, a better understanding of village landscapes will help to improve the works of landscape and architectural artists. We can all choose our starting and finishing places. Personally, having been stunned by the extent of recent rural transformation, I try to see villages in an unemotional way, as intellectual puzzles or challenges spread out across the landscape. This conflicts in some ways with what I said earlier about the human aspect but it does fulfil a need for outdoor challenges. Meanwhile, for those seeking tasks as worthwhile as they are rewarding, the recording of the recollections of old villagers is strongly recommended. Looking back across a couple or more generations, the big events and issues are well recorded and the day-to-day recollections and trivia are what today's historians cherish.

In the course of my career I have met numerous local historians, professionals and amateurs. I was lucky to work on a couple of books with the late Dr Jack Ravensdale, who would dispense

BELOW: *Snow-girt cottages, hedgerow and windmill in Thaxted, Essex*

ABOVE: *The church and cottages that have encroached upon the green at Cavendish, Suffolk: such a scene, like that on the facing page, is a real enticement to take up an interest in village history.*

insights and wisdom in self-effacing whispers. However, I never met anyone, professional or amateur, who was more in touch with his chosen topic than a chap who had retired as a dentist. Professional disregard for amateurs masks the fact that history, geography and archaeology were all born of the efforts of diligent, often obsessive, amateurs. Too much is made of the 'pro/am' distinction. Not only do enthusiasts have a purity of purpose, they also have time on their sides – time to ponder, time to think again, time to go back and have another look.

A fascinating engagement with villages (or other aspects of the rural scene) is an activity that can be individually tailored to fit. It concerns a topic that will prove very hard to exhaust: in the late 1990s, I spent three years studying a township that amounted to just one-third of a parish and it contained one village and, as it emerged, the former village site and two deserted medieval villages. Equally, any trips away from the chosen village will offer opportunities to compare your village with those of other regions or of foreign countries. A village study is something that you can neglect, pick up again,

OVERLEAF: *Muker in Wharfedale, slumbering through winter as it awaits the summer influx of visitors, but no less enticing during the quiet season*

rewrite, cross out, return to afresh and plunge into at the first signs of boredom. It can find you talking to people that you might otherwise never have known. It may lead you, willingly, to acquire skills that you had never thought of possessing. Also, it has its indoor aspects, in the library or at the computer, as well as its out-of-doors fieldwork and recording, so there is never a 'wrong time'.

Let me finish with a quote from C.B. Fawcett, who wrote in 1919, as a member of a movement that was enthusiastically exploring ideas for devolved government:

> … the man or woman who has no love for and pride in his or her home region is not thereby qualified for wider views of life. Provincialism in itself is a good thing, and a necessary factor in the well being of humanity.

This is all true. Most ordinary people of former times were villagers and to encounter them as they have lived through the successive ages is a most civilizing and rewarding affair – far more so than learning about the nobles and generals whose statues glower over the city squares. Today, the village is at something of a crisis point in its existence – but has not it always been so?

BELOW: *Stonesfield in Oxfordshire wears its wares – it was one of the places where stones suitable for roofing could be found.*

ABOVE: *A fine flint-built church at Great Yeldham in Essex*

Take any case and there is no doubt that the village concerned will be better for being studied – and the student may benefit more than he or she imagines. An interest in villages is good for the environment, good for the village community and also good for the researcher and discoverer. On countless occasions I have left my study feeling deskbound, ratty and put upon. I have grumbled and groaned as I hauled on my field boots. But just a few steps down the track and my camera bag lightens, my pace quickens and I see puzzles and clues beckoning from several sides. In no time at all, life seems a whole lot more interesting. It has always been like this for as far back as I can remember. Is it the fresh air, the seasonal tints or the remaining wildlife? I expect these all play their parts, but I think that discovering worthwhile challenges to the mind plays the greatest part. In this way, the village will not disappoint.

1

THE REALLY ANCIENT VILLAGES

*F*OUR OUT OF EVERY FIVE people in the UK live in towns and a third of the British population can be found living in one of the seven great conurbations. For most people, the village has become a rather unfamiliar place – a place associated with romantic myths about country life. It was not always this way. We only have to travel back through time for about a century and a half to reach a stage when half of the British lived in rural settings, mostly in villages. If we could travel back a few more centuries, to the time of Chaucer in the fourteenth century, we would encounter medieval kingdoms in England and Scotland where townsfolk were tiny minorities within populations that were almost entirely rural.

In a large part of England and in the lower parts of Scotland and Wales, villages were very strongly established at the time when the Normans conquered England and then Wales and threatened a conquest of Ireland. However, should we travel back still further, to the Roman invasion of England in AD 43, we would find no towns in Britain, just the few strange, rambling, fortified capitals of the most progressive British tribes. We would see some villages, but the greater part of the tribal populations would be found living in *hamlets* and *farmsteads*.

All this is to say that the prominence of villages in the landscape has changed greatly over the years – as indeed it does across the world today. In the Canadian prairies we find widely scattered farmsteads or ranches and small urban service centres, but very few villages; on the plains of Hungary and parts of Eastern Europe there are some villages as big as towns; on Orkney there are

LEFT: *The outlines of an Iron Age roundhouse beneath a tree at Kestor, Dartmoor*

hundreds of farmsteads but very few village-like settlements, while in most parts of rural France, ancient villages are numerous.

Looking further into the evidence, we can only conclude that the evolution of the village is not always the logical development. They do not *have* to exist. We take them for granted because they are such obvious parts of rural life and national mythology as we know them. However, there are numerous societies that exist with few if any villages and so we must discover why many parts of the world do have them. Here are some possibilities.

DEFENCE

A small community should be able to put up a more convincing defence against hostile intruders than an isolated family living in a farmstead could (though in practice, flight was often a preferred option).

CO-OPERATION

Much of the work in the countryside is more easily done when households can help each other and when equipment and draught animals can be shared.

ORGANIZATION

When numerous households that have shares in the land live closely together they are better able to discuss programmes for the working of the land and accomplishment of tasks. Many tasks, like mowing and reaping on the lord's personal estate (*demesne*) were performed by the massed and regimented labour of the village.

POWER

A village that is organized under a head man or under a committee of chosen council members will have an effective system of authority. The ruling council can impose social norms or can act as a conduit for the demands and decrees of a feudal or tribal overlord.

SOCIAL FACTORS

When households are gathered together in a co-herent community they are more likely to attract or to create useful institutions, like a church, a market and guilds to promote welfare, while centres of population are attractive to artisans and craftsmen who seek customers. Also, the village provides a more stimulating context for conversation/gossip and friendship than does the solitary farm.

HEALTH

Medieval villages were filthy and disease-ridden places, but mortality was even greater in the towns of the day. Epidemics carried off so many townspeople that a town had continually to attract masses of rural settlers in order just to stay the same size.

With such powerful enticements to village life, why did not everyone live in a village? There are other arguments that favour farmstead, hamlet or town life.

CONVENIENCE

The more that people congregate together, the more distant they are likely to be from their lands and so precious time will be wasted in dragging ploughs along lanes and tracks and carrying milk pails around. In the medieval villages, households tenanted lands that were split up and scattered all around the township. The farmers in solitary farmsteads and small hamlets could step out of their doors and straight into their holdings.

INDEPENDENCE

The tenant in an out-lying farmstead was not constantly under the eye of officialdom; in medieval times people to be avoided might include the lord, his steward, the leading bondsmen and the reeve who supervised affairs from within the village. Where the terms and conditions of the tenancy were concerned,

ABOVE: *Yockenthwaite in the Yorkshire Dales is a typical hamlet of the uplands. Its name contains the name of a Celtic landowner combined with '-thwaite', meaning a clearing or enclosed meadow, which suggests this is an ancient settlement.*

the holder of a solitary farmstead might be in a better position to negotiate directly with the lord or his representative.

FREEDOM

During the Middle Ages, most villagers lived in bondage and their best hope of freedom was to escape to a properly constituted town and to live there undetected by their overlord for a year. Towns were anomalous islands of freedom in the ocean of rural bondage.

FAMILY

The isolated farmstead matched the family in size while the hamlet cluster of farmsteads matched the extended family of aunts, great-uncles, nephews and cousins. The village, being larger, was not a family-sized settlement, and this was significant during the many family-centred centuries.

EXTRAS

Away from watchful eyes, the tenant from a farmstead and hamlet might find it easier to poach large and small game, take timber, release livestock into forbidden grazings and generally to exploit the resources of the setting.

HEALTH

Epidemics were less likely to reach the little-visited corners of the landscape, even though the most virulent ones, like the Black Death, most certainly did. Still, in the farmsteads and hamlets there were fewer people to contaminate water supplies with their dung heaps and burials, fewer sneezing or coughing and fewer arriving to introduce a fatal infection.

A closer look at the pros and cons of village life can take us a little nearer to understanding the whys and wherefores of the village.

ABOVE: *Massive construction works of the prehistoric era, like Stonehenge and many others, must have needed special villages for the labour forces, rather like the navvy camps of the canal, railway and reservoir building eras.*

DEFENCE

Strength in numbers only works if numbers, martial skills and armaments are superior. Medieval villagers, who were normally barred from any martial training, certainly knew better than to stay and face any armies or war-bands that happened by. They saved their own skins and as many of their beasts as they could gather and retreated to the woods and marshes in times of trouble. Some prehistoric villages, hamlets and farmsteads were *stockaded* and ringed by defensive banks and ditches, the banks being crowned by a palisade or thorn hedge. The defences, though impressive in many cases, would have been more proof against rustlers than against armies and it is not clear how far these defences were intended to be functional and how far they served as status symbols. Defences were not confined to the larger settlements and between the late prehistoric period and the Middle Ages, *raths* – substantial farmsteads surrounded by circular ramparts – were built in their thousands in Ireland. On any flight across Ireland one will see many of these rampart rings.

The real prehistoric strongholds were the political centres now known as *hill forts*. Hundreds were built in Britain and some of them contained villages and granaries. At Hod Hill in Dorset, Beacon Hill in Hampshire and numerous other places one can recognize the circular depressions that mark the spots where dwellings stood. A few forts, like Crickley Hill in Gloucestershire, seem to have had disciplined, barrack-like arrangements of buildings. Some hill forts on the continent of Europe did contain barracks, while in Scandinavia in historical times, fortresses ringed with earthworks apparently protected invasion bases where Viking raiders were housed in barracks.

A variety of places were defended, but village defences were only effective against robbers and small bands of rustlers. Many medieval villages on the continent occupied defensive sites on hilltops and cliff tops. In medieval England, however, this did not occur. Defence was not a prime motivation for village life.

INDEPENDENCE

Most of us relish freedom, but in ancient and medieval times everybody had an overlord and these overlords, whether an Iron Age petty chief or a medieval knight, abbess or bishop, could control tributes, rents and the lifestyles of communities. If what was required by the masters of the countryside was simply the working of a holding in a way that sustained the tenants and produced a surplus that could be given up as tribute or rent after the harvest, then it might not matter greatly whether the tenant farmers lived in farmsteads, hamlets or villages. Arrangements of this sort were probably widespread in ancient and Roman Britain.

During the Dark Ages, highly complex methods of working an estate evolved. They involved the division and dispersion of holdings, so that the average family might tenant a 'virgate' of around 30 acres (c. 12.1 ha.) of ploughland, scattered around the township in strips of around an acre (0.4 ha.) in area, as well as shared in the meadow and access to the commons. They also involved complicated arrangements for recruiting labour gangs to toil on the lord's demesne and very detailed arrangements for the administration and synchronization of work and the borrowing of plough beasts. On the heaviest clay lands, six or eight oxen were needed to haul a plough and village households owning just one or two oxen had to combine their resources in order to create a plough team. With all this in mind, it would have been impossible to operate this new system of *open field farming* unless people were gathered together in village dormitories where they could interact, cooperate and take direction.

Villages had always been present, but from about AD 800 onwards they became very numerous and developed because they were essential to the operation of a particular new way of working estate farmland. This system largely persisted in most places through the Middle Ages, while village labour forces were needed to operate the large farms of a parish through the centuries of hand tools and crowded fields until the mechanization of farming in the nineteenth century. It was the demands of estate farming that saw villages swell and multiply. Other factors, like health, family or tastes in company were incidental, for until fairly modern times, country folk had little control over their destinies.

VILLAGES OF ANTIQUITY

*I*F WE GO beyond the time of recorded history and then beyond the ages of metalworking and the first age of farming to the closing centuries of the last Ice Age, around 13,000 years ago, we would find no villages that we could recognize as such. People hunting in an arctic-like environment could not cultivate crops or gather fruit and fungi. They depended entirely on hunting game. This game was constantly on the move, heading for northern and upland pastures in the summer and retreating in the winter. The hunters following the game will have made small, temporary settlements – tents supported by mammoth bones (as discovered in the Russian steppes) and igloos or cave-mouth camps in some other places. At certain times of the year – perhaps in midwinter when communities may have been sheltering on sea strands and lake shores – village-sized tent or igloo settlements may have formed as dispersed communities came together to exchange news, trade goods and prospect for partners.

Eventually, the climate warmed and trees returned but the patterns of migration around a hunting territory persisted until a knowledge of farming was introduced to Britain from continental Europe around 6000 years ago. Cultivation then bound people to places. At first, huntsmen may have sown a few cereal seeds and gone off fishing or fowling for a while. Before long, they realized that life-sustaining calories were more easily produced by cultivating primitive strains of wheat and barley than by expending masses of energy, often to little effect, on the chase. From then on, crops and livestock exerted a tyranny over human life. One had to be there to sow and tend them, and then to defend the lush young stems against deer, wild cattle and horses, or the sheep and cows that shared the farm. Next, at just the right time, the crops had to be harvested and then special arrangements had to be made to preserve the food and seed corn until the following round of sowing and harvest. Similarly, domesticated cows had to be milked every day and flocks had to be guarded against wolves. Farming made survival more likely and allowed more offspring to be supported, yet it stole the freedom to roam, follow whims and pursue adventures that humans had enjoyed for around three million years.

During the first age of farming, that lasted until around 2200 BC, in the Ages of Copper, Bronze and of Iron that followed, and then into Roman times, villages claimed a niche in the landscape, but they were always greatly outnumbered by hamlets and farmsteads. Just *why* people in one place should be inhabiting a settlement with, say, half a dozen to 30 or so clustered dwellings that we might consider to be a village, while their neighbours all around were found in smaller settlements seems quite mysterious.

There are some aspects of ancient life that remain unknown, but readers interested in reconstructing pictures of prehistoric or Roman landscapes could keep the following points in mind.

Firstly, we used to be taught that prehistoric people in Britain were very few in number. We were also told that they settled only on the higher, chalky ground, where the light soils supported a less impenetrable tangle of woodland. Now we know this is wrong. Ancient pottery and metalwork have been found on all kinds of ground, and even the heaviest woodland on the sticky clay of the vales was cleared and settled.

Secondly, our reading of the past was dominated by *invasionism*, which claimed that native populations were driven away and replaced each time invaders like the 'Beaker folk' or the 'Celts' or the Anglo-Saxons arrived. The evidence never really supported this and now the DNA-based evidence suggests that Britain has a very anciently established population, with strong Celtic contributions and Saxon and Danish influences on eastern England and eastern Scotland. Celtic-

ABOVE: *A ruined Bronze Age house at Grimspound, on Dartmoor, with the gateway of the compound showing through the mist*

speakers from Central Europe were supposed to have introduced the Iron Age, around 650 BC, but now it appears that any such Celts arrived early in the Bronze Age and from Iberia. Soon, more detailed DNA pictures can be expected, but on the whole, the evidence suggests that invasions brought new ideas, styles and elites rather than overwhelming masses of immigrants.

Thirdly, by the middle of the Bronze Age, say around 1000 BC, the British lowland countryside was densely populated and semi-natural woodland was only found in confined, less-habitable areas. Standing on most hilltops or scarps one would have seen a landscape divided like a great spider's web with hedgerows and walls and with dwellings at least as numerous as the farmsteads that are seen today.

Fourth, we were taught that the population rose gradually but steadily. Now we see that it changed in cycles of optimistic expansion and tragic decline. It has been suggested that an eruption, around 1600 BC, of the volcano Santorini in the Aegean brought an end to the great Wessex culture that gave us Stonehenge. More certain is the fact that a sequence of eruptions of Mount Hekla, on Iceland, after 1200 BC caused a wholesale retreat of people from the uplands of Britain. Unimaginable quantities of fine ash particles were blasted into the upper atmosphere and darkened the skies, causing a cooler, wetter climate. Most affected were the areas of upland farming and complete Bronze Age landscapes of dwellings, trackways and field walls were abandoned, never really to be colonized again.

Finally, we can never understand the ten centuries of prehistoric life in Britain if we entertain the old images of loutish cavemen and interminable woods. The archaeological evidence suggests that by the closing centuries of the Bronze Age, the British countrysides were as heavily populated as they would be when William the Conqueror commissioned his famous Domesday survey in 1086, almost 2000 years later. During this period, however, there had been phases of dramatic growth and over-population, as during the Roman occupation, and phases of devastating disasters with accelerating death rates, as in the aftermath of the Roman retreat from Britain after AD 410.

ANCIENT
PEOPLE AT
HOME

THE NATURE of the prehistoric house remained surprisingly similar, all the way from the ones being built in the short Age of Copper that preceded the Bronze Age and ran about 2500–2200 BC, through to the dwellings being built by the native British during the Roman occupation. These dwellings were very different from the ones that developed and were adopted by country people during and after the Roman era, though they were not necessarily more primitive. Different living spaces reflect different domestic lives, while in terms of their construction, the excavated dwellings of the Ages of Bronze and Iron were more solidly constructed and durable than many of the houses that existed in the villages of the Middle Ages. Ancient houses tended to have the following features.

Firstly, dwellings were almost invariably circular. Traces of square Iron Age buildings supported on corner posts and commonly called 'four-posters' have often been interpreted not as homes, but as granaries and stores that were raised above the reach of vermin. Secondly, the largest component of the ancient house was an enormous cone-shaped roof of thatch supported by poles that converged at the apex of the roof. The conical roof was supported on a circular wall that might have been constructed of stone or of posts, wattle and daub, depending upon local resources. In the larger buildings, an inner ring of upright posts helped to bear the weight of the roof. Thirdly, the house wall was low, often around waist height so that one will have needed to stoop to enter under the roof. Sometimes, in stone-built examples, large upright stone slabs formed the portals, and often, a projecting porch was built to check draughts. Entrances that breached the house wall were often built away from the prevailing winds and towards the rising sun. Fourth, the hearth was placed in the centre of the house and turf (peat) or dung would have been burned, with cooking vessels being supported over the fire and with some cooking being done on *bakestones* (heated stone slabs). Smoke from the hearth formed a pall in the tall roof before filtering away through the thatch and would have been useful for killing insect pests and for smoking meats.

ABOVE: *The Pimperne house at the reconstructed Iron Age farm at Butser Hill, near Petersfield, a wonderful evocation of Iron Age life*

RECONSTRUCTIONS

*D*URING recent decades, authentic reconstructions of prehistoric houses have been accomplished at a selection of places and they provide vivid introductions to ancient life.

SITES INCLUDE:

 FLAG FEN CENTRE, near Peterborough, with Bronze Age and Iron Age houses

CASTELL HENLLYS in the Pembrokeshire National Park, with four roundhouses and a four-poster

BERNERA, linked by bridge to the isle of Lewis, with an excavated Iron Age village and reconstructed roundhouse

BODRIFTY, Cornwall, with a reconstruction of a massive local roundhouse

PEAT MOORS CENTRE, Westhay, Somerset, where three replica Iron Age houses have been built

BUTSER HILL, Queen Elizabeth Country Park, Petersfield, Hampshire, where the reconstruction of the huge Iron Age house based precisely on an excavated example from Pimperne set the standard and precedent for reconstructions

CRAGGAUNOWEN, County Clare, where a defended cluster of Iron Age roundhouses has been built on an artificial lake island or *crannog*, examples of which were common in Bronze/Iron Age Scotland and Ireland

ABOVE: *The remains of an Iron Age dwelling with contemporary field walls in the background at Kestor on the edge of Dartmoor*

READING
THE
ANCIENT
SETTLEMENTS

*A*NY LINGERING beliefs that prehistoric communities were few and widely spread were finally driven away by the events in the final third of the twentieth century. The science of aerial archaeology had come of age and archaeological photographic surveys backed up by expert air photographic interpretation (notably by the Cambridge University team) were revealing new ancient settlement sites almost more rapidly than they could be catalogued.

Meanwhile, the motorway building bonanza and the rapid expansion of towns was resulting in hundreds of 'rescue excavations', with sites being given a rapid survey and dig before vanishing beneath brick and concrete. The rescue work also revealed an unexpected wealth of ancient dwellings and settlements. At present, about 5000 prehistoric dwellings are known on Dartmoor alone, many of them victims of Hekla eruptions.

However, all this is not to say that one can search in any locality and expect to discover ancient house sites. By far the greatest destroyer of the evidence has been ploughing, which will quite quickly level a site. Given that countless ancient house sites have been ploughed, on and off, since the homes were deserted 2-, 3- or 4000 years ago, it is not surprising that in the agricultural lowlands, much of the evidence has been scoured away. However, the local enthusiast can encounter evidence and make discoveries. Here are the main possibilities.

AIR PHOTOGRAPHS

A roundhouse was usually circled by a shallow ditch that caught the rainwater as it dripped from the thatch. Ploughing may scour away the shallower evidence but not bite deeply enough to erase this ditch. As crops grow, those standing above the ditch are nourished by the deeper silts and grow taller, casting a shadow on their neighbours to produce what are known as *crop marks*. On air photographs, rings representing these ditches are frequently revealed, often clearly showing the little break in the ditch that was once the entrance. Sometimes, the outlines of ancient field ditches will be visible, as will the dark 'dots' representing the airtight pits where grain was stored to prevent it from germinating. The local reference library or archaeological/heritage unit are places to enquire about the air photograph coverage for a particular place. Most locations have been photographed on numerous occasions. The Cambridge University Unit for Landscape Modelling air photograph site can be accessed at <u>venus.uflm.cam.ac.uk</u> and the National Monuments Record site is <u>www.english-heritage.org.uk/server/showConWebDoc.4150</u>. The air photograph site for Scottish antiquities is <u>www.rcahms.gov.uk/aerialphotography.html.</u> Vertical air photographs (looking straight down) are available along with the large-scale Victorian maps at <u>www.old-maps.co.uk</u>. Other sites, including ones of local interest, may be found by using a search engine.

HUT CIRCLES

On more rugged terrain, where stone was available for house-building and where later ploughing has not been a threat, the circular walls of ancient houses quite commonly survive to ankle-, knee-, or even waist-height. In the most impressive cases one can see how stones weighing two or more tons were incorporated into a wall or erected upright to form the portals flanking a doorway. These features are known, for obvious reasons, as *hut circles*. Occasionally, they are marked on Ordnance Survey maps, though most are not. They are very frequently seen by ramblers in the British uplands and it is impossible to walk across Dartmoor or Bodmin Moor without seeing a good selection of hut circles. There must be thousands of examples that are still unrecorded.

HUT TRACES

Hut circles with their boulder walls are striking features wherever they show through the heather and rough pasture. Less obvious ancient house evidence also exists, and where dwellings have stood on downlands their former presence may be marked by house-sized dimples of a shape that might be produced by pressing a football into sand. These traces can be well-marked in settings

RIGHT: Earthworks and tumbled stone walls at the former village of Carn Euny in Cornwall, settled by the native Britons during the Roman occupation

ABOVE: *Rings of rubble mark the dwellings inside the ramparts of the Welsh hill fort of Tre'r Ceiri on the Lleyn peninsula.*

such as the interiors of ancient hill forts that stand on chalk scarps. On hillsides, one can sometimes detect little shelf-like notches terraced into the slope, marking the platform that supported an ancient house.

FIELD WALKING

This is a technique used by archaeologists and it involves marking out a regular grid across an area and then having it walked systematically by members of a competent team who mark the position of each pot fragment and other artefact. The heavier concentrations of domestic debris may indicate the location of former settlements. Broken pots would have been trampled into earthen house floors or dumped in a midden outside. Some expert guidance is needed before field walking is practised in the field, but fragments of thick, coarse ancient pottery and items of metalwork often turn up in gardens. When found in gardens the question is that of whether the pottery is in *situ* or whether it has come in with a load of topsoil. The experts at the local museum should be able to provide identifications of any pot fragments found.

ABOVE: *The continuation of hut circles up to the rubble rampart wall (right) at Tre'r Ceiri*

WHAT DID
PREHISTORIC
SETTLEMENTS
LOOK LIKE?

*W*E CAN OBTAIN a fair impression of the appearances of ancient settlements by picturing the roundhouses that have been described, then imagining examples of different sizes and building materials and then thinking of different ways of combining the dwellings together.

Solitary roundhouses, usually with a few associated structures, such as perhaps a granary, a pigsty and some paddocks for lambs, equate to our farmsteads. Groups of up to half a dozen or so roundhouses are the equivalents of hamlets, while larger clusters could be considered to be small villages. In fact all these formations are replicated time after time by the prehistoric evidence seen at ancient settlement sites.

Farmsteads and all the differently sized clusters could be *open* or undefended or else to some degree fortified. The defences of ancient settlements could take the form of a massive wall, like the one that surrounded the Iron Age hut circles at the hilltop settlement of Tre'r Ceiri, near Pwllheli, or the compound of *moorstone* (granite) boulders ringing Bronze Age Grimspound on Dartmoor. In the lowlands it was normal for the fortified places to be protected by a ditch, with the *upcast* from the ditch being thrown

ABOVE: *Part of the small village at Din Lligwy on Anglesey that was contemporary with the late Roman occupation of the British mainland. Large upright stones were the portals that flanked the entrances. This was one of the last generations of settlements with circular houses in the prehistoric tradition.*

inwards to build a rampart bank that may have been topped with a palisade or a living thorn hedge. On air photographs, this enclosing ditch may form a strong crop mark encircling the dwelling traces.

Sometimes it is possible to infer a local social hierarchy from differences in the scale of buildings. When they attacked the dozens of closely packed roundhouses in the village sitting inside the massive ramparts of Hod Hill hillfort in Dorset, the Romans targeted the iron bolts from their artillery of 'ballistas' at a particular dwelling, which is assumed to have been the chieftain's house. At the very well-preserved Romano-British village of Din Lligwy on Anglesey, one massively walled roundhouse is regarded as the home of the local chieftain.

We can recreate most ancient settlement forms using these simple ideas about roundhouse clusters and open or defended settlements. The interesting thing about prehistoric villages is that they *tended not to be structured.* They could be just a scatter of dwellings, like the Bronze Age tin-workers' dwellings on the flanks of Rough Tor on Bodmin Moor. Even when a compound wall or a ditch imposed some sort of form there were never the distinctive village-shaping components like greens, back lanes, parallel plots (or *tofts*), marketplaces and so on that we associate with medieval and later

BELOW: *A hut circle with its portals still standing, part of a settlement of Bronze Age tin workers near the summit of Rough Tor on Bodmin Moor*

villages. The Romans did introduce some more organized and specialized villages, some heavily industrialized areas and some settlements serving travellers, and it was in the Roman era that the norm of the house that was square rather than circular was introduced. Whether more than a handful of the Roman villages survived into the medieval heyday of the village is uncertain. This is usually referred to as the question of continuity.

Readers of the village will usually struggle to establish a link between the villages in an area today and the settlements of the prehistoric/Roman eras. A devastating sequence of traumas and transformations divides the different ages of settlement. Roman routeways, power centres and boundaries certainly did exert influences in the Dark Ages but for a village to survive the chaos and epidemics that followed the Roman withdrawal without being greatly changed would be surprising.

The most compelling fact to be remembered is that those who created ancient villages seem never to have intended that their settlements would persist. Permanency was an attribute that was neither sought nor achieved. The archaeological evidence shows that farmsteads, hamlets and villages might have been occupied for several generations, perhaps a couple of centuries or more, but sooner or later their populations would drift off and settle somewhere else in the locality. Quite why they did so remains a puzzle. Rather than being over-ambitious and seeking to discover evolutionary history that never existed it is perhaps best simply to bear in mind that the villages of late Saxon, Viking and Norman times were founded in countrysides that already sagged under the weight of history. People had been working, changing, building and dying in them for 10,000 years or more. The villages that we now occupy, visit or drive through stand upon a landscape that is banded with layer upon layer of human history. Beneath the fields, the woods and the housing estates lies the wreckage of innumerable settlements from the Ages of Iron, Bronze, Copper and Stone, even though their lineages may very seldom link up directly with those of any living villages.

2

WHERE DID VILLAGES COME FROM?

S UDDENLY, VILLAGES WERE APPEARING across the countryside. We have seen that in prehistoric and even in Roman times, villages were very much in a minority amongst the hamlets and farmsteads. Even those that existed tended to endure for just a few generations or centuries before being abandoned. Our quest to understand the origins of our heritage of villages has, until quite recently, been undermined by persistent but deeply flawed ideas about settlements and their founders.

HOW DID WE GET IT WRONG?

A NYBODY who studies the history of explanations will know that once a bad idea finds its way into print it can soon become conventional wisdom and then come to be regarded as irrefutable fact. People simply assume that because everybody seems to accept it and because it is quoted in all the books the idea must have been shown to be true. In the case of villages, a magnificent edifice of interpretation was built on the sands of fallacy.

It was assumed that after the Roman departure from Britain in AD 410, great hordes of Anglo-Saxon settlers arrived, drove out the native peoples and began to clear the dense woodland that 'covered the country'. However, even when trees returned after the close of the last Ice Age (it ended around 10,000 BC), a continuous woodland cover was never established. Any woods that the Saxons

LEFT: *The moated manor of Kentwell Hall in Suffolk. Much earlier manor houses could be the nuclei around which villages developed and they were usually the control centres for village development.*

found would largely have been smallish fragments, remnants of ancient woodland enduring within working countrysides. The countrysides that existed in Britain in the late Bronze Age and Roman times were much more heavily populated than any that our Saxon pioneers created.

It was said that the Saxon settlers introduced their 'three-field' system along with their villages. In fact, this complex system of farming was unknown in the Saxon homelands. In England, they entered places devastated by political turmoil, economic decline and, probably, by plague and no innovative agricultural initiatives took place for around four centuries after these pagans arrived. It was believed that the sudden dominance of the Old English (Anglo-Saxon) language and place-names demonstrates the slaughter and eviction of the indigenous Celtic speakers. However, English today is almost universally understood in places as far apart as the Netherlands, Kenya, India and the West Indies. This does not show that English invaders exterminated all the native people of these places. It is a cultural phenomenon that we can easily explain.

BELOW: *The reconstructed pagan Saxon village at West Stow in Suffolk, with dwellings standing exactly on the sites of excavated originals*

Soon, the DNA evidence will answer the questions about British ancestry. Thus far, and as described, it seems to show a very anciently established British population that was affected along the North Sea shores by Anglo-Saxon and Viking settlement (Saxons and Danes had fairly similar homelands and their migrations were only a few centuries apart, so DNA work has difficulty in distinguishing between them). So far the DNA results have been contradictory, early studies underlining the 'Celtic' integrity of Wales and Cornwall but suggesting a dominant Germanic (Anglo-Saxon and Viking) presence in England and eastern Scotland. More recent work shows a strong Celtic or very ancient influence throughout Britain, with smaller Germanic contributions.

Much 'evidence' was derived from place-names. Many of our names contain the element '-ing', as in Reading or Birmingham. It comes from 'ingas', which means 'people of'. Thus, Paddington would be 'the "ton" or farm of Padda's folk' and Birmingham is 'the home place of Beorma's people'. It was assumed that because these names seemed to reveal groups of settlers led by patriarchs or war-band leaders, they must date from a time of active migration and conquest. Now the '-ing' names are no longer regarded as being the earliest of the Saxon names, and some regard the names that refer to topographical features, like hills and streams, as being earlier.

Thus, the Saxons or English did not arrive in great waves and begin to introduce villages and three-field systems right away. Their numbers are debatable, but they did produce some ruling dynasties and the spread of the English language was a great political and cultural triumph. This may have been assisted by the demoralization of the more civilized British natives after the collapse of the Roman Empire. The Saxon/English settlers had less to lose, but more to gain, while strong government may have made the British inflexible. It was several centuries after the Roman retreat and the English arrival that changes were set in motion that spawned and nurtured villages in their thousands. Research by archaeologists in the English Midlands has revealed that in the period AD 400 to 850, approaching the eve of the so-called 'Big Bang' of village creation, landscapes were covered by a multitude of hamlets that differed in all respects from the large, compact villages of the Middle Ages and present day. Some larger settlements must also have existed, but these villages were far fewer.

How to
Make a
Village

*V*illages that were ancestral to those of today began to appear in the middle centuries of the Saxon era and continued to be formed right through the Norman period and on until the great population decline of the fourteenth century, when climate changed and the Black Death arrived. The arrival of villages both intended and destined to survive took place in unlikely circumstances of political turmoil and division and they were parts of a great package of changes that transformed the faces of most countrysides.

Excavations have shown that some villages were created in the early centuries of the Saxon era, the fifth, sixth and seventh centuries. These places tended to be rather small and to have the form of loose and unstructured collections of farmsteads set in paddocks. They lacked the organization of dwellings around roads and greens and churches that typified most medieval villages. There was frequently a

ABOVE: *The turbulent character of the centuries following the Roman withdrawal was captured on this Pictish symbol stone at Aberlemno, near Forfar.*

distinction between the 'halls' or dwellings and the smaller buildings with sunken floors. The latter are thought by some to have been weaving sheds. A few early villages on the North Sea coast may have served as immigrant camps for new arrivals. A Saxon village of the pagan centuries has been reconstructed directly upon the sites of the original houses at West Stow in Suffolk. Perhaps the main point of difference between it and prehistoric settlements was the use of dwellings that were rectangular rather than round. It is a most evocative site and well worth visiting (see p.40).

The archaeological evidence suggests that the ancient habit of desertion directly followed by resettlement nearby persisted into this age. However, some of the hamlets seem to have provided nuclei for the permanent villages that developed. In various places, pottery from the eighth or ninth centuries found around an old village church site will identify the ancient core of the settlement. Black, hard to spot and 'tempered' using grass, this pottery looks unexciting, but it serves as a glorious fanfare heralding the first stages in the foundation of durable villages. Such places of worship and local centres of power may have acted like magnets, sucking settlers in from other hamlets in the locality. *Royal vills* – the headquarters of estates owned by the king – were important places that could have grown into villages (or into towns, like Luton and

Aylesbury). Minster churches (see Chapter Five), other monasteries and lordly residences must also have been magnets.

The first era of village invention and creation in the ninth to tenth centuries was a time of diversity and turmoil. In the lowlands of England, English speakers dominated most places, but names containing 'Wal' show where some 'Welsh foreigners' or Celtic speakers lived. The north-west of England, the Welsh Marches and the far west were still Celtic-speaking areas, while along the English Channel and North Sea shores, raiding and eventual settlement by Danish Vikings would threaten the Church, disrupt communities and create Old Danish-speaking localities in northern England. Similarly, Norwegian Vikings, moving between stepping stones in the Northern Isles, Scottish Highlands and Islands, the Isle of Mann, Ireland, Cumbria and the northern dales of England, would introduce another cultural strand, including the Old Norse language. Britain during the genesis of villages was anything but a homogenous and well-ordered place.

The population had been growing for some centuries, partially recovering from a frightful decline around the time of Rome's withdrawal. To support more people and to encourage

BELOW: *Change could be both unpredictable and comprehensive — how large a settlement might have grown around the monastery on Holy Island had not the Vikings burst from the North Sea mists.*

commerce there would have been a need to produce more calories – and this would have required new systems of farming. Somehow, an extremely elaborate system of communal farming was developed, though it required the wholesale reorganization of estates. It is wrongly called the 'three-field system' in most classrooms ('open-field system' would be more accurate). The 'fields' concerned were vast expanses of ploughland, divided into blocks or *furlongs* and sub-divided into a multitude of ribbon-like *strips* (also known as 'lands' or 'selions'). Fields often numbered three, but in different places there were numbers between two and nine – occasionally even more. The system may have allowed a more intensive use of the ploughland, perhaps releasing some land as valuable pasture and meadow, but it demanded intense levels of disciplining and organization of the labour force. People had to work according to precise calendars of cooperation and households had to help each other, for example by pooling their oxen to produce teams of six or eight beasts needed to haul a plough across heavy clay ground.

Given a rewarding but labour-intensive method of farming that depended on discipline and synchronized working, the establishment of centralized labour pools in dormitories was essential. *These dormitories were the new villages.* Who pulled the strings of change? As the changes unfolded, Britain was still divided between numerous warlike kingdoms; different dynasties and beliefs competed in England and then came the turmoil of the Viking raids. No one king had the dominion or authority to impose the changes. Also, it is impossible to imagine that households living in some form of bondage would readily have surrendered their remaining independence to live in a dormitory labour pool. So it seems most likely that the transformations were developed by some influential estate owners and imitated by countless others. Village life was not the creation of the mythical Saxon bands of free colonists. It was imposed from above, transforming existing countrysides and burdening ordinary countryfolk with onerous obligations.

Archaeologists talk of a 'mid-Saxon shuffle', for in the middle phase of the Saxon era, the bases of life seem to become topsy-turvy, with the abandonment of old-style settlements and the establishment of new ones. Part of the process was the introduction of Christianity and later, the superseding of the early minster-type churches by estate churches planted in villages by their landlords. Had some beautiful princess fallen asleep some time around AD 750 and slept for a couple of centuries then, at least in the English lowlands, she would have awoken to seen the main facets of the landscape – the settlements, the farming patterns and the organization of worship – completely transformed. By the time of the Norman Conquest, most of the villages existing then, exist today and a majority of the villages existing today, existed then. If we listened carefully to the heavy Old English drawl of villagers when we asked them the names of their villages, we could navigate around the eleventh-century English lowlands with a map torn from a modern school atlas.

OVERLEAF: *The minster church at Kirk Hammerton, near York. Its name suggests a distinction between it and the other settlement on the estate, identified as Green Hammerton.*

The village and its open fields:
Gamlingay, Cambs. As mapped in 1601

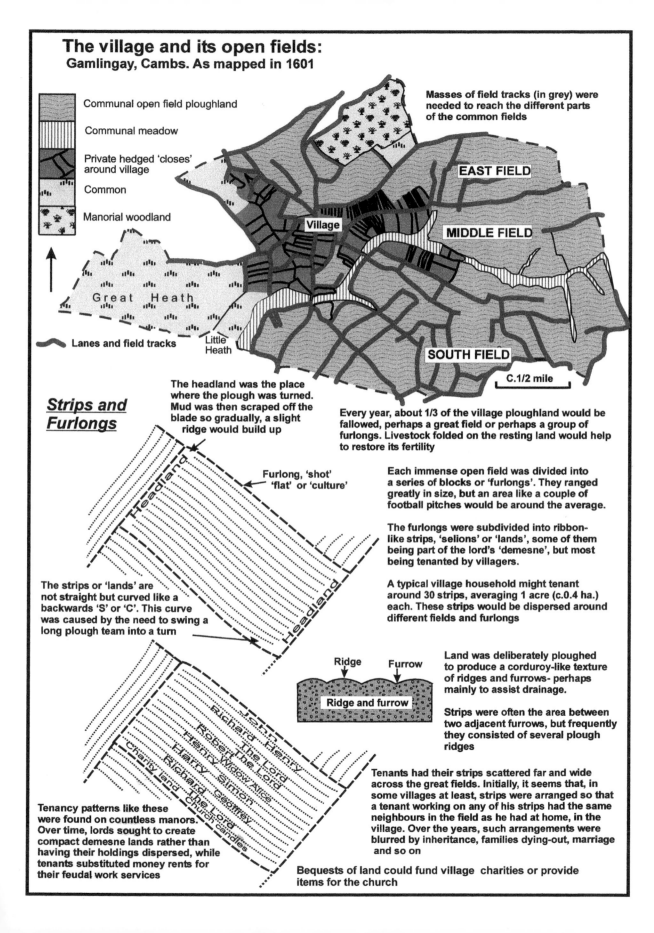

Communal open field ploughland

Communal meadow

Private hedged 'closes' around village

Common

Manorial woodland

Lanes and field tracks

Great Heath

Little Heath

Village

EAST FIELD

MIDDLE FIELD

SOUTH FIELD

Masses of field tracks (in grey) were needed to reach the different parts of the common fields

C.1/2 mile

Strips and Furlongs

The headland was the place where the plough was turned. Mud was then scraped off the blade so gradually, a slight ridge would build up

Furlong, 'shot' 'flat' or 'culture'

Headland

Headland

The strips or 'lands' are not straight but curved like a backwards 'S' or 'C'. This curve was caused by the need to swing a long plough team into a turn

Ridge   Furrow

Ridge and furrow

John
Richard Henry
Robert The Lord
Henry Widow Alice
Harry Simon
Richard Geoffrey
charity land The Lord
Richard Church candles

Tenancy patterns like these were found on countless manors. Over time, lords sought to create compact demesne lands rather than having their holdings dispersed, while tenants substituted money rents for their feudal work services

Every year, about 1/3 of the village ploughland would be fallowed, perhaps a great field or perhaps a group of furlongs. Livestock folded on the resting land would help to restore its fertility

Each immense open field was divided into a series of blocks or 'furlongs'. They ranged greatly in size, but an area like a couple of football pitches would be around the average.

The furlongs were subdivided into ribbon-like strips, 'selions' or 'lands', some of them being part of the lord's 'demesne', but most being tenanted by villagers.

A typical village household might tenant around 30 strips, averaging 1 acre (c.0.4 ha.) each. These strips would be dispersed around different fields and furlongs

Land was deliberately ploughed to produce a corduroy-like texture of ridges and furrows- perhaps mainly to assist drainage.

Strips were often the area between two adjacent furrows, but frequently they consisted of several plough ridges

Tenants had their strips scattered far and wide across the great fields. Initially, it seems that, in some villages at least, strips were arranged so that a tenant working on any of his strips had the same neighbours in the field as he had at home, in the village. Over the years, such arrangements were blurred by inheritance, families dying-out, marriage and so on

Bequests of land could fund village charities or provide items for the church

*P*LACE-NAMES do not provide the magical solutions that were claimed. Even so, they are valuable clues to the early days of the village. The first generations of durable villages will, if successful, lie inaccessibly stratified beneath the relics of more than 1000 years of continuous occupation. Deserted medieval villages may sometimes be excavated to reveal their formative days.

In general, it is impossible to know exactly how a living village looked in its early days. Houses were rebuilt within their plots on dozens of occasions, though road patterns and property boundaries have tended to be more permanent.

The pioneers of our subject were fascinated by 'continuity', often wondering how many settlements are rooted in Roman times. Some villages have been seen to coincide with Roman sites – though this is hardly surprising given the multitude of places occupied in Roman times. There are striking examples of the continuity of power centres. Several Welsh churches are associated with

BELOW: *Ashwell has a name that is easily translated: 'the spring overhung by ash trees'.*

ABOVE: *The 'ing' word part does not always mean 'people' and the name of Finchingfield, Essex, is quite easy to translate — it is probably 'the field where the finches are caught'.*

Roman sites and York Minster stands directly upon the headquarters of the huge Roman fortress at York. However, it seems doubtful that many settlements experienced an unbroken continuation of life from Roman into Norman times.

Its name can tell us something about the early days of a village. An example is Ashwell in Hertfordshire, which must have been established by a spring shaded by ash trees — and there are thousands of similar examples. The majority of names do not describe the *village*, but relate to the *setting* in which it was established. The host of names ending in '-ton' relate to a farm or an estate and not, as is commonly said, to a village. The villages must have grown in the farm or estate setting.

Each translation is a guess and different old words can produce the same word parts. Faringdon in Oxfordshire may derive from an Old English word for a fern and another for a hill (*fearn-dun*) though many would think that the '-ing' part must refer to 'the people of', as described earlier. Similarly, Birthwaite near Knaresborough might be regarded as the 'burgh' or stronghold in the 'thwaite' or meadow clearing. Actually, early versions of the name show it to be Birkenthwaite or 'birch wood clearing'. It is best to use the *earliest recorded version* of a name that can be found.

A great many words turn up frequently in village names. Leaving out the most obvious examples, like '-wood', '-brook' or '-water', some of the most common are set out in the table opposite.

Discovering
More

B Y THE TIME that William the Conqueror sent his assessors out to compile Domesday Book in 1085, the village revolution was around a quarter of a millennium old and still creating new settlements. People imagine that Domesday Book is a comprehensive historical description of the English countryside in Norman times – until they consult it. It was a guide to the King's assets and dues and the pattern of tenancies: the notion of leaving an enduring record of Norman England for the generations of scholars to follow would never have entered William's hard head. Tersely, the assessment moves from estate to estate, recording some features and disregarding others. Villages as such are not really mentioned and attention is fixed on

BELOW: *At Appletreewick in the Yorkshire Dales, a thin snow cover brings out old farming patterns and house plots. The corduroy pattern below the dwellings is ridge and furrow, which terminates at the old headland.*

The meanings of some common village names

Name part	Original language	Meaning	Name part	Original language	Meaning
Ac	Old English	Oak tree	-mill, miln	Old English	Mill
Afon/avon	Welsh	River	-mouth	Old English	River mouth, estuary
Ash	Old English	Ash tree	-muir	Gaelic	Moor or sea
Barton	Old English	Barley farm/outlying settlement	-newydd	Welsh	New
			Over	Old English	Slope, scarp
Betws	Welsh	Chapel	Parvus	Latin	Small
Bólstaðr/bister	Old Norse	Homestead	Pen	Welsh	Hill, head
Bridge/brig	Old English	Bridge	Pit	Pictish	Portion of land
Burgh/borough	Old English	Stronghold, often just a manor site	-porth	Cornish	Harbour
			Pwll, -pool	Welsh/Old English	Pool
-by	Old Norse	Farm, hamlet (many became villages)	Rath	Gaelic	Ring fort
			-scale	Old English	Hut on summer pasture
Caer	Welsh/Cornish	Fort	-stead	Old English	A place (hall-stead is manor site)
Capel	Welsh	Chapel			
Carl-	Old English	Place of the churls	-stock	Old English	Place with stumps or logs
Chester	Old English	Roman military site	-stoke	Old English	Small settlement or holy place
Cotes, coates	Old English	Cottages			
-cumb, -combe	Old English	Valley, hollow	-staithe	Old Norse	Landing place for sea/river craft
-don	Old English	Hill			
-dun, -don	Gaelic	Fort	-stow	Old English	Religious site/gathering place
-ey	Old English	Island			
-field, feld	Old English	Open field land, unenclosed land			
			-street	Old English	Roman road
-ford	Old English	Shallow crossing place on a river	-toft	Old Norse	House plot
			-ton	Old English	Farmstead, estate
-haven	Old English/Norse	Anchorage	Thing/-thing	Old Norse	Assembly place
-ham (1)	Old English	Water meadow	-thorpe	Old Norse	Hamlet
-ham (2)	Old English	Homestead (often becoming a village)	-thwaite	Old Norse	Clearing, meadow
			Tre, Tref	Cornish	Homestead
-ing (1)	Old English	People of a patriarch	Wal/-wal	Old English	Stranger, native Briton
-ing (2)/eng	Old English	Meadow or plant community	-wald	Old English	Wooded hills
			-ware	Old English	Occupants of a place
Kil	Gaelic	Church, churchyard	-well	Old English	Spring or well
-kirk	Old Norse	Church	-wick, wickham	Old English	Cheese farm/Roman roadside village site
Llan	Welsh	Church			
-ley	Old English	Trees – present or cleared!			
			-worth	Old English	Enclosure
Magnus	Latin	Great(er)	Ysbyty	Welsh	Hospital/hospice

estates, their value and assets. So far as their Norman masters were concerned, the conquered people and the nature of their habitations were of no concern. It did not matter who or where they were so long as they performed their feudal obligations.

When such factors are properly taken into account, Domesday Book is a fascinating source of information, revealing the relative importance of ploughland, wooded pasture and so on in the different manors, and showing which places had prospered since the days of Edward the Confessor (1042–66), and which had been wasted by the invading Norman army.

The Domesday assessors set out to record: 1. the name of the place; 2. the identity of the owner in 1066; 3. the number of hides (a loose land measure of 60–120 acres or around 24–48 hectares) and the number of ploughs there; 4. the number of tenants of different grades; 5. the amount of pasture, meadow and woodland there; 6. the number of mills and fishponds; 7. the valuations of the place in 1066 and 1086, and 8. the owner of the estate in the time of Edward the Confessor. This information is listed in a terse, almost shorthand, Latin form, with some headings sometimes being missed and some features that existed (like many mills) being overlooked. Here is a typical entry from Barton-under-Needwood, Staffordshire:

> *Land of the King in Offlow Hundred [an administrative division]. The King holds Barton. Earl Algar held it [before]. 3 hides. Land for 18 ploughs. In the lord's demesne 2 ploughs. 2 slaves [slavery was more a Saxon than a Norman institution]. 17 villeins and 8 bordars [different grades of bondsmen, the villeins being the powerhouse of rural society] with 9 ploughs. Meadow 20 acre [c. 8.1 ha.]. Woodland or wood pasture 2 leagues by 1 league [about 6 miles by 3 miles]. A mill [worth] 6s [about 30p]. In the time of Edward the Confessor value £6. Value now £7.*

This is the sort of staccato listing of facts that readers researching their villages and localities should expect to encounter. The abbreviated Latin involved can be followed fairly swiftly. Domesday Book has recently become available online at www.nationalarchives.gov.uk/domesday.

Place-names, particularly those of the villages, have a useful part to play in recreating the countrysides that existed at the time of village creation. Dictionaries of place-names are available at all good reference libraries. Though village landscapes have changed profoundly since Saxon times, amazingly the organization of fields surrounding villages often retained all its essential features for more than 1000 years. Many village open field systems were dismantled in the dying days of the Middle Ages and in Elizabethan times. Other strip fields, commons and shared meadows endured into the eighteenth or nineteenth centuries, before being destroyed by the Parliamentary Enclosure of common lands. Many features that allow a reconstruction of the old medieval open fields still existed when Ordnance Survey workers were drawing their maps in the second half of the nineteenth century. Map resources vary between different parishes and manors, the best being the detailed Elizabethan estate maps. The little book *The Logic of Open Field Systems* (Russell 1995) uses the evidence of maps to reconstruct the medieval field patterns of some 47 Lincolnshire parishes. Similar projects can be undertaken for other settings. Ask your reference librarian or county archivist about the parish maps

ABOVE: *The Norman conquerors demonstrated their domination in a grandiose campaign of church building. At Little Ouseburn, near Boroughbridge and close to a Roman road, the builders of the early Norman church seem to have employed some large, squared stones from Roman ruins.*

that may have been drawn *before* and *after* the Parliamentary Enclosure of parishes in your area; about the English/Welsh 'tithe maps' of 1837–52, with their detailed portrayals of the fieldscape; the eighteenth-century military and other surveys of Scotland – and especially the excellent First Edition 6 inches to 1 mile Ordnance Survey maps of Britain (available online at www.old-maps.co.uk). Further ideas about discovering the old village setting are given in the chapter that follows.

3

TAKING SHAPE AND MULTIPLYING

*T*HE GOLDEN AGE of the village in England spanned from the times of the later Saxon kings – those who ruled over a united English realm – to around the fourteenth century, when the growth and spread of villages was reversed by disasters. (In Scotland and Wales, villages were never as prevalent: hamlets, farmsteads, local strongholds and capitals were more prominent and so a golden age of villages is much harder to recognize there.) During the heyday of villages, those that existed tended to grow and to bud off daughter villages into a countryside that became ever more crowded. 'Village England' was born, though these early villages looked nothing like those depicted on fancy biscuit tins or in Robin Hood movies. They were dormitories for populations that were mainly composed of households in bondage to a feudal lord and they often consisted of nothing more than a collection of rather ramshackle dwellings greatly overshadowed by a church.

The documents of this time are devoid of colourful descriptions of these places and consist largely of taxation records, lists of feudal dues and manor court rolls that record the punishments inflicted for petty infringements of the estate codes. Some more information comes from the landscape and from archaeological excavations as well as from the indirect evidence of place-names.

For all its gaps and shortcomings, the picture that takes shape is of a hopeful and vibrant society. It was a society that had blithely cast aside all the lessons of previous experiences of the consequences of environmental abuse and was packing every habitable corner of the countryside with people. The people were tough, but so were the bacteria, viruses and hardships ranged against them. A few folk

LEFT: *A view of Cerne Abbas in Dorset. Many claim that the village developed in the shadow of the explicit chalk-cut giant on Giant Hill, nearby. But since there is no recorded mention of the figure until the medieval era was well passed and gone, this is most unlikely.*

ABOVE: *Thaxted in Essex takes its name from the place or 'stead' where material for thatching was cut.*

would live to a fair old age, but plague, the diseases of contaminated water sources, tooth infections, child birth and the crippling consequences of working in the rain and living in a cold and draughty dwelling ensured that the lucky ones who survived infancy were unlikely to reach what we now regard as old age. These villagers of late Saxon, Norman and Plantagenet times must have lived for the day, knowing that tomorrows would probably be few.

When we look at the evidence, we do not seem to encounter communities bowed down by fatalism. Rather, great reserves of energy and endeavour seem to have been released as societies rediscovered the hopeful vitality that had been lacking since the early days of the Roman occupation. Villages were founded, they grew and often took on new shapes. Land-hungry settlers probed the unoccupied niches in the countryside. Could a few families survive in this rather uninviting spot or that one? This was the time of the *Medieval Warm Period* of unusually salubrious climates, so the answer to the question was probably, yes, for a little while. But by the time that our age of expansion ended in deteriorating climate, economic disorder, border raiding and plague, the villages had become too big and too heavy and many would have to go. However, a pattern of villages had come into existence that, with some gaps, persists to this day.

*A*T THE TIME when villages were expanding, writing was an accomplishment reserved for a small minority of the population, mainly clerks in holy orders. They wrote to reproduce texts or to set down religious polemics or to record economic and legal data for landowners. Hardly anybody felt a mission to record the appearance of places, the thoughts of ordinary people or the details of day-to-day village life. The landscape of a surviving village can be full of information but many villages have no remaining medieval buildings, while most that survive are heavily modified or date from the last century or so of the Middle Ages. So how can we find a porthole on the times of village founders in AD 900, AD 1100 or AD 1250? Some might say: 'Domesday Book?' But as we have seen, a look at actual estate entries in Domesday shows that it may make a couple of terse remarks about the amount of ploughland and the amount of wooded pasture for swine – but give little information that would allow a reconstruction of a Norman village setting as it existed when the Book was compiled in 1086. However, as we have touched upon in Chapter Two, there is one abundant source of evidence that is available to the

BELOW: *The communities of a thousand years ago had a much richer vocabulary of words to describe settings. This led to more economical place-names, so that Burnsall in Wharfedale means 'Bruni's nook of river bend land'.*

unskilled enthusiast: place-names. They are present on every map and there are lots of dictionaries that offer informed attempts at their translation. In beginning a survey of names around a village the following thoughts may prove helpful.

Imagine that you had to name (re-name) a favourite spot in the countryside. What would you call it? High Hedges? Orchid Dell? The Birches? It is very probable that you would choose a name like these – one that *described* the outstanding feature of the place. In the past, people did exactly the same. However, places change. There may be no trees or badgers left in Badger Wood while Salbeck may have lost its sallows (willows) and its beck due to excessive water use. Physical settings are transformed, but place-names are remarkably durable. They can persist long after their meaning has been forgotten. In this way, the place-names that are found in the area surrounding a village may paint a much more accurate picture of the setting as it existed around the time that the village was founded than does the countryside in its current form.

BELOW: *Place-names can reveal unsuspected aspects of local history. Kersey means 'watercress island'.*

ABOVE: *Some names still ring true. Austwick in the Yorkshire Dales is 'eastern dairy farm' and the limestone here still supports emerald pastures.*

The years when villages were spreading were also a very fertile time for place-name creation. In the Saxon era, names inherited from the Celtic-speaking British were often difficult for English speakers to articulate, and so they were anglicized or replaced. Also, the proliferation of villages meant that there were countless new settlements needing names – and the little features in the expanding village fields also needed names.

Most of the names adopted were of an environmental nature and they describe features of the surroundings as they were when the names were given. A significant number of names are personal and they usually identify an early patriarch or estate-owner. Few of the earlier people mentioned can be identified as people appearing in historical archives. Many names relate to farming. The communities steeped in agriculture and working with very basic technology had immensely rich vocabularies for aspects of farming. Most of the words referring to areas of land of different shapes, qualities and ownerships have been forgotten, so we have to refer to a dictionary to discover their meaning. Some pieces of land were associated with clergy, with raising funds for church charities or with funding aspects of ritual and regalia, like a 'Chalice Field', whose profits paid for communion wine.

Languages evolve. Confronted by a text in fourteenth-century English, like Chaucer's *Canterbury Tales*, our reading is halting and our comprehension full of gaps until we get a feeling for the plodding rhythm of the work. Faced with a document like an Anglo-Saxon charter of AD 1000 we might recognize some words, but struggle much more. If we could hear it being read, a few more

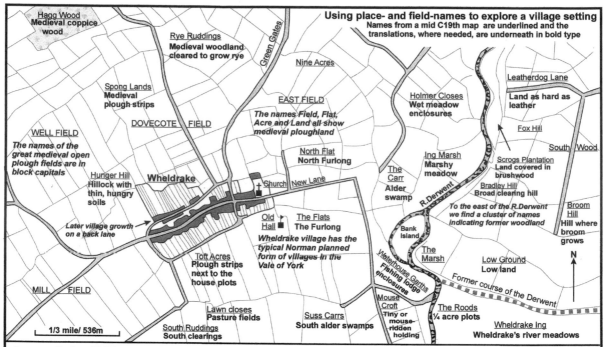

Using place- and field-names to explore a village setting
Names from a mid C19th map are underlined and the translations, where needed, are underneath in bold type

Hagg Wood
Medieval coppice wood

Rye Ruddings
Medieval woodland cleared to grow rye

Green Gates

Nine Acres

Leatherdog Lane
Land as hard as leather

Spong Lands
Medieval plough strips

DOVECOTE FIELD

EAST FIELD
The names Field, Flat, Acre and Land all show medieval ploughland

Holmer Closes
Wet meadow enclosures

Fox Hill

South Wood

WELL FIELD
The names of the great medieval open plough fields are in block capitals

North Flat
North Furlong

Ing Marsh
Marshy meadow

Scrogs Plantation
Land covered in brushwood

Hunger Hill
Hillock with thin, hungry soils

Wheldrake

The Carr
Alder swamp

Bradley Hill
Broad clearing hill

Broom Hill
Hill where broom grows

Church   New Lane

R.Derwent

To the east of the R.Derwent we find a cluster of names indicating former woodland

Later village growth on a back lane

Old Hall

The Flats
The Furlong

Wheldrake village has the typical Norman planned form of villages in the Vale of York

Bank Island

The Marsh

N

Toft Acres
Plough strips next to the house plots

Waterhouse Garths
Fishing lodge enclosures

Low Ground
Low land

Former course of the Derwent

MILL FIELD

Lawn closes
Pasture fields

Suss Carrs
South alder swamps

Mouse Croft
Tiny or mouse-ridden holding

The Roods
¼ acre plots

Wheldrake Ing
Wheldrake's river meadows

South Ruddings
South clearings

1/3 mile/ 536m

As mapped in the mid-19th century, Wheldrake parish had undergone a relatively recent transformation, when its common lands were privatised by Parliamentary Enclosure. Some new, straight-sided fields appeared and the old through-road to the east of the village was straightened and realigned. Even so, old boundaries and field names had survived the changes. They contained enough information to allow a reconstruction of the medieval setting in which Wheldrake took shape.

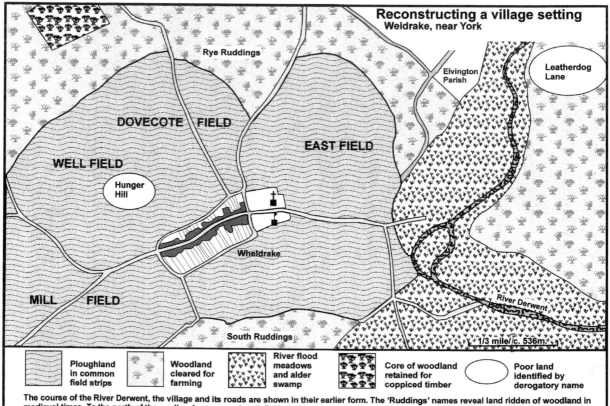

Reconstructing a village setting
Weldrake, near York

Rye Ruddings

Elvington Parish

Leatherdog Lane

DOVECOTE FIELD

EAST FIELD

WELL FIELD

Hunger Hill

Wheldrake

MILL FIELD

River Derwent

South Ruddings

1/3 mile/ c. 536m.

Ploughland in common field strips	Woodland cleared for farming	River flood meadows and alder swamp	Core of woodland retained for coppiced timber	Poor land identified by derogatory name

The course of the River Derwent, the village and its roads are shown in their earlier form. The 'Ruddings' names reveal land ridden of woodland in medieval times. To the north of the medieval common plough fields it was removed to produce extra ploughland, apparently for growing rye, while to the south, it was removed to create 'lawns' or pasture. Four main open fields are indicated and shown in bold block capitals, though perhaps Well Field and Dovecote Field were once one field. The damp meadows beside the Derwent will have yielded hay, grazing, fish and fowls. In Norman times, Wheldrake housed around 6 families and had increased about ten fold by the 14th-century. Its name might mean 'Cold stream' but this is very debatable. As the village is on a slight ridge, 'Wheel ridge' or 'Death ridge' are more likely interpretations.

words would seem familiar. Gradually, the meaning of some words has been forgotten and over the years those who have encountered them have either turned them into gibberish or tried to convert them into something that seemed more meaningful. In this way, a field that had contained a Saxon pig sty or *hlōse* could become 'Loose Field' and then 'Lucy's Field' and it might end up as 'Lucky Field' – with fallacious rumours of treasure found there.

Place-name translations are not set in stone. All those provided in the dictionaries are guesses. Usually the probability of accuracy is very high but a portion of the translations will be wrong, for most of the names are open to more than one interpretation.

RECREATING THE VILLAGE SETTING

*V*ILLAGES were established in long-worked countrysides rather than in pristine wildernesses. However, these countrysides usually looked very different from those of today. The descriptions of land boundaries in Anglo-Saxon charters show that well-maintained hedgerows were more numerous, while woodlands, though not so very much more extensive than they are today, were well maintained and carefully organized to produce timber and to provide woodland grazing for cattle and pigs. Land drainage was far less developed and water was not extracted from watercourses and boreholes for irrigation, so wet places were more numerous and extensive.

To reconstruct a village setting you will need a map, such as those published by the Ordnance Survey, and a place-name dictionary: the local reference library should have several examples. The OS 1:50,000 maps by no means show all the names in a locality and the larger the scale of a map employed, the more names will be revealed. Other maps, held in the reference library or county record office, like the nineteenth-century tithe maps or First Edition 6 inches to 1 mile Ordnance Survey maps will show additional names.

Equipped with the map, these tables and a good place-name dictionary, you can now recreate the setting in which your village was founded. In medieval and earlier times, rivers were unruly and unconfined, so you would not expect to have found dwellings on their floodplains. Areas around clusters of woodland names can be shaded as woodland, and those around wetland names as marsh, with the agricultural names showing former ploughland, pasture and meadow. Extensive commons were a part of the medieval scene and they can often be recognized at a glance from the straight walls and hedgerows of the geometrical field patterns of Parliamentary Enclosure that privatized and carved them up in about 1750–1850. Your plotting map can be a photocopy of a library map (but ask about reproduction rights first) or a tracing. The 6 inches to 1 mile map can make a good base map if it is enlarged as necessary on a scanner or photocopier.

OVERLEAF: *Villages take their identity from their settings and Holy Island is a product of the encircling sea, the strands, dunes and early Christian foundations.*

ABOVE: *Watendlath hamlet in a relatively remote part of the Lake District — one of thousands of settlements that lacked the resources and good fortune to become villages*

PLACE-NAMES ASSOCIATED WITH FORMER WET PLACES

NAME	ORIGINALLY	LANGUAGE	MEANING	NAME	ORIGINALLY	LANGUAGE	MEANING
Carr	kjarr	Old Norse	Alder tree swamp, marsh with brushwood	Marsh	mersc	Old English	A marsh
				Mere	mere	Old English	Pool, pond or lake
				Mire	*mýrr*	Old Norse	Swamp
-ey, -y, as in Thorney, Denny	eg	Old English	An island	Moor	mõr	Old English	A sodden lowland heath as well as an upland moor
Fen	fen	Old English	A watery place or fen	Moss	mos	Old English	A boggy area
				Pool/pwll	pwll	Welsh	A pool
Ham	hamm	Old English	Water meadow, land surrounded by marsh — but 'ham' more frequently comes from a word for 'homestead'	Sal-	sealh	Old English	Place with willows (sometimes place linked to salt trade)
				Weir	wer	Old English	Dam or fishing pool
Holme(s)	holmr	Old Norse	Water meadow or island	Wham	whamm	Old English	Marshy hollow

Place-names associated with rivers and streams

Name	Originally	Language	Meaning	Name	Originally	Language	Meaning
Beck	*bekkr*	Old Norse	Stream	Den	*denu*	Old English	A valley
Bridge, Scots brig	*brycg*	Old English	A bridge	Force	*fors*	Old Norse	Waterfall
				Ford	*ford*	Old English	A ford
Brook	*broc*	Old English	A brook, but if there is no brook nearby then perhaps Mr Brock the badger	Gill	*gil*	Old Norse	Ravine with a stream
				Glen	*glennos, gleann*	Old Welsh and Gaelic	Upland valley
Cumb, Combe	*cwm, coomb*	Old Welsh/ Old English	Cup-like hollow or a trough-like valley	Slack	*slakki*	Old Norse	A shallow valley
				Slade	*slæd*	Old English	A short valley
				Strath	*srath*	Gaelic	Broad valley or river plain
Dale	*dalr*	Old Norse	A valley (also from an Old English word for a pit or hollow)	Wath	*vath*	Old Norse	A ford

Place-names associated with the local terrain

The village founders used a much richer vocabulary for topographical features, so this is a selection of the commoner names.

Name	Originally	Language	Meaning	Name	Originally	Language	Meaning
Bank	*banke*	Middle English	Sloping ground – often a hillside	Law	*hlāw*	Old English	Hill or ancient burial mound
Brae	?	Old Norse	A Scottish word with a Scandinavian origin for a steep slope	Link	*hlinc*	Old English	Bank or ledge but developed into the golf links of the sandy seashores
Dale	*dalr*	Old Norse	Valley	Lith	*hlíth*	Old Norse	A slope
Dun	*dun*	Old English	A hill, but can also come from the Celtic *duno*, which can mean a fort as well as a hill	Ness	*naess, nes*	Old English/ Old Norse	A headland
				Pen	*pen*	Old Welsh	Hill or headland (Penicuik near Edinburgh is 'Cuckoo Hill')
Fell	*fjall*	Old Norse	Upland hill or slope, mountain side				
Head	*heafod*	Old English	Head or hill	Side	*side*	Old English	A long slope

PLACE-NAMES ASSOCIATED WITH WOODLAND

Woodland was carefully managed in different ways and had many forms and uses, giving rise to a much richer vocabulary than the one that survives.

NAME	ORIGINALLY	LANGUAGE	MEANING
Bere	*bearu*	Old English	Grove – but some *bere* words come from an OE word for barley
Coed	*coid*	Old Welsh	A wood
Coille	*coille*	Gaelic	A large wood
Copy/coppice	*copis*	Mid.English	A coppiced wood
Den/dene	*denn*	Old English	Wooded grazing for swine
Frith	*fyrhth*	Old English	Woodland
Grove	*graf*	Old English	A grove
Hagg	*hogg*	Old Norse	Division of a coppice
Hay	*(ge)haeg*	Old English	A small wood or a hedged clearing
Hollins	*holegn*	Old English	Holly wood giving leaf browse for livestock
Holt	*holt*	Old English	Thicket
Hurst	*hyrst*	Old English	Wooded hilltop
Ley	*leah*	Old English	An awkward word referring to trees that are either there or else removed

NAME	ORIGINALLY	LANGUAGE	MEANING
Lund/lound	*lundr*	Old Norse	A fairly small wood
Ridding/ridden	*ryding*	Old English	Same as Sart
Royd/royd	*rodu*	Old English	Same as Sart
Sal-	*salh*	Old English	Place with sallow (willow) trees
Sart	*assart*	Old French	A clearing made for farming or settlement
Shaw	*sceaga*	Old English	A small wood
Spring	*spring*	Old English	A coppiced wood
Stock/stocking	*stocc/stoccing*	Old English	Cleared woodland with tree stumps
Stubb/stubbing	*stubb*	Old English	Same as stock
Thwaite	*thveit*	Old Norse	Enclosure, perhaps a clearing
Tree	*treow*	Old English	A tree or a heavy timber
With	*vithr*	Old Norse	A wood
Wood	*wudu*	Old English	A wood

Place-names associated with farming

The village in question will almost certainly have depended entirely, or almost so, on agriculture during its first centuries of life. The village founders had a remarkable array of words associated with the land and with working it, of which but a small fraction are in usage today. These are most of the words that frequently crop up in place-names.

Name	Originally	Language	Meaning	Name	Originally	Language	Meaning
Acre	æcer	Old English	A land measure; it usually denotes arable land	Lawn/ launde	launde	Old French	Glade, woodland pasture
Baulk	balca	Old English	Narrow belt of land for access and grazing within great plough fields	Leas/ leasows	Læs/læwe	Old English	Enclosed pastures
				Lin-	lin	Old English	Place where flax was grown
Croft	croft	Old English	A small enclosure	Mead	mæd	Old English	Meadow
Den	denn	Old English	Woodland swine pasture, similar to the word for a hollow	Park	park	Old French/ Mid. English	A deer hunting park, but can also be a paddock or just an expanse of pastures
Field	feld	Old English	A field in the sense of unwooded, dry country. Later, cultivated land	Rigg	hrycg/hryggr	Old English/ Old Norse	Ridges of plough-soil produced in making ridge and furrow ploughland
Furlong	furlang	Old English	A block of plough strips, known by other names, like 'shot' and 'culture' in different regions	Scale(s)	scela	Old English	Hut on summer grazings; shieling
				Setter	sætr	Old Norse	Same as scales
Garth	garð	Old Norse	Small enclosure, paddock	Ship	sceap	Old English	Sheep, sheep pasture
Hads/ heads	hæfod	Old English	Land at the head land between two furlongs				
Hay, haya	haga	Old English	Hedge				
Land	land	Old English/ Old Norse	Ploughland, sometimes a plough strip				

LEFT: Llanddewi Brefi, the 'church of St David' in central Wales, surrounded by the fields that have sustained it through all its history.

PLACE-NAMES ASSOCIATED WITH HUMAN-MADE FEATURES

As the village communities grew, so the creations of the human-made environment became more prominent. Examples that can appear in the place-name record include the following.

NAME	ORIGINALLY	LANGUAGE	MEANING
Betws	betws	Welsh	A chapel
Borough	burh	Old English	A fortified place – often just a manor house
By	bý	Old Norse	Farm or hamlet
Chester	ceaster	Old English	A place the English associated with Roman military camps
Church	cirice	Old English	Church land
Cot/court	cot	Old English	Place where there are cottages – often the homes of the poorest members of the community
Ham	hām	Old English	Homestead – some of them developed into villages
Ingas	-ingas	Old English	People – presumably those associated with a local patriarch
Kill	cill	Gaelic	A Christian place or burial ground
Kirk	kirkja	Old Norse	Church/church land
Laker	leikr	Old Norse	A place for games
Llan	llan	Welsh	A church or an enclosure
Mark	mearc	Old English	Boundary land
Path	pæð	Old English	A path
Pit-	?	Pictish	A share of land
Playstow	Pleg-stow	Old English	A place for games and, in some cases, for meetings

NAME	ORIGINALLY	LANGUAGE	MEANING
Rath	ràth	Gaelic	A round fort/defended farmstead
Shire	scïr	Old English	Shire, boundary
Stoke	stoc	Old English	Holy place or small settlement
Stow	stow	Old English	Gathering place or holy place
Street	stræ	Old English	A word the English settlers used to describe Roman roads
Temple	temple	Mid. English	A property of the Knights Templar. In Celtic lands the word can come from the Gaelic teampull, a church
Thorp	Þorp	Old Norse	Hamlet or minor settlement linked to a larger one
Toft	topt	Old Norse	A house site or a house plot
Ton	tun	Old English	Can refer to a farmstead, an estate or enclosed land. Many tuns grew into villages
Tref, tre	tref	Welsh	Farmstead, homestead or hamlet
Wal/walh	walh	Old English	Relates to indigenous British ('Welsh') communities in areas dominated by English speakers

RIGHT: *The market cross in Lavenham, Suffolk, a village-sized settlement with the medieval status of a town*

THE
GROWING
VILLAGE

*A*s we shall see, many villages originated in a decision by someone in authority and were planned and built to a specified size and form. Most, however, began small and responded to favourable conditions by growing. Like raindrops, such villages needed nuclei to grow around, but many, perhaps most, villages resulted from growth around two or more nuclei or growth poles, with the originally distinct smaller settlements merging into one as they expanded. Such villages are agglomerations of different little clusters, but identifying these original cores can be quite a challenge.

Power in the countryside was largely in the hands of landlords – people like Anglo-Saxon nobles or *thanes*, Norman knights and aristocrats, bishops, abbots, abbesses and priors. These people were more likely than the villagers themselves to determine where on an estate the village should be. We

RIGHT: *Many villages bear the imprint of a strong master. At West Tanfield, in Wensleydale, the church is packed with monuments to the Marmions, the kings' champions in medieval times, and the status-seeking tower of the dynasty stands alongside that of the church. East Tanfield is a deserted village.*

have seen that open field farming required the concentration of the feudal land workers in village-sized settlements. Just where such settlements should be was not always obvious, for apart from some attractive situations on market roads and some negative ones, on flood-prone or swampy ground, the rules seem to have been quite vague.

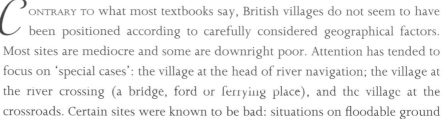

THE WHYS OF WHERE

*C*ONTRARY TO what most textbooks say, British villages do not seem to have been positioned according to carefully considered geographical factors. Most sites are mediocre and some are downright poor. Attention has tended to focus on 'special cases': the village at the head of river navigation; the village at the river crossing (a bridge, ford or ferrying place), and the village at the crossroads. Certain sites were known to be bad: situations on floodable ground or on wet, often waterlogged ground are obvious, while there seems to have been a case for avoiding the best ploughland if an alternative perch was available. *Bad sites* were sometimes adopted.

BELOW: *The halls of medieval lords, sometimes marked by 'burgh' or 'hallsteads' place-names, would often be moated, in imitation of the great castles. This is the old moat at Foxearth, Essex.*

The ports of Lynmouth and Boscastle on the North Devon coast were exposed to flash floods cascading down the valleys from Exmoor, and these resulted in the disastrous modern floods of 1952 and 2004 respectively. The medieval village of Cublington was on a poor, damp site and when villagers resettled the parish after it had been devastated by the Black Death, they chose a better-drained site on higher ground.

Probably the most important determinant of a village site was the quest for a position astride a reasonably lively *through-road*. Villagers did not like to be stranded in backwaters and local commerce depended on trade goods circulating between village markets and fairs. Siting on a pre-existing routeway is probably the most common factor in village foundation. In examining a village site it is useful to try to reconstruct the Roman, Dark Age and medieval road patterns. (I eventually made sense of the location of three villages in my native Nidderdale when I realized that their churches were all positioned beside a Roman route that had largely sunk back into the countryside.) The importance of a road link is exemplified by the cases of medieval villages that abandoned their original sites in order to exploit livelier roadside situations, as with Comberton in Cambridgeshire. Not all the best siting opportunities were snapped up by village founders. Royston, in Hertfordshire, has an exceptional location at the intersection of the ancient routeway, the Icknield Way, and the Roman Ermine Street, but it did not become an independent market centre until 1540.

ABOVE: *At Earls Barton in Northamptonshire, the nucleus is the Saxon church, which seems to occupy an older fortified position. It might itself have begun as a defencework, consisting just of the tower, which may have been used both as a refuge and place of worship by the local dynasty.*

One should never overlook the importance of *water transport* in medieval and Roman times. Land routes were often too rutted or boggy to allow the transport of bulky goods, like building stone, and a large portion of commerce in general travelled on waterways. The boats employed could be very narrow and what may seem today to be scarcely more than a ditch could have been the lifeline that gave a medieval village its reason for being. Village names and road names that include the elements '-staithe', '-hithe' or '-hythe' indicate old landing places.

The *village church* is explored in Chapter Five. As the estate (parish) churches partly took over from the first minsters in later Anglo-Saxon times, so the main founders of churches were the estate owners, who provided places of worship for their family and retainers, and then for their estate tenants. A village might grow around the nucleus of such a church – or else the church might be positioned within an existing village. Various churches, such as those at Okeford Fitzpaine in Dorset or Masham in North Yorkshire have been associated with finds of Anglo-Saxon pottery nearby, showing that the original village was huddled around its church.

In looking at the site of a village one can consider the local geology and the quality of natural drainage (some Fenland villages were judiciously sited on slightly raised islands of well-drained gravel). One can also look at the network of roads and dip into local history books to identify any Roman roads and the places that had markets, thus allowing the old pattern of commerce to be reconstructed. Then one might look for special advantages, like access to waterways that were navigable by narrow boats or proximity to a safe river crossing. *Fording places* (sometimes with '-ford' or '-wath' names) were particularly attractive and many later gained bridges. Adverse factors can also be considered, like liability to water-logging and flooding, remoteness from thoroughfares, altitude and exposure, and so on. If villages were scored out of ten according to the excellence of their situations I suspect that most scores would be clustered in the four to seven zone!

BUILT TO PLAN

*D*RIVE THROUGH a place like Castleton in Derbyshire, Boroughbridge in North Yorkshire, or scores of others and you will find that you are proceeding by a series of dog-leg turns. What does this remind you of? Not the winding Olde Worlde villages of the picture books, but rather the brash, young mega-cities of the New World. Straight lines and right angles do not populate the picture books, but they cover the desks of planners. Countless medieval villages *were* planned. This is to say, they were coherent visions that were transferred intact from the mind of the planner, usually the landlord or his agent, and then brought to life in the landscape.

BELOW: *The straight lines of medieval planning in the stunted town of New Buckenham*

Villages are beguiling and deceitful places. Their gnarled trees and mellow, lichen-encrusted stone may whisper messages about antiquity and random, piecemeal growth. However, when we take a dispassionate look at a great many villages, we find the half-hidden lines, angles and symmetry that tell of complete or partial planning.

Planned villages were the solutions that a lord or his agents produced in answer to particular problems. These challenges could be the removal of a population that was spread across an estate and its concentration in a purpose-built village, or the rehabilitation of an estate that had been badly disrupted by war. The best example of this concerns the hundreds of planned villages built in the reign of William the Conqueror (1066–87) to repopulate estates in the North East of England that had been devastated by the evil Harrying of the North in 1069–70.

Other reasons for a planned village include the establishment of a market village or the demolition and rebuilding of part of an existing village to accommodate a market, as at Sheriff Hutton, North Yorkshire and many other places.

BELOW: *The great house at Harewood: the development of its park resulted in the eviction of communities and their rehousing in a planned village beside a nearby turnpike road.*

Alternatively, the new village may have resulted from the need for a settlement for tenants, traders and retainers to accompany a castle, as at Corfe in Dorset, where the East Street and West Street run roughly parallel, each one directed towards the great castle.

THE HALLMARKS OF PLANNING

No village landscape should be explored without bearing in mind the possibility that the place may have been built to a plan. If this occurred in, say, Norman times then dwellings will have been rebuilt and converted on dozens of occasions and nothing of the original fabric will remain. However, planning tends to become fossilized in road patterns and property boundaries, and in the 'straight line and block' patterns that these form. Houses come and go but property lines live on.

Perhaps strangely, it is very often easier to glean the basic facts from a map than it is in the real place. Maps dispense with the 'noise' of colour and details and give a bird's-eye view of the simple geometry of layouts. They show which lanes are parallel, which junctions are at right angles and which property, lane and boundary patterns are 'rectilinear' or formed like a gridiron. The following hints should help.

Firstly, the motorist has the worst view, being low down, responsible for driving and seeing a rapidly shifting scene. You can drive through a village and see nothing but rows of dwellings fronting the high street and standing lengthwise on to the road and wall-to-wall. You are quite blind to the fact that each dwelling has a long plot running back at right angles to the high street as far as a back lane. Such an intricate and *integrated* pattern of street and lane, house and plot could not possibly have formed by prolonged, spontaneous growth. It has to have been built to a single plan.

Secondly, the commonest form of village planning, seen in thousands of examples, is the one that involves dwellings set closely along the through road, with plots or 'tofts' running back to a common boundary. Imagine that a village was built to such a plan in Norman times. By the end of the Middle Ages, each house might have been demolished and rebuilt on a dozen occasions. Each might have undergone three or four further rebuildings since the Middle Ages (houses becoming more durable with time). It is remarkable that so many village plans survive and that one may make a reasonable attempt at describing how one may have been set out perhaps 800 or even 1000 years ago. Roads, lanes and property boundaries have proved far more durable than houses. A less common plan is that of the square or triangular green, flanked on each side by dwellings. Milton in Cumbria (square) and Nun Monkton, North Yorkshire (triangular) are examples.

Thirdly, where gridiron plans are found in villages, they often indicate settlements that were created by ambitious landlords in the expectation that they would become trading towns. Hedon near Hull and New Winchelsea in Sussex became stranded half way, with building development proving insufficient to fill the grid that had been marked out on the ground. At Newtown (Francheville) on the Isle of Wight, hedgerows mark out the grid that the thirteenth-century plantation borough was hoped to fill. Medieval plantation towns were most numerous in Wales and New Radnor was a thirteenth-century fortress town which now displays a grid-based layout, a

Villages built to medieval plans
Examples of features to look for

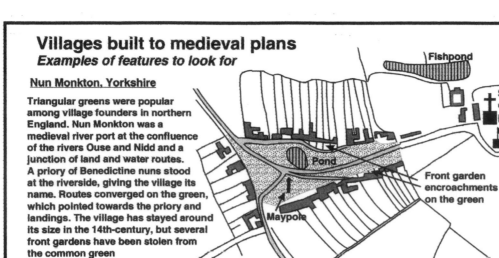

Nun Monkton, Yorkshire

Triangular greens were popular among village founders in northern England. Nun Monkton was a medieval river port at the confluence of the rivers Ouse and Nidd and a junction of land and water routes. A priory of Benedictine nuns stood at the riverside, giving the village its name. Routes converged on the green, which pointed towards the priory and landings. The village has stayed around its size in the 14th-century, but several front gardens have been stolen from the common green

New Radnor, Powys

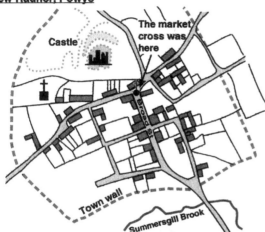

Several villages are failed planned medieval towns. In the mid-13th century, a new castle town with a protective wall was built at New Radnor. Commerce declined and by the end of the Middle Ages the borough was much decayed, but the remnants of the original 'grid-iron' lay-out of a main street intersected by three other streets is still apparent

Kimbolton Bedfordshire

The original village was unplanned and it straggled along its way past the church. In 1200, Geoffrey Fitz Piers bought the right to hold a market beside his castle. The section of the village between the church and the castle was completely redesigned and the road was diverted into a new, neatly planned commercial area flanking the Main Street

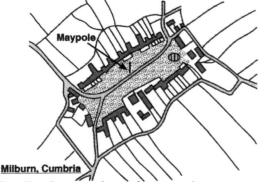

Milburn, Cumbria

The village is arranged around a rectangular green. Front gardens encroaching on the green are the only significant changes to the medieval plan

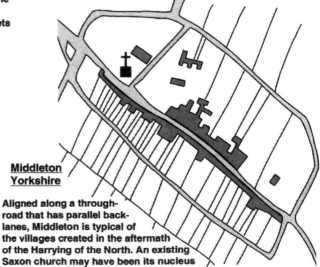

Middleton Yorkshire

Aligned along a through-road that has parallel back-lanes, Middleton is typical of the villages created in the aftermath of the Harrying of the North. An existing Saxon church may have been its nucleus

market street pointing to the mound that once carried the castle but the dimensions are those of a village. New Buckenham still preserves the grid layout created in the twelfth century by William Daubigny II. He placed it beside his motte and bailey castle which commanded the road between Norwich and Bury St Edmunds. It had a market green and gained a church, but the probable 80-house plots that were intended for households in what was essentially a new town may not have been filled. The place never expanded beyond the square ditch that surrounds it.

Fourthly, parts of existing villages could be demolished and built to a planned form. This was most common where markets or castles were inserted into a layout and where other features, like schools, almshouses or chapter houses, were introduced.

Finally, the planning motifs developed in medieval and earlier times were sometimes adopted by the Georgian and early Victorian crafters of 'villages of vision'. Often, their village creations were built to house populations dislodged by making landscape parks – like neatly planned Harewood outside the gates of the great house near Leeds.

BELOW: *Part of the replacement village at Harewood, where it was hoped that a position on a turnpike and a ribbon factory would stimulate employment.*

O F THE THOUSANDS of villages that were created between the reigns of the Anglo-Saxon kings and the disasters of the fourteenth century, a sizable minority would perish. Most, however, would grow. Even so, growth was not simply a matter of getting bigger, and various distinct and different patterns of growth are embedded in the landscapes of British villages.

Very frequently indeed, growth involved the merging of separate communities that had accreted around different cores. Often, careful examination of the village map will suggest that the village is a composite made up of, say, a community that lived around the village church; a community that had been established to serve a manor house or castle; a community associated with a monastic house, perhaps a priory or nunnery, or else a community of ecclesiastical officials; and finally, perhaps a community comprising tenants or retainers associated with a different manor in the locality. 'Lumpy' layouts, like stew with dumplings, can reveal these patterns on maps, where distinct clusters are seen within the village map.

BELOW: *The ruined church at Segenhoe in Bedfordshire. The congregation migrated across the village fields to a Norman castle site at Ridgmont.*

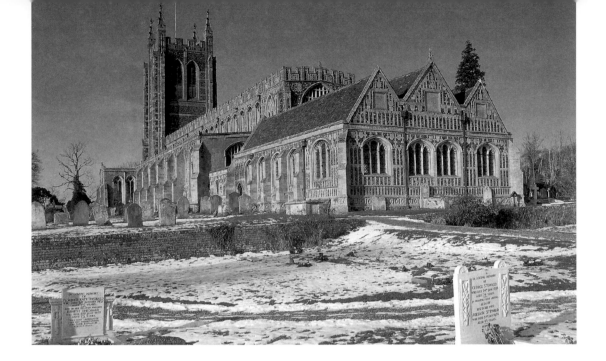

ABOVE: *Long Melford church bears witness to the importance of patronage by wealthy sponsors. Most was gained from the cloth merchants, the Cloptons, but other local dynasties, like the Peytons, also played a part in creating a magnificent palace of a church in the fifteenth century.*

OVERLEAF: *Abbotsbury: like many villages it experienced cycles of misfortune and recovery.*

Growth could take surprising forms – including that of the village that turns itself around. In the early days of Village England, small villages and hamlets seem quite often to have formed on ancient trackways and Roman roads at the places where these approached river crossings. Such trackways might later be overtaken by routeways running in different directions, *along* a valley rather than *across* it. The old settlements might then turn themselves around, growing to follow the along-valley rather than the cross-valley routes. Hampsthwaite in Nidderdale and several settlements in the River Cam valley near Cambridge are among the numerous examples.

According to the evidence of the datable pottery that they left behind, some villages migrated, caterpillar-like, across their townships, growing in one direction and decaying at the other. In Norfolk, the lure of common grazings seems to have caused the moves. Still more surprising are the cases of villages that leapfrogged their own fields in order to claim what seemed to be more desirable sites. For example, the village that had grown around its church at Segenhoe, Bedfordshire, in late Anglo-Saxon times was attracted to the site of a hilltop castle that was built in the locality at Rougemont (meaning 'red hill') in Norman times. Segenhoe was abandoned, while centuries later, Rougemont, by then Ridgmont village, was redeveloped as an estate village by the Duke of Bedford.

Many villages embody a history of wildly changing fortunes. Badly scarred by the Black Death, Abbotsbury in Dorset was already in decline when Henry VIII dissolved its monastery in 1538. The fabric of the village was damaged in a Civil War encounter and then in the early eighteenth century

the western section of the settlement burned down. However, in the nineteenth century there was a revival associated with basket- and rope-making industries and the railway link to Weymouth arrived in 1885. Severe misfortunes followed, with very high casualties being suffered amongst the village menfolk serving in the 1914–18 war. Today Abbotsbury survives in modest prosperity.

The growth or shrinkage of a village can be discovered from taxation records, but this involves difficult archive work. Much of the information is embedded in the village church. As a congregation grew, it needed a bigger church. This growth could be expressed in a heightening of the tower, the construction of one, and then two, side aisles to increase the capacity of the nave, an enlargement of the chancel, the raising of the nave roof and the creation of a clerestorey up above to admit extra light, and so on. Each phase is accomplished in styles of architecture that can be dated, so the church really is a vital source of village history.

OVER TO YOU

WE HAVE EXPLORED the village in its setting, discovering the character of the countrysides in which villages were founded, and have gone on to see how information about the history of the settlements is locked into their shapes.

For the reader who has never attempted to interpret a landscape or home place, historical and archaeological landscape research might seem a most daunting venture. Excavating sites or deciphering medieval Latin documents are, indeed, undertakings that demand skill and training. However, a great deal can be discovered without any prior training.

Doggedness is of great value, but another attribute will seem less obvious: the ability to make sense of *shapes*. It is the alignments seen in a village plan that suggest different possibilities, while a sensitivity to shapes can be acquired and developed. This helps in innumerable ways. You might see a road that seems out of alignment with a village, but which then 'dog-legs' and enters it. Who caused the road to divert into what must have been a new village and why was the village erected where it is rather than on the existing roadside? Lots of other useful questions like this could stem from the investigation of shapes.

It is the questions rather than the answers that build towards discoveries. With a working life devoted to geography and landscape archaeology I still cannot deliver *answers* to every query. But the *questions* that I ask of a landscape or a map have got better and better. So will yours.

The following tips may help.

TIP DISCOVERING THE VILLAGE OF THE FOUNDING FATHERS

1. Use the hints given earlier to attempt a reconstruction of the setting in which your village was founded. If you can use several books of place-name translations pick the translations that seem best to fit the topography and vegetation of each place concerned. Remember that what are on offer from the authors are guesses.

2. Make the maximum use of maps. The older the map you use, the further it takes you back in time. The last 50 years have seen stupendous rural changes. The Industrial Revolution began in about 1760 and it has been associated with accelerating urbanization and transformations. If you can find a map dated about 1750 it is likely to show a place far closer to its medieval appearance than to the setting as it appears today.

3. Question the staff at a record office or reference library for all you are worth – this is what they are there for. You should expect to see the very useful First Edition 6 inches to 1 mile Ordnance Survey maps that were produced in the years around and after 1850. There may be some slightly older and larger-scale tithe maps, but the remainder is largely a lottery. Privately drawn eighteenth-century maps at a scale of 1 inch to 1 mile or even large-scale estate maps dating back to Elizabethan times may exist. If there are any of the latter they will open a fantastic porthole on the past of the village.

4. Postcards and old photographs may reveal the Victorian and Edwardian village landscapes. Most villages had taken shape by then, but many fishing villages (beloved by photographers) were still growing.

5. You might ask yourself how Sherlock Holmes would have tackled a problem. Logical deduction has an important place. If a group of houses is seen standing on a green it is most unlikely that the green was formed around them and highly likely that they have encroached upon the village common.

6. The first time that you crack a little problem, the world may not care less. Yet you will feel a little glow, your confidence will surge and you will feel encouraged to tackle another problem. These things are enough in themselves to make it worthwhile.

4

THE VILLAGE GREEN

*W*HAT COULD BE more evocative of Olde Worlde England than the village green? The mere mention of the words conjures up pictures of maypoles, of milkmaids flirting with their shepherd swains and of the village sages seated under the spreading boughs of a chestnut. All this was once a part of the world of the village green – but a pretty minor part. Greens offer plenty of interest, but not much of that interest is of a romantic nature. When we take a more dispassionate look at the village green, we find a number of puzzles and contradictions. Villages were traditionally rather hungry places and all the local features had to merit their places in the scene. That being the case, no community could afford to have an extensive area of grassland just lying around waiting for May Day dances and a few trysting couples. Greens must have earned their keep; they must have had significant, *practical* functions – otherwise they would have been ploughed up or built upon.

When we look at the actual greens, we find that they all shared one essential feature: *they were all common land.* This is to say, they were shared among all those village tenants who had rights to plough or graze livestock in the common fields. As a result, one might expect that the manor court and the hallowed customary practices that were so important to the old communities would have preserved village greens for all time. Sadly, this was not the case. As we shall see, many greens were eroded by encroaching dwellings, while the Parliamentary Acts of Enclosure that 'privatized' so many strip fields, meadows and grazings also took swipes at the other commons in the countryside – the village greens. Quite a few village greens ended up in the squire's back yard in the Enclosure era, *c.* 1750–1850. Some

LEFT: *The maypole on the green at Aldborough; the ribbons around the pole show that it was recently used for dancing.*

ABOVE: *Cricket on the vast green at Eltisley in Cambridgeshire*

greens became the squire's garden. Most unusually, the process was reversed on one occasion: at Whittlesford in Cambridgeshire, a green was acquired quite recently, it being formed about half a century ago from derelict land that had been a garden in Georgian times.

Other than all being kinds of commons, our village greens prove on inspection to be a very mixed bunch indeed. Some are of vast, park-like dimensions; some are irregular; some are neatly defined triangles or rectangles; and some are just tiny pockets of land that take up a little space at a road junction. It is stretching the imagination to believe that an expanse of, say, 20 acres (c. 8.1 hectares) of grassland might be the same kind of thing as an island at a road junction, the whole of which could be shaded by a single tree. They may both be *commons* in *villages*, but there the similarity surely ends.

Therefore, we conclude that while commons known as 'greens' were features of a great many villages, they cannot all have had the same function. We must be meeting several different forces that created 'public lawns' within village landscapes for different purposes.

THE OLD CORRAL THEORY

One of the earliest attempts to explain village greens suggested that in unsettled Anglo-Saxon times, the greens had functioned as protective enclosures into which cattle were driven at night. These greens were ringed by dwellings, just as the covered wagons circled a defended area in the old western movies. This oft-quoted idea does not quite stand up to scrutiny when we take into account the following points.

Firstly, the little that we know about villagers' reactions to approaching war-bands suggests that, very sensibly, they would drive their cattle into remote woods or marshes and disperse them there, making it harder for foragers to find and steal the whole village herd. Then the immense variation in the size of greens tends to refute the theory. Some were far too large to serve as compact corrals and could have supported a multitude of wildebeest and some were so small that they could scarcely have pastured a couple of guinea pigs. Moreover, the ideal shape for such a compound would be circular, as many prehistoric examples show. However, few greens approach the circular form: irregular and angular shapes proliferate while it has been seen that numerous greens were deliberately set out to square and triangular shapes.

Let us not rule the old theory out entirely. There are some rectangular greens in the areas of England exposed to medieval Scottish raiding that were plainly created by an act of deliberate planning by the village founders. With controlled approaches to the green via lanes entering at the corners and cottages and farmsteads forming fairly continuous perimeters, it might just be possible that village greens like the one at Arncliffe in the Yorkshire Dales or Milton in Cumbria had defensive aspects.

THE MAYPOLE ON THE GREEN

Maypoles do not belong in the realms of romantic fiction: some villages had them, but given the perishable nature of the timber pole and the decline in folk customs in the Industrial Age, the maypoles seen on greens today – as at Aldborough and Nun Monkton, both near Knaresborough, or Ickwell Green in Bedfordshire – are likely to be modern replacements.

The village green, with or without a maypole, would tend not to be the only nor even the main venue for village recreation. The larger of the medieval fairs tended to be held in great open spaces, often *between* rather than *within* settlements. That ritual dancing took place in special fields rather than on greens in villages is evidenced by lots of field names, like 'Dancers' Meadow' or 'Dancing Plain', where dancing may have been associated with the great landmarks and festivals of the village year. 'May Field' is another common field name along with ones like 'Maypole Hill' and 'Maypole Ground', which show that maypoles were sometimes set up in fields rather than on greens.

OVERLEAF: *Fimber in the dry chalk country of the Yorkshire Wolds. Ponds like this one in the village green would have been useful for watering livestock moving on the hoof.*

There is also good evidence that village games, generally of a rather brutal and parochial complexion, were held in fields and grounds beyond the village designated as *plaistows* (i.e. 'place for games'). This is another common field name and survives in numerous places, as do similar names like 'Playing Close', 'Playsteds' and 'Pleasure Grounds'.

So far as dalliance was concerned, it appears that more pledges were made (and more villagers conceived) in the churchyard rather than on the green. Despite the best efforts of the authorities, the churchyard was the main venue in village affairs. It was there that villagers dashed with hot news and gossip; there that deals were struck; there that folk played board-type games and ball; and there that couples courted – without any gravestones then to deflect a ball or conceal a kiss.

The old records do not tend to offer very much information concerning maypoles – though one never knows one's luck. In my native township of Clint, in Nidderdale, it is recorded that in the early eighteenth century the maypole was dismantled after the local squire's son had some sort of accident playing on it.

There are some related place names, like Maypole Meadow, Newnham, Gloucestershire, and I have shown that the names show that poles could be erected on a hill or in a pasture outside the village area. The appearance of the old poles is uncertain though modern ones tend to be white with contrasting bands or spirals. Conifers, like those that provided straight masts for ships, were alien to England and it is not clear what would have been used for the straight upright shaft. The pole would have been slotted in a heavy stone base – of which there are probably quite a few lying part-buried and forgotten on greens. It would be easy to confuse them with the socketed stone plinths that held the shafts of market crosses.

Dancing at May was part of a collection of originally pagan, fertility-related rituals, which included the bringing of foliage from the greenwood and amorous nights spent there by the youngsters. Whitsuntide, May Day or Midsummer were the times for such festivities, different dates being preferred in different communities. Perhaps the maypole custom derived from the ancient and widespread practice of felling a tall, slender tree in the woods and erecting it in front of the homestead, where its greenery would symbolize rebirth. Occasionally, such specimens may have caused confusion, for a bush was the sign of a village ale-house. (The morris dancing tradition is described in the chapter that follows.)

THE VILLAGE POND

The pond could be an important adjunct to village life, and many lay within greens. In dry countrysides, like most chalk downlands, the presence of a natural supply of surface water could serve as a great magnet for settlement. Ashmore in Wessex is an ancient example, taking its name not from a moor, but from its mere.

Some ponds are fed by springs, but many village ponds are artificial, and such ponds seem to have been created since Iron Age times. *Dew ponds* were created – often by professional pond-makers – by excavating a hollow and then lining it with water-retentive puddled clay. Dew plays little if any part in filling these ponds; some have natural supplies, but surface run-off is usually the water source.

ABOVE: *Newton on Rawcliffe, where the pond might go back to the Norman foundation of the village*

Even medieval villagers familiar with typhoid, dysentery and plague may have hesitated to drink pond water, but it might safely have been used in brewing. Village ponds were probably most useful in providing watering places for livestock on the move. Attractive ponds like the one at Newton on Rawcliffe in the North York Moors, which may be Norman in age, or the example lying just across the Vale of Pickering at Fimber in the Yorkshire Wolds, are examples.

The lord of the manor raised his freshwater fish in a private fishpond away from village poachers, and while domestic ducks and mallard hybrids usually colonize village ponds, proper *duckponds* should have an island where the birds can roost free from predators. The presence of a pond within a green shows that they were both common resources, shared by the village community, while farmers often had their private stock ponds on the boundaries between fields.

TREES

Some greens boast several trees, some have but one, while many have none. One might be tempted to conclude that any green must be at least as old as the tree(s) growing on it – but let us be wary. My own research in northern England suggests that an oak there can reach an age of 800, so such a tree might have been standing before there was a green, or even a village.

ABOVE: *A tree and bench on the green at Aldborough*

In the Middle Ages and for a while afterwards, trees were habitually pollarded, especially those growing on commons. Crops of useful poles or fronds for animals to browse on were harvested every five to fifteen years or so from the crown or 'bolling' when the trees were repollarded. In most places, pollarding seems to have ended at least two centuries ago, leaving trees to grow in top-heavy form with ever-thickening branches springing from the old crown. Any large trees of this description seen on a green are likely to be at least two centuries old, and might even date back to the Elizabethan or Tudor eras.

Oaks, ashes and hornbeams may often be seen on greens with limes occasionally appearing. The wonderful old elms have largely disappeared, while beeches are too shallow-rooted and prone to fall to survive to great ages. Horse chestnuts were favoured as imposing trees offering expanses of shade and mature specimens are sometimes seen ringed by benches. Conkers for the young folk are an added advantage.

A few village trees have attained celebrity on account of their great ages (frequently greatly exaggerated) or their associations with famous people or events. A sycamore growing on the green at Tolpuddle in Dorset is the famous Martyr's Tree. It was the meeting place of the Friendly Society whose members attempted to organize against rural injustices, became the Tolpuddle Martyrs and were transported to Australia in 1834. Less celebrated is the horse chestnut on a little road junction green at Morton in Derbyshire. It is said to have been moved from the nearby churchyard and planted at the spot where a stagecoach overturned on a sharp bend.

Even with the most refined techniques, the ages of specimen trees are hard to deduce. As a tree grows, it becomes hollow and therefore it loses the heartwood that might be used for annual ring counts or carbon-14 dating. Its girth is influenced by its species and genes, the ground it is growing in, the local climate and the way it is managed. Being less affected by competition from neighbours, a tree on a green should grow more rapidly and in a more spreading manner than one in a wood. (There are trees beside some industrial villages that seem quite slender and young, but the hardships of pollution have held them back and insignificant-looking specimens may in fact be up to 300 years old.)

CONCLUSION

Village greens *could* be useful, but were not essential, for communal romps and rituals. They *might* harbour useful ponds, while any trees growing on them were not without their value. This does not amount to a compelling case for the existence of village greens and the real clues seem to lie in the enormous variation that is displayed. We need to look at the different sizes and shapes and ask how each type of green might have been so very useful as to be preserved through centuries of village history.

MAKING SENSE OF WHAT WE FIND

*N*O THEORY will stand up unless it explains why the different kinds of green should have been so important to the old village communities. Here are some suggestions.

THE REALLY BIG GREENS

There are many greens that are completely surrounded by their villages and which occupy but a fraction of the village area. At the other extreme, there are the vast expanses of grassland that have a village attached at one side. At places like Barrington in Cambridgeshire, a cricket field is almost lost in the green while at Long Melford in Suffolk, the spectacular and gigantic church is utterly dwarfed by the adjacent green.

If we look at the many varied maps that were drawn in the Elizabethan to early Georgian era – before the great commons were sliced up and put into private ownership by Parliamentary Enclosure – then we will see numerous strings of dwellings that straggled along the edges of commons. The builders of these houses must have seen a real advantage in living on the margin of a great, shared grazing resource. All the neighbours will have had their own animals on the common, mingling in the common herd. There is no reason to suppose that common pastures were any less attractive when the majority of villages formed in the eighth to the thirteenth centuries. Living on the edge of a green or common made good sense for the stockman. There is good evidence that pasture and meadowland were in short supply during the Middle Ages. Now, archaeological evidence has emerged from Norfolk to show that several communities actually abandoned their established homes and churches, leaving them behind in order to set up new homes beside precious commons.

This was proved on the basis of *field walking*, already mentioned. The technique requires that the land concerned has been tilled and that the field walkers can recognize the distinctive pottery produced in successive eras. Over the years, a thin general scattering of fragments from broken pots is formed as pottery discarded on the midden is spread on the fields along with the farmyard muck. However, a much heavier concentration of shards builds up in and around the village houses, as when fragments of broken pots are trampled into earthen floors. Now, if an archaeologist finds a concentration of Saxon pottery in one spot, Norman pottery nearby in the next and thirteenth-century pot fragments in the next, he or she may decide that these concentrations of broken pots chart the migration of the village. This is how the Norfolk discoveries were made.

BELOW: *One corner of the enormous green at Long Melford*

So the very big village greens seem likely to have originated as common pastures that attracted households to settle around their margins.

THE COMPACT MARKET GREENS

A great many village greens have compact forms, and some display quite distinct geometrical forms. Now, as explained in Chapter Three, wherever we find straight lines and neat, regular shapes we must think of planning. And whenever we think of planning then we think of some lord who had the clout to exert an influence on the landscape – which takes us to another explanation for many village greens.

Some medieval lords were very wealthy with numerous scattered manors, but many had inherited holdings that amounted only to a 'knight's fee': an estate just large enough to raise the income needed to arm and support a knight. The lord had a part of his estate that was worked by the bond tenants as a *demesne*, and he also had rents and various other dues – a couple of eggs here and the odd hen there. Opportunities for self-betterment were not very many, but one was extremely popular: *holding a market*. Village markets in themselves were not very exiting, but they did produce a handy trickle of income from fines and tolls: traders who came to market and broke the rules could be fined, as could 'forestallers', who traded illegally before they reached the authorized venue.

In twelfth- to fourteenth-century England one did not need to be a very imaginative lord to launch a market – everybody was doing so. As a result, the trade was spread too thinly and few markets really prospered. Within any region there was an attempt to protect market precincts and prevent a gross overstocking with mutually competing markets, though some areas, like Wensleydale, had far too many of them. Also, market days were staggered, so that neighbouring villages traded on different days.

Obviously, a market needed a venue. A very few were held in celebrated but detached settings, but the great majority took place in villages and towns. There were good reasons for this: there were captive communities of customers, albeit rather penniless ones; long-established road networks that already converged on these centres of population; and a church to cast its sanctifying eye on proceedings.

SO HOW DID THE MARKET AFFECT THE VILLAGE LANDSCAPE?

The first stage in the establishment of a market would occur when the landowner, bishop, noble or whoever was seeking to establish a market paid a 'fine' (really a fee or tax) to the monarch for the privilege of founding a new trading centre, though sometimes it was the monarch himself who launched a market. In 1282, for example, one Robert de Plumpton paid the king £10 for the right to hold a market at Grassington in Wharfedale. This was a large sum at the time and one may wonder whether Robert ever got it back.

The market-owner would already have a good idea about how the chosen village would be adjusted to accommodate its new market. The market might be tagged on to one end of the village. It might be slotted into a gap between rows of buildings. On the other hand, a wholesale demolition of houses might be involved in order to fit the market into the selected slot, say beside the

ABOVE: *The green that originated as a new town market place at New Buckenham*

churchyard, in front of the manor house or at a convergence of local roads. A customary market, held, say, in the churchyard might be given a new venue when its existence was formalized through the purchase of a charter.

The size of the market green might reflect the size of the market – or an optimist's view of its future size, as at New Buckenham. Many market greens are far larger than the market could have covered, but market charters usually included the bonus of an annual fair on the day of the saint to which the village church was dedicated. Fairs were much more fun than workaday markets – and some contained so much fun that they had to be housed outside the village, in a field. As the day of the fair (sometimes two days) approached, there would be a mounting sense of anticipation, for this would be the only time in the year when dealers in exotic goods came near the place.

Where the establishment of a new market was part and parcel of the planned creation of a village, the market green or square would often have the form of a tidy rectangle or triangle, with the dwellings arranged around the sides and plots or *tofts* running back from the dwellings. When the monks of Jervaulx abbey in Wensleydale founded the village of East Witton, just after 1300, and bought the right to hold a market there, the green had the form of a much elongated rectangle, with

RIGHT: *The stocks on the green at Aldborough*

roads arriving from different directions and entering at each corner. The monks of Byland abbey founded Old Byland village as lines of farmsteads arranged round a more compact, squarish green.

Another layout that was popular in northern England was that of the triangular green that was inserted into the acute angle at the intersection of three roads, often the place where a main road bifurcated, as at Hampsthwaite near Harrogate. Sometimes, a *headrow* (i.e. the row of dwellings at the head of the village) crossed the top of the forking 'Y'-shaped road layout. The famous Headrow in Leeds is a relic of what was still a village layout at the start of the nineteenth century. In some Scottish layouts, a *town house* stands at the head of the market triangle.

Market greens and market squares both originated in market charters purchased from the Crown by their landlords. When the trading area of a green was cobbled to give a hard surface, the term 'square' tended to be adopted. This happened when a successful market village was promoted to become a town but it was infrequent in villages.

Markets also had social effects on village populations that went beyond commerce and economics. As venues for meeting and mixing, they could always spawn the parochial excesses that coloured old village life. The presence of strangers could spark fights while ruffians were easily attracted. At markets in the vicinity of Ripon, foresters (often thugs and nuisances) from the Forest of Knaresborough were feared as trouble-makers.

LANDSCAPE RELICS OF A MARKET GREEN

The state of survival of old markets and market greens varies considerably. At Ripley, chartered in 1357, the triangular market square (really an elongated triangle) between the medieval church and castle is still well cobbled; the market cross is complete from its restored lantern head down to its stepped plinth, and the stocks at the cross base are still functional. In other cases, the market green has been built upon, while numerous other villages with greens were completely deserted. Relics of well-preserved markets and market greens include the following.

These marked and hallowed the place of the market and had designs similar to those of other crosses seen in churchyards or marking the boundaries of church lands. Instead of carrying a cross, they normally had lantern-shaped heads and they were supported on a shaft which might be stumpy and just waist-high or much taller than a man. The shaft would be slotted into a raised stone base, which was often polygonal and stepped. Sometimes the affairs were so arranged that wrong-doers could sit on the cross plinth with their feet, or feet and wrists, sticking out of the *stocks*.

Not all crosses were of this type. In the seventeenth century, a 'typical' market cross at Cheddar in Somerset was subsequently surrounded by a hexagonal arrangement of arches carrying battlements and at Abbots Bromley in Staffordshire, the six stout posts of the *butter cross* (associated with a market for butter) supported a pyramidical roof, thus giving some shelter to traders. A butter cross supported by eight posts and crowned by a weathervane can be seen at Harrold in Bedfordshire (where there is also a cylindrical stone *lock-up* on the green). At Tickhill, South Yorkshire, the cross has the splendid form of a cupola with a domed roof and a weathervane and it stands on a plinth of five steps. Perhaps the most charming example is the octagonal timber-framed market cross at Wymondham in Norfolk, with diamond-paned windows in each face, eight posts to support it and a pyramidical tiled roof.

Following the decay of a market, the cross would normally be reduced by stone-robbing. Protestant zealots would often vandalize market crosses just as they destroyed other crosses. Lantern heads rarely survive in place and a few have been replaced with crosses. Sometimes the stumps of shafts remain and the survival of cross bases is more common. Any overgrown slabs found on a green could easily be the last relics of a village market cross.

Market crosses are not the only crosses found on greens, for greens and squares are popular situations for village war memorials, which often adopt traditional cross-like forms, as at Ripley, or Finchingfield in Essex.

THE ELEANOR CROSSES

The most distinguished of village crosses had nothing to do with commerce. These are the Eleanor crosses, originally 11 in number and forming a chain from Harby in Northamptonshire to Westminster, each marking a place where the funeral cortege of Queen Eleanor rested in 1290. Examples survive at Geddington and Hardingstone in the county where she died and at Waltham Cross in Hertfordshire.

MOOT HALLS, MARKET HOUSES, GREEN HOUSES AND COURT HOUSES

Markets were also associated with buildings, *moot halls* or *market houses* or *green houses*. These were places where the 'court of pie powder' (named from an Old French reference to the dusty feet of those going to market) would meet on market days to settle disputes and exact fines. They were also places

RIGHT: *The cross in the market triangle at Ripley*

LEFT: *The stream and green at Finchingfield*

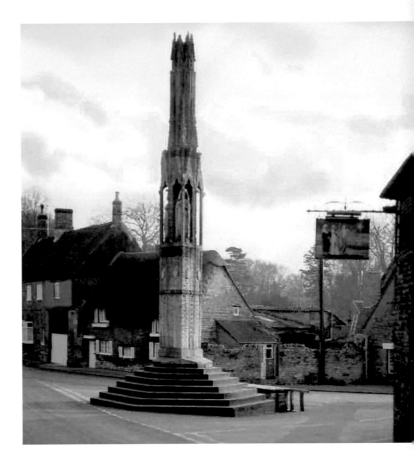

RIGHT: *The Eleanor cross at Geddington, Northamptonshire, marking one of the places where the funeral cortege of Queen Eleanor rested*

where the trestles and boards and other bits and pieces that were assembled to form stalls and the *shambles* where butchers worked could be stored under the courtroom between markets. (The famous Shambles in York was the street of the city's medieval butchers.)

A different type of *court house* is a less common survival: the court houses employed by the local manor courts. The fourteenth-century court house at Long Crendon in Buckinghamshire originated as a 'staple hall' or wool store but became the court room of the Queen's stewards, who controlled the local manor in the fifteenth century.

GUILDHALLS

Often similar in appearance are the *guildhalls*, usually built for village guilds involved with the village church and for local societies concerned with mutual assistance in times of illness and hardship. The guilds were generally linked to particular churches, so that a large village with more than one church might have more than one guild and more than one guildhall. A smaller proportion of these places were guildhalls used by trade guilds, and these places needed closer access to the market square or green.

The various public buildings associated with greens varied in appearance, some being rectangular and rather 'house-like', like the green house at Elstow in Bedfordshire. They can be very imposing structures, like the one at Winster in Derbyshire or the towering medieval cutlers' guildhall at Thaxted in Essex (see Chapter Three) and they can have unusual shapes, like the hexagonal house for the yarn market at Dunster in Somerset. Some display high-quality late medieval timber-framing, like the guildhalls at Stoke-by-Nayland, Suffolk and Whittlesford. Winster market house was carried on an arched base of stone and at Stoford in Somerset, the original guildhouse of 1353 may have been of timber but the surviving successor is a thatched building with fine stone mullioned windows and it dates from the sixteenth century.

As failing village markets fell out of use in the sixteenth, seventeenth and eighteenth centuries, so any remaining market houses became redundant. By the ending of the legal powers of trade guilds in 1835, most trade guildhalls had become obsolete, though some continued to be used by church societies. Many of the old public buildings stumbled on as schoolrooms or venues for church and parish meetings. Eventually, they have tended either to be conserved as local antiquities or refurbished as private houses. When they have passed into domestic use, the more heavy-handed conversions can make the old market house or guildhall hard to recognize.

GREENS OF THE SMALLEST SIZE
There are many bits of common land that cover a smaller proportion of the village area than a stamp does on an envelope. Either these greens have been greatly reduced or they are quite different from the grazing greens and market greens described so far. There are various ways in which these greens might form.

ROADSIDE GREENS
The tracks or 'drifts' entering a village might have broad, grassy verges, allowing livestock that were being driven on the hoof to slow down, spread out and nibble at the turf. Some *roadside greens* may amount to no more than the remains of former verges.

LANE GREENS
Several small villages are approached by ribbons of common land and these *lane greens* seem to have originated in a lane and its associated broad verges that at some time came to be regarded as a green.

THE LOCK-UP, WHIPPING POST AND STOCKS
The old village had various public structures that stood on pockets of public land. The lock-up where the constable banged up the local drunks and felons, the wretched *whipping post*, and the stocks all had their surrounding patches of ground. The structures often disappeared, but the patches of public ground might remain.

THE PINFOLD OR POUND
In the old days of open fields, unfenced commons and areas of private farming, the straying of beasts from the commons into cultivated strips or enclosed 'private' fields was a constant nuisance. Most farming communities employed a pinder who would 'arrest' trespassing animals and keep them in the

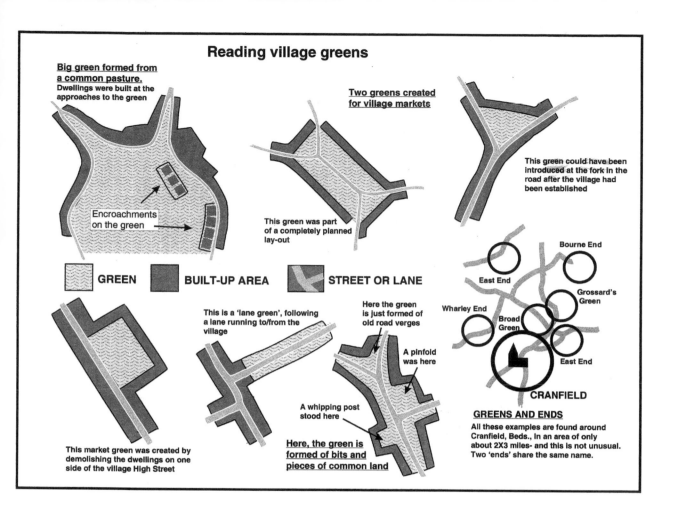

Reading village greens

Big green formed from a common pasture.
Dwellings were built at the approaches to the green

Encroachments on the green

Two greens created for village markets

This green was part of a completely planned lay-out

This green could have been introduced at the fork in the road after the village had been established

▓ **GREEN**   ▓ **BUILT-UP AREA**   ▓ **STREET OR LANE**

This is a 'lane green', following a lane running to/from the village

Here the green is just formed of old road verges

A pinfold was here

A whipping post stood here

Here, the green is formed of bits and pieces of common land

This market green was created by demolishing the dwellings on one side of the village High Street

Bourne End
East End
Grossard's Green
Wharley End
Broad Green
East End

CRANFIELD

GREENS AND ENDS
All these examples are found around Cranfield, Beds., in an area of only about 2X3 miles- and this is not unusual. Two 'ends' share the same name.

village *pinfold* or *pound* until their owners paid a fine and redeemed them. The pinfolds were small enclosures, usually much smaller than a school playground, but their fall from use and removal could lead to the existence of a patch of ground regarded as a green. Empty house, school or chapel sites might also become informal greens. Closely mown greens are relatively helpful places on which to search for buildings and structures – cross bases, dame schools (run by a village housewife, spinster or widow), former houses and pound walls might all be found as earthworks, protruding slabs or parched grass.

CONCLUSIONS

If these suggestions that greens of different shapes and sizes have distinctly different origins are valid then we might hope to be able to look at a green, on the ground and on the map, and identify its origins. This could well be true if these tricky packages of common land had maintained their original forms. Most have not, and the most widespread cause of the transformation and reduction of a green resulted from *encroachments*.

OVERLEAF: *The green house at Elstow: note how brick rather than wattle and daub is used to fill the panels in the timber frame.*

ENCROACHMENTS: WHITTLING AWAY AT THE GREEN

In theory, the existence of the green as a common open space should have protected it against incursions by individual house-builders: one can hardly start building in a public park. In reality, in times when the population was growing and needed new village houseplots, in times when there were more homeless paupers than the community or authorities could cope with, and in times when the value of the green to the community had diminished, the building of new dwellings or lines of dwellings on the green could occur.

Greens could be entirely devoured by encroachments, or the intrusions might affect just a corner of the green. At Barrington and many other places, the encroachment forms an island of housing on the green. The village sleuth will not find it difficult to recognize some encroachments: the island of dwellings stranded in the green, the part of the village's built environment that juts right out into the green, or the solitary house among the lawns are all quite easy to identify. Other encroachments can be recognized when the smooth property line of house frontages suddenly jigs to carry the houses towards the heart of the green.

Encroachments could, indeed, devour a village green. At scores of villages, including some famous picturesque examples, like Lower Slaughter in Gloucestershire and Okeford Fitzpaine in Dorset, the expansion of building on to some or all of their greens has changed the village landscape. However, this was not necessarily an irreversible process. An inspection of old maps will reveal some encroaching buildings that have now gone – like the six homesteads shown forming a broken line running down the middle of the green at East Witton in a map of 1627.

When a green has been closely mown, it is not unusual to detect slight steps, ridges and level platforms denoting places where buildings have stood. Sometimes, the edges of stones may be peeping through the turf, while in times of drought, the parching of the grass growing over buried stonework can be quite distinct. The buildings detected might be former encroaching houses, or perhaps an old market house or lock-up, though if the traces are very localized, the buried relic might be a market cross or maypole base.

Front gardens in old villages are very usually the products of the enclosure of an old green. Before the development of a 'cottage garden whimsy' in the nineteenth century, cottages and farmsteads did not have front gardens. Sometimes, land would be taken, piecemeal, from a green to become a private front garden, and sometimes Parliamentary Enclosure would carve up the whole green. There are scores of examples, like the front gardens of Fearby and Cold Kirby, both in North Yorkshire, and of Knock in Cumbria. Greens tended to be pinched to become front gardens when their original uses had been devalued so that the community did not resist the privatization of common property. Lines of front gardens seen strongly suggest that neighbours had agreed a carve-up of their green.

SOME INTRIGUING ODDMENTS

By looking at the big grazing greens, the market greens, the tiny greens and encroachments, we have covered the main themes that the village sleuth should be aware of. However, Britain would not be Britain if we could not boast a wealth of intriguing exceptions. Here are some of them.

ABOVE: *Front gardens bordering a green, as at Fearby, near Masham, are almost invariably encroachments on the old common.*

There are a small number of villages that have greens associated with much earlier archaeological features. At Piercebridge, County Durham, the green corresponds to the layout of a Roman camp, while at Aldborough the attractive, sloping green covers part of a lost Roman town.

Throughout England, particularly in wooded country, settlements called 'Green' and 'End' abound. Nobody is quite sure where they all came from or whether they are older or younger than the larger villages. Often, *greens* and *ends* seem to be satellites of larger villages, lying at, or just beyond, their extremities. The 'ends' seem to be so called because they lie at the end of a village or the end of a township, so that Park End, Green End and Town (the old word for a village) End were at the end near the park, green and village respectively. The greens were hamlets or small villages that were so called because a little green was a key component of the settlement. Many of them must have resulted from a drift of households to settle around a peripheral patch of common grassland.

In some localities associated with anciently wooded country, the ends and the greens become the basic units of settlement rather than larger, plump villages. Quite often their names include a surname, perhaps of the person who had been the leading landowner or farmer in the locality when the little village or hamlet was forming?

We usually think of greens as lying at the heart of villages, where the roads coming in from different directions intersect, but there are a number of greens that are peripheral to their villages, as at Llanwda, near Pembroke. Lanes with wide verges could exist as the lane greens (see p.104) running to and from villages, as was the case with Youlthorpe, East Yorkshire.

5

THE VILLAGE CHURCH

*T*HE FIRST GLIMPSE of a village that the traveller sees from afar is often the steeple of its church. Imagine what a towering symbol of community this must have been in earlier medieval times, when the village dwellings were insubstantial, single-storey hovels and the church that loomed over them was usually the only stone building in the settlement. Churches were concerned with the formal organization of worship, but the village church became much more than this. It was the favourite venue for proclaiming news or danger and exchanging gossip, a focus for wide-ranging social activities and it was charged with awesome responsibilities to 'speed the plough' and secure an abundant harvest. It was the true focus of communal life in days when churchgoing was almost universal and often obligatory.

Most of the literature on village churches has tended to be written by art historians and architects, who are concerned with the architectural styles employed and the quality of their execution. Here, the emphases are on the church *within* the village community and the church *within* the village landscape. With good books on church architecture and the layouts for liturgy abounding, here I have focused on the church in its place and among its people.

LEFT: *The Saxon tower of the church at Barton on Humber, with typical round and triangular headed windows and raised band or 'strapwork' decoration. The visible architecture provides no hints of several important rebuildings as evidenced by the excavation of the church.*

WHERE DO
CHURCHES
COME
FROM?

*C*HURCHES DISCLOSE some of their history very readily to any visitor who can recognize the Saxon, Norman and Gothic styles that are portrayed in so many books. But there are other secrets that they hang on to and the early phases in the lives of most of the older village churches are usually shrouded in mystery.

An imaginary but not unusual church might reveal a twelfth-century nave, a thirteenth-century tower and some windows inserted in the early fourteenth century. However, if we were able to *excavate* the nave we might discover the bases of rubble-filled Norman pillars. Then, if we could analyse the stains in the adjacent soil, or perhaps discover finely wrought fragments of metal from the binding of an ancient bible, we might find evidence of one or more timber-walled Anglo-Saxon churches, the existence of which was totally unsuspected by later generations. Barton on Humber church is famous for its Saxon tower, but excavation revealed an earlier Saxon church and six major building phases in the centuries that followed the building of this tower. In terms of its age and history, the church is like the iceberg that only shows a portion of its mass. Often, the chancel arch was the most stable feature that remained as rebuilding succeeded rebuilding.

The first generation of Anglo-Saxon churches, some in villages and some not, were the *minsters* (from the Latin, *monasterium*). The name endures in cases like York Minster, Wimborne Minster and Ripon Minster and minsters were established from the seventh century onwards. In the case of Wimborne Minster, the church can be traced back to a double monastery founded for monks and nuns around AD 700. These were not parish churches as we understand them. Rather, they were staffed by a body of clergy, and the priests or monks would travel from the minster to preach, often in the open, at settlements and places where people congregated. In Wales from the tenth century there were *clasau*, which were staffed by an abbot and canons and resembled the minsters of England, while in Ireland and Scotland, the Celtic church was based on the monastery and was introspective rather than evangelical.

Some minsters may be revealed by dedications to obscure saints – in Cornwall and Wales such saints may often have been their founders. A popular early dedication, often associated with English minsters, was to St Mary the Virgin, as with the parish church on Holy Island, Northumberland, which may stand on the site of the church founded by St Aidan.

The Anglo-Saxon minsters of England can be surprisingly hard to identify and many examples must remain undiscovered. A rebuilding in one of the centuries after the Norman conquest leaves a building indistinguishable from parish churches. However, in some cases, daughter churches maintained a relationship with their minster or mother churches. The Rogation Days in spring (the Monday, Tuesday and Wednesday before Ascension) were, in ancient customs, 'Gangdays', from the old word, still used in North East England, associated with walking. Villagers would follow their priest as he beat the bounds

RIGHT: *Look about three-fifths of the way down the tower and then a little to the right. Can you see a string course? Perhaps you do not know what a string course is. Well, it is a sort of projecting band of stone. No, not the one that is running into the lancet. The sloping string course – no, that is the eaves. Look down a bit ...*

Bell tower added in 1836

The minster church of the Cs 7th-8th was rebuilt in the C12th by monks from the nearby priory and then again in the C13th, creating the pointed arches

Trace of former roof

Head of former window

of the parish and sometimes villagers would process to the old mother church in a neighbouring parish. Evidence of such Rogationtide or Gangday ceremonies may unveil an old minster.

A very high proportion of minsters were sited on royal estates – not least because kings needed literate people to record rents, obligations and their estate economies. Thus it was sound practice to establish priests – the only literate people around – on a royal estate. Churches located on estates or *vills* that Domesday Book of 1086 shows to have been owned *directly* by the king have a much higher probability of being minsters. Sometimes the old minster links persisted through centuries of trauma and change. Medieval churches in the Knaresborough area had links with the ancient minster in the declined Roman focus of Aldborough, even though the patterns of settlement and trade had greatly changed. Research into medieval links with other churches, the provision of priests and preaching in outlying places could unveil a minster and its daughters.

Minster names, like Little Minster or Minsteracres, are very obvious, but there are other clues to very early churches: the 'Eccles' names. Eccles, Eaglesfield, Exley and so on could derive from the Latin *ecclesia*, 'a church', and reveal very early centres of worship.

Later in the Anglo-Saxon era, estate owners tended firstly to provide churches for the use of their families and immediate retainers. They needed only tiny naves and services could even be held in the bases of their towers. Then these churches expanded to serve the whole estate. The *estate* became the *parish* and the new churches, sometimes called 'field' or 'proprietorial' churches by the experts, became *parish churches*. Thus, a different system of parish churches, rectors and vicars and diocese came into being, with a single clerk presiding over the church and with the congregation being the population of its parish or estate. Now people came to church rather than having the church come to them. As ancient estates fragmented, so different churches served the portions. These divisions might be distinguished by names like 'Great'/'Little', 'East'/'West', 'Magna'/'Parva', and so on, as with East Meon and West Meon near Petersfield. Sometimes they took the names of their respective churches, like Stoke Holy Cross with a dedication that distinguished it from Upper Stoke, Ashby St Mary, Rockland St Mary, Thwaite St Mary and Caistor St Edmund, all near Norwich.

In the early days of conversion in the Celtic-speaking west, all the monks or missionaries were 'saints' and they normally came from the nobility. We know nothing or next to nothing about most of them, but we do know that churches dedicated to obscure Celtic saints are usually very early. A few such saints extended their work into eastern England, where Celtic dedications, to St Cedd, for example, tend to suggest ancient foundations.

THE
CHURCH
AND THE
DEVIL

*T*HIS IS AN AGE OF LURID, fantasy history, full of stories of witchcraft, Knights Templar, paganism, Holy Grails and nonsense that the facts can never support. The idea that the countrysides of the medieval British kingdoms were permeated by witchcraft and satanic practices is quite false. There are a few connections with paganism, some inevitable, but some rather surprising and the most important points follow.

CHRISTIANITY AND PAGANISM

During the conversion era, in the middle centuries of the Anglo-Saxon era, the Christian missionaries found it expedient to take over the sites used for pagan worship and 'Christianize' them, thereby appropriating their mantles of sanctity. Throughout Britain, *holy wells* were taken over and given Christian rather than pagan patrons, so that the well of the pagan goddess Annis would often become St Anne's well. Similarly, in Ireland and Wales, pagan *standing stones* would be inscribed with the sign of the cross. The most dramatic instance is that of the church at Rudston in the Yorkshire Wolds, which stands right beside a prehistoric monolith that is 8 m (*c*. 26 ft) tall. *Solitary churches* with topographically dramatic situations are always likely to have pagan precursors.

Witchcraft was not endemic in medieval England and witch burning was not a practice. The few who were accused were likely to be people with an inheritance that was coveted, people with mental or physical disorders that were not understood at the time, widows who might be thought burdens

BELOW: *The prehistoric monolith that attracted the siting of the church at Rudston in the Yorkshire Wolds*

on their community or family or those prone to deviant or violent behaviour. Judged by modern conceptions of witchcraft, the majority of medieval villagers, particularly the women, might be considered witches or wizards. They all had profound knowledge of herbal medicines and many were influenced by superstitions. Many of the remedies worked and were all that was available to a village by way of medicine. Many of the superstitions were entirely ridiculous and were seen as such at the time by the more rational people in the community.

There seems to have been a few scattered instances of pagan practices, explaining the practice of locking font covers so that holy water could not be stolen for use in pagan rites. Far more remarkable is the often quite blatant use of pagan symbols in Christian churches. *Sheila-na-gigs* are lewd and blatant female images that seem to be fertility symbols linked to pagan traditions. An example can be seen on a possibly older slab built into the tower of the church at Whittlesford in Cambridgeshire, where a woman is shown with a goat. Though pagan, these symbols need not be older than the conversion to Christianity and might be associated with local cults. Pagan symbols have also been found under the altars of some Welsh churches.

Far more numerous are *green men*, also fertility symbols but less sinister, which are usually depicted as an elfish head that has a pair of large vines issuing from its mouth. Crowcombe in Somerset, Melbourne in Derbyshire and Landbeach in Cambridgeshire, which has at least three green men, are among the many churches containing green men, which may be carved on stone or on wood. Plenty of examples were perfectly obvious to the medieval incumbent of the church and to the bishop on his visitations. One can only conclude, therefore, that they express the church's burden of responsibility for the fertility of the village lands and embody an attempt to hedge bets by invoking any pagan and cultish help that might be going. Green men can be found in all sorts of places – carved into the stone capitals of pillars, on woodwork or far up and largely out of sight in the roof timbers. There is always a chance that a hunt will turn up something, even if the green man and his cult remain partly mysterious.

The church had its own Christian symbolism. For the villager, medieval worship was not an intellectual exercise. The Latin masses were largely incomprehensible. Religion was about fear and retribution but it also provided the rituals that gave comfort and meaningfulness to birth, marriage and death. The walls of churches were brightly painted and emblazoned with images of the saints. Most prominent was likely to be a *Doom painting*, which gave an uncompromising message about the torments awaiting sinners in Hell.

We must remember that medieval, Elizabethan and later congregations had rich understandings of *symbolisms*, both Christian and lay. Images that seem no more than pictures to our eyes conveyed quite specific meanings to our forebears. The instances run into thousands, but, for example, a hammer was an instrument of Christ's passion, a saw was a symbol of Joseph, Mary's husband, and

LEFT: *A green man is included in the vibrant Norman carving around the door of the church at Kilpeck, near Pontrilas. He is directly beneath the end of the arch.*

RIGHT: *The church at Whittlesford where a slab depicting a blatant sheila-na-gig is incorporated immediately below the clock*

ABOVE: *A restored panel in the facade of Lincoln cathedral provides a warning of the fate in store for sinners.*

also of melancholy, a lily symbolized purity and a flag like the cross of St George symbolized the Christian victory over death.

Harmless rituals that must have been partly related to the cult of fertility survive in our many *morris dancing* troupes. In England, these experienced a great revival with the rediscovery of folk music and dance traditions during the last century or so, though it is not widely known that dozens of similar troupes have been established among English-speaking communities overseas. The origin of the name is controversial: it might come from 'Moorish' or from the Latin, *mores*, associated with customs. The antiquity of the tradition is not in doubt and the earliest record known is from 1448.

EVIDENCE OF
CHURCHES
PAST

A CHURCH NEED NOT outlive its community, while congregations could dwindle away to leave a church abandoned and derelict. As we have seen, communities may drift away and new church sites can be exploited. There must be hundreds of early church sites still awaiting recognition by archaeologists. A technique for recognizing the former presence of a church that is available to all is one that is based on the evidence of place-names. Thus, Llandovery was *Llanddyfri*, which is the *llan* or church by the stream, Llanddewi is the Church of St David, while Kilbride is the church or priest's cell dedicated to St Bridget. The following table gives the commonest of names linked to places of worship.

Place-names associated with places of worship

Name part	Language	Meaning
Betws	Welsh	Chapel
Capel	Welsh/Old French	Chapel
Carn	Cornish/Welsh	Stone pile, sometimes ancient tomb
Celli	Welsh	Grove, sometimes sacred
Cill/kill	Gaelic	Church, burial ground, priest's cell
Cirice	Old English	Church
Crois	Gaelic	Cross
Cross	Middle English	Cross
Crows	Cornish	Cross
Cruc	Old Welsh	Burial mound
Eccles/eagles	Vulgar Latin	Early church
Episcopus	Latin	Bishop
Ermitage	Old French	Hermitage
Frater	Latin	Monk or friar
Funta	Old English	Spring, sometimes holy
Graf/grove	Old English	Grove, sometimes holy
Gwydfa	Welsh	Ancient burial mound
Haugr/how	Old Norse	Burial mound
Hob	Middle English	Association with the Devil (or with tussocks)
Holy-	Old English	Holy (-wood, -well, -head, etc.)
Hlaw/law	Old English	Burial mound
Kirk	Old Norse	Church
Llan	Welsh	Church, church enclosure
Lund	Old Norse	Small wood or sacred grove
Men/maen	Cornish/Welsh	Stone, often a standing stone
Minchin	Old English	Refers to nuns
Minster	Latin/Old English	Monastic church
Quoit	Cornish	Stone Age tomb with massive capstone
Stock	Old English	Sometimes a holy place (or tree stumps)
Stow	Old English	Place of assembly or worship
Teampull	Gaelic	A place of worship
Temple	Middle English	Place associated with Knights Templar
Tump	Old English	Ancient tomb
Well	Old English	Spring, sometimes holy
Weem	Gaelic	Cave, sometimes home of a saint
Winn	Old English	White or holy

THE CHURCH AND ITS SITUATION

CHURCHES ARE FOUND in a wide manner of locations relative to their villages. Any exploration of the position of the church is likely to yield useful information about the history of the village.

Churches situated in the heart of a village could be the nucleus (or one of the nuclei) around which a village has grown. Alternatively, the church could have been provided to serve an existing young settlement. The area around a

OVERLEAF: *The village church in the biscuit-coloured local greensand stone at Denver in Norfolk*

'core' church may be built up and the houses may be quite old, but even so they could represent encroachments on an earlier church green as at Okeford Fitzpaine, Dorset and many other places (see Chapter Four).

Numerous villages, usually the larger ones, have more than one church. This might simply reflect the size of the population and congregations, but in other cases it reflects the fact that a village was divided between more than one manor, with each manor supporting a church. In the extreme case of Swaffham Prior in Cambridgeshire, St Mary's and St Cyriac's share the same churchyard. The village was split between two parishes and so it had two parish churches.

Some rural churches are isolated. These are always interesting and the following possibilities should be considered:

1. The church may have served a village that came to be deserted (see Chapter Seven). Often, the village was evicted from a new landscape park, leaving its church behind.
2. The church could have been attracted to a pagan sacred site – *holy springs*, a prominent hilltop, an ancient standing stone or prehistoric earthwork, etc.
3. Perhaps the area has a long settlement tradition of hamlets and farmsteads rather than villages, so the church is positioned at a convenient mid-point.
4. The village may have migrated from its original location and the site of its church, as at Weasenham St Peter in Norfolk or Caxton in Cambridgeshire.
5. There remains the possibility of bizarre and unique choices. In Cornwall, a church is said to mark the place where the cart carrying the body of the hermit-princess, St Endellion, stopped and she was buried. Legend claims she was murdered by the owner of a field into which her goat had trespassed.

Occasionally, wealthy patrons who paid for the building of a church would position the building roughly at some mid-point between their mansion and the estate village that provided the congregation, as at Birstwith in Nidderdale.

Hilltop churches are fascinating. They are often dedicated to *St Michael*, the archangel. The hilltops were often associated with pagan worship and St Michael may have been seen as an apt replacement for the equivalents of Hermes and Mercury in the British assemblage of pagan deities. The most dramatic example stands inside the Iron Age hill fort on Brent Tor (also spelled Brentor), Dartmoor.

A number of churches are associated with foundation legends concerning satanic interference. In the case of Brentor, it was believed that local people who were building a church at the foot of the tor (hill) were continually frustrated by the Devil, who moved the stones to the top. Eventually, they decided to give in, but he still interfered with their church building. So they called upon St Michael, who hurled a boulder that hit the Devil between his eyes and ended the altercation.

Reading village church settings (1)

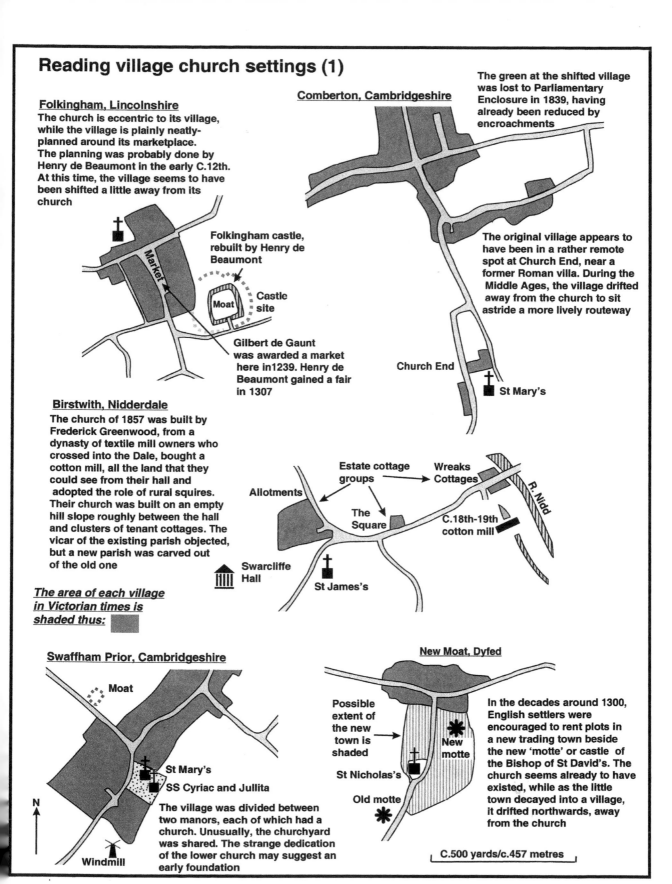

Folkingham, Lincolnshire

The church is eccentric to its village, while the village is plainly neatly-planned around its marketplace. The planning was probably done by Henry de Beaumont in the early C.12th. At this time, the village seems to have been shifted a little away from its church

Folkingham castle, rebuilt by Henry de Beaumont

Moat

Castle site

Market

Gilbert de Gaunt was awarded a market here in1239. Henry de Beaumont gained a fair in 1307

Comberton, Cambridgeshire

The green at the shifted village was lost to Parliamentary Enclosure in 1839, having already been reduced by encroachments

The original village appears to have been in a rather remote spot at Church End, near a former Roman villa. During the Middle Ages, the village drifted away from the church to sit astride a more lively routeway

Church End

St Mary's

Birstwith, Nidderdale

The church of 1857 was built by Frederick Greenwood, from a dynasty of textile mill owners who crossed into the Dale, bought a cotton mill, all the land that they could see from their hall and adopted the role of rural squires. Their church was built on an empty hill slope roughly between the hall and clusters of tenant cottages. The vicar of the existing parish objected, but a new parish was carved out of the old one

Estate cottage groups

Wreaks Cottages

Allotments

The Square

R. Nidd

C.18th-19th cotton mill

Swarcliffe Hall

St James's

The area of each village in Victorian times is shaded thus:

Swaffham Prior, Cambridgeshire

Moat

St Mary's

SS Cyriac and Jullita

The village was divided between two manors, each of which had a church. Unusually, the churchyard was shared. The strange dedication of the lower church may suggest an early foundation

N

Windmill

New Moat, Dyfed

Possible extent of the new town is shaded

New motte

St Nicholas's

Old motte

In the decades around 1300, English settlers were encouraged to rent plots in a new trading town beside the new 'motte' or castle of the Bishop of St David's. The church seems already to have existed, while as the little town decayed into a village, it drifted northwards, away from the church

C.500 yards/c.457 metres

Reading village church settings (2)

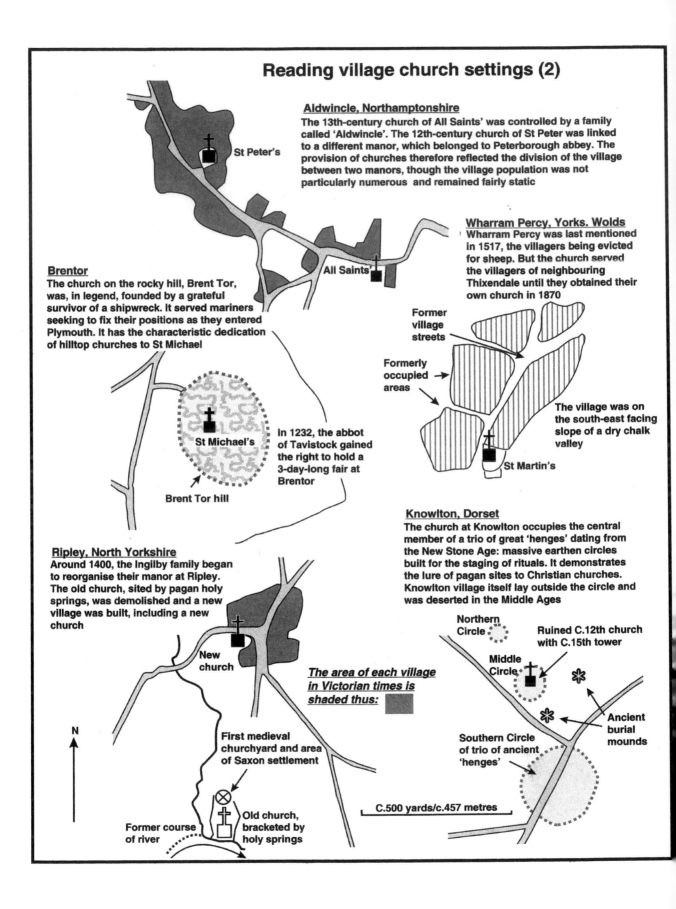

Aldwincle, Northamptonshire
The 13th-century church of All Saints' was controlled by a family called 'Aldwincle'. The 12th-century church of St Peter was linked to a different manor, which belonged to Peterborough abbey. The provision of churches therefore reflected the division of the village between two manors, though the village population was not particularly numerous and remained fairly static

St Peter's

All Saints'

Wharram Percy, Yorks. Wolds
Wharram Percy was last mentioned in 1517, the villagers being evicted for sheep. But the church served the villagers of neighbouring Thixendale until they obtained their own church in 1870

Former village streets

Formerly occupied areas

The village was on the south-east facing slope of a dry chalk valley

St Martin's

Brentor
The church on the rocky hill, Brent Tor, was, in legend, founded by a grateful survivor of a shipwreck. It served mariners seeking to fix their positions as they entered Plymouth. It has the characteristic dedication of hilltop churches to St Michael

St Michael's

In 1232, the abbot of Tavistock gained the right to hold a 3-day-long fair at Brentor

Brent Tor hill

Knowlton, Dorset
The church at Knowlton occupies the central member of a trio of great 'henges' dating from the New Stone Age: massive earthen circles built for the staging of rituals. It demonstrates the lure of pagan sites to Christian churches. Knowlton village itself lay outside the circle and was deserted in the Middle Ages

Northern Circle

Ruined C.12th church with C.15th tower

Middle Circle

Ancient burial mounds

Southern Circle of trio of ancient 'henges'

Ripley, North Yorkshire
Around 1400, the Ingilby family began to reorganise their manor at Ripley. The old church, sited by pagan holy springs, was demolished and a new village was built, including a new church

New church

The area of each village in Victorian times is shaded thus:

N

First medieval churchyard and area of Saxon settlement

Former course of river

Old church, bracketed by holy springs

C.500 yards/c.457 metres

Various church towers around the British coast served as useful sea marks, helping vessels to navigate into harbour. Some towers may have been positioned for this purpose. The one on the volcanic crag of Brent Tor was used by navigators entering Plymouth and legend claims that the church was provided by a grateful shipwreck survivor. The church tower at Happisburgh in Norfolk was a very important sea mark. That it was not always effective is evidenced by the numerous shipwreck victims buried in the churchyard.

CHURCH AND PEOPLE

THE RELATIONSHIP between the village church and its congregation changed greatly over the centuries but it was always important. The days of mystification and the Latin mass, the terrifying Doom painting and the fining of villagers for non-attendance are long gone. However, most village churches date back to the medieval era, or even to the middle Saxon period. The church is a magnificent repository for village history that sometimes spans more than 1000 years; churches have shared their fates with their village congregations, growing in good times and sometimes being reduced when times were hard.

RIGHT: *Morris dancing has regained its popularity and can be seen on many village greens. Members of The Poacher team are shown here.*

ABOVE: *At Branston church in Lincolnshire the fabric of the church can be 'read'. The door and its flanking arches are Norman but the alternating upright and horizontal slabs stacked vertically near the right-hand margin comes from a Saxon corner made with 'long and short work'. In the side wall of the tower between the above features one can see a round-headed or Romanesque arch that was subsequently blocked.*

OVERLEAF: *Kilham has one of many misfit churches, with congregations declining when Driffield, nearby, captured much of the village's commerce.*

THE CHURCHYARD

It is said that churchyards that are oval rather than square denote ancient foundations. Such yards were said to be associated with the enclosures of Celtic monasteries and they are most common in the Celtic lands but may be found elsewhere, as at Bramham and Sherburn in Elmet, near Leeds. This 'shape–age correlation' should not be over-stretched.

Medieval churchyards were free of gravestones, but amongst the mounds and odours people would play, deal, gossip and pet, sometimes to extremes and to the consternation of their priest. Gravestones give us the names of former villagers – family names that may still be common in the population – and they tell us about life expectancy in former times (though the graves of infants were seldom marked in this way, so the high levels of child mortality are not revealed). As they age, stones become patterned with the circular white, green, orange and grey colonies of lichen. The dated stones show the growth rates of lichen, which may be compared to lichen growths on undated masonry to provide very rough estimates of age.

The churchyard is likely to contain a cross to hallow the ground, while other crosses may be housed inside the church, or even be built into the fabric of its walls. Their origins are often problematic. A cross with Anglo-Saxon or Anglo-Danish decoration could well be a relic of times before the church was built, when monks preached in the open. It could have stood at the site of its successor church, but it could easily have been imported from some distance away – perhaps giving service as a gatepost for some intervening centuries.

Some churches house relics from abbeys plundered at the time of the Dissolution, like the rood screen loft at Hubberholme church in the Yorkshire Dales. Several churches, like Kirkdale minster in the North York Moors, have crosses that predated the church incorporated in their walls by their builders, while Little Shelford church, near Cambridge, has a Saxon grave slab in its wall, showing a pre-existing cemetery.

Some Scottish churchyards, especially ones near the old universities with medical schools, contain 'mortsafes'. These are metal cages placed over burials in the hope that they will prevent exhumation for dissection.

THE EXTERIOR

Much has been written about church architecture, but from the point of view of the village sleuth there are many useful pointers suggested by the exterior of the building.

The various lay and ecclesiastical benefactors built a church to fit its congregation. Bursts of building very often coincide with surges in local prosperity based on flourishing industry creating affluent patrons. The most important stimulus to the rebuilding of churches was money from the wool trade, which flooded in during the later part of the Middle Ages at the time when the Perpendicular style was in vogue. From Norfolk to Devon it underwrote some spectacular building works, not least the Somerset church towers at places like Westonzoyland and Batcombe.

If times were good and population swelled, as it did quite rapidly between 1066 and 1348 (the Norman Conquest and the arrival of the Black Death), then the building would need to be enlarged,

ABOVE: *Westonzoyland church on Sedgemoor has one of the finest towers in a part of Wessex renowned for its Perpendicular towers. Wool-based prosperity in the fifteenth century underwrote many such projects.*

perhaps by lengthening the nave or adding side aisles. When the congregation declined and those remaining were left with part-responsibility for an over-large church there was a great temptation to cut maintenance costs by reducing the building. The nave might be lowered, the chancel sacrificed, side aisles shed, and so on. In the case of Kilham in the Yorkshire Wolds, the large and flourishing village had an appropriately large church. However, its commerce gravitated to Driffield, a few miles away, when the Driffield Navigation was cut and completed in 1775. In its heyday, Kilham also supported six schools, though there is only one today.

Some of the evidence for the reduction will be apparent in the building (for example in a 'V'-shaped 'crease' or scar on the tower wall that marks a formerly higher nave roof). Very dramatic evidence for the wholesale reduction of churches can be seen in some East Anglian coastal villages, like Covehithe, where most of the villages concerned have been lost to the sea. At Wharram Percy, a deserted village in the Yorkshire Wolds, archaeologists have marked out the walls of the once larger church around the shell of the remaining church.

Church patrons, congregations and builders were largely at the mercy of the natural availability of building materials. In the Cotswolds and Northamptonshire, top-grade limestone was present in abundance, while in the chalk country, builders worked with the local flint, as described below.

THE INTERIOR

Church interiors are packed with subtle clues concerning the village congregations over the centuries. There is far more inside the village church than the eye may see. Beneath the visitors' feet may be the bones of various priests as well as members of the local nobility who 'bagged' the choicest resting places. Also beneath the floor are the archaeological remains that provide the only clues to a full understanding of the history and evolution of a building that may have experienced a dozen or more major rebuildings.

In the side aisles or lying beneath the floor may be the tombs of the medieval local nobility. From the tomb effigies one can usually see the evolution in the armour of knights and in the fashions of dress worn by the ladies, while some figures may be shown wearing the robes of the important state offices they held. These were the masters of the village and as the medieval era yielded to that of Elizabeth and the Jacobeans, so some churches became so packed with freestone, marble and alabaster monuments that one might imagine that it was local nobility rather than God that was the object of worship.

Ornamentation was often quite bucolic, even vulgar, and we might wonder if the faces in the gargoyles and other carvings were former villagers? Sometimes day-to-day items are portrayed, like musical instruments or the trade tools of farriers or carpenters.

After the Reformation, and particularly during the Commonwealth, the rejection of Roman practices was evident in the vandalization of the many images that had been associated with the church of Rome and the limewashing of walls that had been brightly painted and illustrated with subjects from the gospels. Today, we can see the empty niches that had held statuettes, the disfigured images, including some tomb effigies with their chins and noses bashed off, while it is very rare indeed for wall paintings to survive – though many must lie masked behind the whitened walls.

One can never be sure what treasure may be stored in a church, or where it came from. Stone crosses of the pre-Conquest era quite often come to rest inside churches, though their places of origin can be uncertain. Several northern English churches house Dark Age hogback tombstones, very heavy blocks of stone that stood over a burial and which are carved to resemble a Viking-age house which may be clasped at each end by bears.

Close inspection of the church fabric can be revealing; for example, the rood screen in Ripley church can be seen to have been cut down to fit before installation, proving that it had been removed from the earlier church, one that I know was situated between holy springs.

ABOVE: *A wonderful heritage of village church wall painting disappeared in the Reformation and its stormy aftermath. At Little Missenden in Buckinghamshire a fragment, showing John the Baptist and the infant Christ, has survived.*

Through good times and through bad, from the plague pit in the churchyard to the soaring Perpendicular tower, churches mirror the fortunes of their villages. If the bursts of rebuilding or expenditure on expensive fittings can be dated they may indicate the periods of prosperity in the life of the congregation. Churches built on the buoyant Tudor wool trade have been mentioned, while in the Yorkshire Dales, a later phase of wool-based wealth produced charming little churches in the 'Pennine Perpendicular' style.

THE
CHURCH AT
HOME

*J*N CHAPTER SIX I explain how cottages, being built of local materials and according to local traditions, fit so snugly into their settings. This was largely due to the poverty of land transport and the inability to haul in building materials from far afield. Very much the same was true of churches. While wealthy cathedrals, like Ely, and well-endowed monasteries could afford to import stone, usually, as far as was possible, by ship or narrow boat, the average parish could not afford the choicest of stone unless it happened to stand on it or close to a resource. Much that is seen results from the need to use what was available and affordable. However, other vital inputs were local tradition and whimsy, so that a church of limestone rubble in one part of the country can look quite different from one of similar materials in a different region.

It is fairly easy to match a village church to its local resources. For example, in the chalk country of Norfolk, Cambridgeshire or Sussex one will see churches walled in flint. The chalk containing the

BELOW: *Barrington church is unusual in being built of local chalk clunch, normally only thought suitable for interior carving.*

seams of flint nodules is normally too soft to be used externally, but it was used internally as 'clunch' and might line towers and provide excellent material for internal carving (and village graffiti!). Flints, picked up from the litter in the fields of the downlands villages, would not do for corners ('quoins'), lintels, jambs and other dressings, so a decent sandstone or limestone will be seen to have been imported – narrow bricks pillaged from ruined Roman sites being used, if available. In the Norfolk chalk country the extreme poverty of materials resulted in flint churches being built with cylindrical flint towers to save the cost of buying stone for quoins. At Barrington in Cambridgeshire, the chalk 'clunch' in the parish was just tough enough to build a durable white church that contrasts with its flint-walled neighbours.

Roof pitches can reflect the nature and weight of roofing materials. Many churches were thatched for centuries and needed steep-pitched roofs. A few thatched churches still remain, like Woodbastwick in the Norfolk Broads. Many steep-pitched nave roofs were originally thatched in wheatstraw or reed and were later tiled.

Local geology can be discovered at any outcrop or bedrock exposure in the parish. Geology maps can be bought or ordered from good stationers or book shops. (Ask for a map of *solid geology* rather than *drift geology*, for the latter shows the loose deposits overlying the hard rock that might have interested builders.) It should be possible to link a village church to a nearby quarry that furnished its materials.

Churches, or rather congregations and parishes, tended to compete with each other. Attitudes were parochial and rivalries with adjacent communities could be intense. These pressures encouraged villagers to vie to produce better carving and carpentry and taller towers than those boasted by their neighbours.

In ways that can seem unfathomable, different regions developed their own styles of church architecture that were partly independent of environmental assets and shortages. The list of examples is very long, but we can mention the churches on the Sussex–Hampshire border built under Norman influence in the reign of Edward the Confessor *before* the Norman conquest; the timbered towers and the wholly detached towers seen in Herefordshire and Worcestershire; the wonderfully carved bench ends on pews in Somerset churches; the East Anglian hammer beam roofs and the South West's love affair with embossed barrel-vaulted roofs and churchyard crosses. Churches are born of their localities and communities. Century upon century of local history is embedded in their walls – and at least some of it can be discovered and extracted.

RIGHT: *In Norfolk, towers, like this one at Roydon, were built in a cylindrical manner because stone for corners was not to hand.*

6

COTTAGES AND FARMSTEADS

*S*EEN IN ONE WAY, the village is a collection of houses. Actually 'a jumble' of houses might be a better phrase, for it is the diversity of sizes, styles, colours, shapes and ages of its dwellings that make the village landscape so appealing. Today, architects may win prizes and builders may have qualifications yet none of their housing developments attract the throngs of visitors that can be seen in scores of villages built by illiterate rough masons, prospective owners, housewrights and neighbours – none of whom had either seen a plan or could have recognized what it was for if they had seen one. Old village houses were craftsman-built, not architect designed. There were no building regulations to determine the heights of rooms and innumerable other dimensions and no specifications of required safety features. There were no planning officers to arbitrate on what could and could not be and what things materials should be made of. Usually, the result of all this anarchy was a visual confection of sheer delight. To be fair, however, the results also included spectacular conflagrations when entire village streets burned down.

Houses, and especially village houses, are not specimens to be appraised and preserved. Rather, they are continually evolving essays on how our expectations of houses have changed through the ages. When some working-class houses were provided with baths in the first half of the twentieth century, nasty little jokes were made about mythical families who were using them as storage for coal. Medieval villagers certainly had no knowledge of baths and their closest acquaintance with them may have been to spy on well-to-do ladies as they bathed in tubs in the open air. Now, a bath

LEFT: *The cottage idyll exemplified at Castle Cary in Somerset*

is taken for granted and virtually all houses have a room set aside as a bath- or shower room. Many people now regard a shower as another essential and may look askance at any dwelling that does not boast bedrooms with en suite bathrooms. Our expectations of houses change, and so do our expectations of rooms. Could we visit a seventeenth-century family, we would surely be confused by the clutter in their home and by the way that any designation of rooms as bedrooms, workshops, kitchens and living rooms seemed very blurred and ill-defined. Beds could be found in 'living rooms' and looms in 'bedrooms'. In my native dale, cheese-making seems to have permeated every corner of the village houses – and we can only imagine the smell. Similarly, could we visit a medieval cottage, we would be surprised by the lack of furniture except perhaps a bench or form, a tressle table, a stump to sit on and iron devices for cooking over the open hearth. Beds would usually be sacks of straw lying on the floor and seething with insect life, while items like chests of drawers or wardrobes had no place in the scene – there was little to put in them had they been there.

BELOW: *The use of local honey-coloured limestone from the Cotswolds for walling and roofing provides Lower Slaughter with its visual personality and charm.*

Our ideas about the functions of rooms change drastically over time, but in the context of a village, space is very restricted and houses are usually jammed together side by side. Expansion was constrained by the corset of the house plot, so as needs and expectations changed it was not always possible to add a new range or wing to a house. Old rooms often had to be reorganized to cope with the changes.

As the centuries passed by, houses tended to become more durable and more permanent as well as more elaborate. In a village founded in Norman times, the first few generations of dwellings were probably of such poor quality that they had to be very substantially rebuilt every 20 to 30 years. Gradually, the durability of houses increased, but it was normally not until Tudor times in the south of England or the eighteenth century in northern England, Scotland and Wales that numerous villagers obtained homes that, if maintained, would last indefinitely. No villages of any real antiquity will contain any dwellings that were erected in the lifetimes of the village founders and most house sites have witnessed rebuilding on up to a dozen or more occasions.

Remarkably, and as we have seen, the *house plots* themselves have proved remarkably persistent and innumerable villagers live in houses with parts dating from different eras that stand in a plot that does go right back to the dawn of the village. Boundaries do not go up in smoke when the house burns down.

WHY SO
MANY
VILLAGES
LOOK SO
PLEASING

*T*HE SINGLE MOST important reason that explains the attractive appearance of so many village scenes is that from Georgian days through to the expansion of the railway network in late Victorian times, conditions for transport in Britain were fairly bad, while from Georgian times back to Anglo-Saxon times, the land transport system was appalling.

These deficiencies may have caused all manner of difficulties, but they meant that houses had to be built of materials that were available locally. Money was lavished on cathedrals, but buildings like York Minster, Ely Cathedral and Canterbury Cathedral relied upon the shipping in of bulky cargoes of stone by ships and barges. With water transport expensive and road transport incapable of moving materials en masse, people were obliged to build their homes of materials that were readily to hand.

In this way, it was convenience rather than artistic taste that resulted in buildings that combine thatch, rubble, mud and timber with such amazingly attractive results.

For much of the medieval period, villagers were largely their own house-builders. As members of a manorial community they would enjoy certain rights to take house-building materials from the common and perhaps from hedgerows and the manorial wood. Stones and clay and ling for thatch could be obtained from the common and the customary right of *husbote* allowed house-building timbers to be taken, although these would have been of modest dimensions. (Through to the start of the nineteenth century, the timber-framed cottages of the poor were distinguished by the skimpy dimensions of their timbers. Today, estate agents' superlatives are lavished on skinny-timbered Georgian and Victorian cottages that had housed the rural poor.)

RIGHT: *Cruck-framed cottages at Ibsley in Hampshire*

Because the materials employed were local, they blended with the surrounding setting. Thatch was echoed in the grain fields; coarse walling stone was exposed in streambeds, field walls and rock outcrops as well as in the village dwellings, and the tones of local mud and clay pits and the limestone quarry were repeated in the daub on house walls. Where dwellings were painted, the local earth hues were employed.

Woods were often worked as *coppice with standards* to meet needs for construction and fuel. Standards, cut as they approached a century in age, produced heavy timber for posts and beams, while the coppice of hazel, oak, elm and other timbers growing on the woodland floor was cut every ten to eighteen years or so and yielded light timber for wattle and laths. Massive, curving braces to reinforce corners could be cut from the bending boughs of old hedgerow pollarded trees. Because of the difficulties of transporting felled trees, village houses were generally prefabricated as shaped and jointed components in the woods where the timbers were felled. Numerals were cut on the beams, posts and braces to ease reassembly and so the house could be rebuilt on its site in the village. With the mortice and tenon and cross halving joints assembled, holes were drilled in the joints and pegs were hammered home to secure a rigid assemble.

There were phases of decline, as when the plague struck a village and empty houses might go abegging, and also phases of optimism and confidence in the countryside, when people were encouraged to build. But there were no short, disruptive periods when massive estates of houses

BELOW: *A charming Wiltshire brick cottage with a West Country pie-crust type thatch. Housing such as this was provided for farm and estate workers in late Georgian and Victorian times.*

ABOVE: *Thatching a cottage in the West Midlands. The timbers are of a size associated with humbler housing and the cottage can be seen to rest on rubble footings that raise its beams above the damp ground.*

appeared all at once. Therefore, the houses in a village tend to be of a multitude of ages, each dwelling having its own history, and as a result, they seem fascinatingly diverse. Also, once built, a house could develop in all manner of different ways, depending on its owners, their occupations and needs, their affluence or poverty, their desires to 'make a show', as well as changes in fashion and aspirations. So these factors exaggerated the differences wrought by differences in ages. The result: a bizarre architectural confection, a landscape of varied house sizes, dates and finishes.

THE AGES OF VILLAGE HOUSES

*V*ILLAGE HOUSES are more difficult to date than the village church. The church was designed to serve fairly standardized rituals, but domestic life was far more complex. Households had different occupations, levels of status and ambitions, while families come in many different sizes. Churches employed distinctive styles of ecclesiastical architecture – the Transitional, Early English, Decorated and so on – that were part of a universal system of architectural conventions. The functional, local 'vernacular' styles employed in old dwellings are far harder to recognize. Also, houses – or their former owners – can be distinctly misleading. Owners often 'buried' styles that had come to be regarded as unfashionable and there is many an irregular medieval timber-framed frontage that is masked by a fashionably symmetrical Georgian facade.

The first house to occupy a village plot might have stood on a beam resting directly on the moist earth. Such beams, even those of weather-resistant oak, would fairly soon rot. Therefore, frames might be placed on *padstones* to stand a little above the damp. The next house might have been raised upon footings of rubble and would therefore have lasted rather longer. The next might have been more damp-resistant still, but have been partly destroyed by fire. Its surviving timbers might then have been reused in the next house, which might, in turn, be succeeded by a dwelling of stone – and so the story would go on.

Although most villages had come into existence by the thirteenth century, it would be most unusual for a thirteenth-century village house to survive, and what might be advertised as such might really only include just a fragment of a doorway or a beam or two of this period. Old village houses tend not to have true ages; they are assemblages of structures and fragments from the passing centuries. Now, techniques like carbon-14 dating and tree ring dating (*dendrochronology*) can provide reasonably accurate dates for house timbers. However, one cannot always be sure that these timbers were not reused from older structures. Squarish beams that were on view in a house tended to have their right-angled edges chambered up to a couple of inches or so of their ends, where the 'end-stops' were left square. Where original timbers are *in situ*, these end stops can be recognized, but if the chambering runs straight through into the wall, the timber has probably been reused from an earlier building.

Roofs tell part of the story of the house beneath. Thatch was very popular in medieval and later times and for the straw or reed to drain freely, a steep pitch was needed. Since thatch is relatively light, it did not matter that such roofs had large areas. Kiln-baked red tiles also need a fairly steep roof slope in order to drain properly. In places like the Cotswolds, Northamptonshire and the Yorkshire Dales, sandstones that were readily split ('fissile') could be quarried to provide false slates for roofing. However, these stone roofs were very heavy, particularly those of the slab-like *thakstones* (thatch stones) of the Dales, and so the lowest possible pitch was employed. Villagers at Stonesfield in Oxfordshire exported roofing slabs that were split from larger stones or *potlids* that would split up after being exposed to frost. *Pantiles* were less heavy than stone, though heavier than thatch and this is reflected in their angles of pitch. When slender sheets of roofing slate were exported far and wide from Cumbria and North Wales on the Victorian railways, they offered lighter roofs that drained well, and roof pitches between the thatch and stone standards were used.

Quite often, one can see how a steep, originally thatched roof has been raised at a shallower angle and re-roofed in tiles or slate, with the extra space resulting from raising the eaves allowing the

RIGHT: *Jettied upper storeys claimed a little extra floor space in towns, but when used in villages the projecting upper storeys seem more like status symbols. These houses are in Thaxted.*

insertion of an upper storey. Similarly, stone-roofed cottages may have their roof ridges raised and be reclad in slate. Sometimes, roof angles were preserved, and tall, really steep roofs were generally thatched, even if the thatch has gone.

Virtually all the medieval village houses that survive largely intact in the south of England date from the *Great Rebuilding* which represented an upturn in the prosperity of many ordinary village households in Tudor and Elizabethan times. Many villages were transformed in a matter of decades by rebuilding as the yeomen and better-off tenants aspired to build family homes that would survive indefinitely. The solidity of the houses, which consumed vast quantities of timber, still testifies to this aim – as well as to the efficient organization of the woods that yielded all the structural timbers.

In other areas, the revolution arrived up to three centuries or more later. Medieval dwellings are rarely glimpsed in the villages of the North and West and the growth of wealth and ambition is displayed in improved stone houses of the seventeenth and eighteenth centuries. Some houses in the northern uplands of England are deceptive, for while they display stone walls to passers-by, these walls encase buildings based on timber framing, usually the old *cruck-framing* style, where each bay is defined by an 'A'-shaped frame of structural timbers.

Upper storeys were slow to arrive. In the modest medieval village cottage, life was lived at ground level and the house was open to the rafters. Later in the Middle Ages, some of the more favoured

BELOW: *Square framing in Weobley, near Hereford. A building using the alternative cruck-framing technique can be seen directly below the church.*

households were provided with raised sleeping shelves or lofts that were reached by a ladder, with proper upper storeys and staircases eventually being acquired. The arrival of the upper storey might be marked by a raising of the roof or the insertion of dormer windows in the tiled or thatched area.

Any chimney stack associated with a very old village cottage will be a later addition. The medieval homes had smoke-holes at the top of their gables, through which the smoke from the hearth on the floor below, which had been hanging in a pall among the rafters, could gradually escape. At the end of the Middle Ages, the grander dwellings were acquiring smokestacks and chimneys, these being built of brick to showy designs that proclaimed a pride in ownership. Then numerous though more functional chimneys began to break up the village skyline.

The importance of flaunting status should not be overlooked. In the village landscape, the house of a successful merchant might be built with 'jettied out' upper storeys – though a jetty only made sense when seeking to gain a little extra upper floor space beside a narrow lane in a congested town. Similarly, the rising yeoman might build far more expensive oak posts (upright timbers) into the frontage of his house than structural needs ever required. The more thick, costly timbers that were displayed in a frontage, the greater their status value. The desire to seem fashionable permeated villages as well as towns. The Georgian desire for symmetry and stone or rendered frontages resulted in the concealment of many a timber-framed street frontage behind a symmetrical, plastered facade. One can walk along a stretch of village street where all the medieval facades are masked. Now, fashion places a higher value on exposed timber frames, even when the timbers are of a low, spindly quality that would have shamed earlier owners.

THE VILLAGE
AND
FARMING

*T*ODAY SOME VILLAGES exist largely as home bases for commuters working in adjacent towns; others are places that become almost dormant when the owners of their second homes have departed. It is easy to forget what the village was and how close were its ties to its setting. Almost all villages began as dormitories for feudal landworkers, and agriculture has dominated their roles for most of their existences.

The typical homesteads in villages established in the centuries around the Norman Conquest were often small, single-storey dwellings of the *longhouse* type. A front door opened onto the road passing through the village and a short passage ran from it to a back door. This passage divided the dwelling into two halves; to one side, a single family room and to the other, a byre, where the family milk cow and perhaps a sheep or two sheltered. While not freshening the air, at least the animals would have raised the temperature. The village house was a farmhouse in the sense that, as bond tenants, the members of the household worked partly on the holding that they rented from their lord, and also worked without payment on the demesne.

As the centuries passed, houses became a little larger and gained more elaborate layouts, but the great bulk of the population in a typical village remained landworkers. Even though feudalism and the old habits of village cooperation declined, the village remained the base for operations on the surrounding land. Gradually the villagers would struggle to stitch together more compact and consolidated holdings, but most of them remained in the village, even though they might have had to walk some way to their scattered fields.

With the passing of the Middle Ages, village artisans with their own workshops gradually took over the crafts, like smithing and joinery, that bondsmen had performed part-time on their manors. As the village population became more diverse, so did the houses. The ones occupied by tenant farmers and yeomen would contain barrels and vats, the clutter of cheese- and ale-making and hams smoking in the wood smoke. The village smith lived beside his smithy and the cartwright had his shed and timber yard as well as his yard, where scorching iron ribs were shrunk upon wheels of wood. While the spinners might sit at their doors, carders and combers of cloth worked among their household clutter and weavers worked by their windows surrounded by yarn and bolts of cloth.

Between around 1750 and 1850, Parliamentary Enclosure transformed hundreds of village settings. In the many parishes affected, the old commons were carved up and reallocated to individuals. Now the village did suffer a severe blow to its old links. Some villagers, having seemingly done well from Enclosure, chose to leave the village and set up home on the new, compact holdings that they had been awarded. This is why the farmsteads standing amongst the geometrical Enclosure field networks are generally of the eighteenth or nineteenth centuries. There were countless other villagers who did badly from the changes and, after briefly struggling to work the inviable holdings that they had been given, chose to quit the village and the countryside forever. Parliamentary Enclosure meant that there were fewer farmsteads on the village street, with many of those that had existed being converted into ordinary homes or workshops.

ABOVE: *Villages do not have just one vernacular building tradition and styles changed according to time and choice. Here at Steeple Ashton in Wiltshire are variations using stone, brick and timber framing.*

To find out about the occupations of people in a chosen village in early modern times one can check the census information from 1841 onwards, or consult nineteenth-century trade directories in a local reference library. The readers will be surprised at the diversity of employment that existed among Georgian and Victorian villagers. Not only are tailors, smiths and joiners, and shopkeepers like grocers, butchers and bakers, likely to have been present, there were often several of each, while the village that now has just one inn may have supported three or four of them in former times.

WHAT CAN
YOU
DISCOVER?

*A*RMED WITH the spirit of enquiry, the untrained enthusiast can discover quite a lot about the village housescape. Detailed interpretations of the evolution of individual houses is a subject that does demand a good measure of expertise and experience but much can be learned about the character of the village and the changing patterns of domestic life.

VILLAGE CHARACTER

Anyone who has travelled across the seemingly interminable uniform landscapes of many of the world's regions will be amazed by the diversity of the British villages. A journey of just a few miles can take us from places of timber-framed cottages with thatched roofs to another with walls of honey-coloured limestone rubble and roofs of red pantiles, and then to one of flint walls, brick dressings and slate roofs. The vernacular architecture of Britain is remarkably varied and each region is remembered and celebrated, in good measure because of the distinctive local styles in the architecture. The thick,

TIP DISCOVERING VILLAGE CHARACTER

1. We have seen that the tyranny of bad roads meant that villagers built their dwellings of those things that were readily to hand – so how did your village gain its visual identity?

2. You might attempt a survey of the older village houses, noting how they were built and the building materials employed. (It is as well to explain what you are doing there in the village street, for there are few things more unsettling than to see a stranger with a clipboard outside one's home.)

3. The ideas suggested in Chapter Three for discovering the village setting will be useful here. If the village has timber-framed houses, the posts and beams will have come from a local wood, with the woven wattle that filled the panels between the frame timbers coming from a local coppiced wood – perhaps the same wood as the posts if it was worked on a coppice-with-standards system. The daub that was plastered on the wattle was made of mud, often reinforced with cow dung and chopped cow hair. Similarly, roofs were covered in local materials, though the repertoire employed included heather, turf and oat straw as well as the wheatstraw and reed seen today. All these landscape features are likely to be embedded in the lists of place-names. Fairly detailed maps, like the Ordnance Survey First Edition 6 inches to 1 mile series, should give the place-names that allow identification of former woods, alder swamps, reed beds and so on.

4. It was a poor village that could not draw on the resources of a local quarry. Village buildings of flint used the flint nodules gathered from the local ploughlands. Usually they were split or *knapped* to present a flat, lustrous face and sometimes they were set in chequerboard patterns. Quarries can be discovered on maps, while on the ground they are marked by depressions or by areas of hummocky ground where dross has been dumped. Medieval quarrymen preferred to work back at a ridge-top exposure of stone and then sledge the stone away downhill rather than become involved in digging deep pits. Samples of stone found at a local quarry site can be matched against village buildings, including the church, to identify the origin of the building stone.

limewashed walls of clay 'cob', topped by piecrust roofs of thatch, remind us of Devon, just as Millstone Grit or limestone rubble walls and stone flag roofs tells us we are in the Yorkshire Dales, while thatch secured by a net weighted with stones and draining into the earth packing of a double stone wall is characteristic of the black houses of the Scottish Highlands and islands. If robbed of its heritage of vernacular houses, the identity of any region would be greatly damaged.

Much can be learned by interrogating a locality or environment. The box below looks at the sorts of things that you might bear in mind.

5. Where there was no building stone to be had, as in the chalk downlands or on the vales coated in deep ice or river sediments, church builders had to use flint or poor local rubble and import good structural stone from further afield. The Barnack quarries near Peterborough sent stone southwards, far into the Fens. Village houses may have walls of a poor or mediocre local stone and lintels, 'quoins' (corners) and door jambs of a better quality imported material. In places near the northern North Sea shores one can see houses walled with seashore boulders with doors and windows framed in a local sandstone.

6. Thatched roofs came from the nearby fields and reed beds, the latter yielding darker, rather more durable materials. Nowadays thatching-grade long straw is harder to obtain and most old reed beds have been drained, through old-style reed cutting beds can be seen at Wicken Fen in Cambridgeshire. In Ireland and the Scottish Islands, oat straw provided a more hummocky-looking thatch. Pantiles might have come from a local tile works, though many arrived from the Low Countries as ballast and were used in coastal areas.

7. Bricks were introduced by the Romans, though the art of brick-making was later forgotten. Bricks reappeared in the townscape of medieval Hull, and by the Elizabethan era, high-status mansions and palaces were being built of brick, then a most prestigious material. Gradually, brick diffused down to village homes. Firstly villagers employed sun-baked bricks of local clay, then the varied products of local brickworks were used, and finally mass-produced bricks. The earlier bricks were uneven in size and their colours and textures were the results of local clay and the differing techniques used to fire it. Old maps and directories may well identify the local brickworks that were destined to be put out of business by the big producers.

8. Undulations and great pockmarks on a former common may show where clay for potting, walling and brick-making was dug. Field names, like 'Clay Pits', 'Brick Field', 'Brickkiln Close', 'Potters Field', 'Tilekiln Field' or 'Kiln Field' are quite common. In the Midlands, the less common field name 'Potlids' can describes the thick cake-like formation of stone suitable for splitting into stone roofing slates.

ABOVE: *Houses in the golden limestone of the Cotswolds at Bourton-on-the-Water in Gloucestershire*

A survey of village character could involve, firstly, an inventory of the different local materials that are displayed in the village landscape. Then you can seek, as far as possible, to link each of these materials to a source of supply – the local woods, quarries and clay pits. Secondly, when this is done you will be well placed to distil the essence of the village character. Much is determined by the shortcomings of the local transport system, but space must be left for human quirkiness. Several locations responded to a shortage of decent building stones by developing clay walling techniques,

ABOVE: Boulders from the nearby beach, local stone and perhaps some stones pillaged from the ruins of the medieval priory combined with pantiles, that were probably brought across the North Sea as ballast, contribute to this house in the south-eastern extremities of Scotland.

The home of William Coates of Burnt Yates hamlet near Knaresborough, who died in 1673

Inventory information about the contents of William's home when he died in 1673 is shown, room by room, in italics

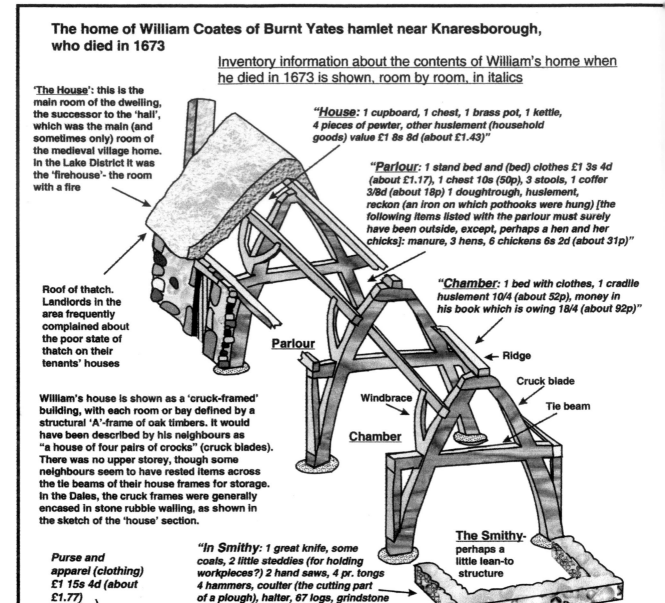

'The House': this is the main room of the dwelling, the successor to the 'hall', which was the main (and sometimes only) room of the medieval village home. In the Lake District it was the 'firehouse'- the room with a fire

"House: 1 cupboard, 1 chest, 1 brass pot, 1 kettle, 4 pieces of pewter, other huslement (household goods) value £1 8s 8d (about £1.43)"

"Parlour: 1 stand bed and (bed) clothes £1 3s 4d (about £1.17), 1 chest 10s (50p), 3 stools, 1 coffer 3/8d (about 18p) 1 doughtrough, huslement, reckon (an iron on which pothooks were hung) [the following items listed with the parlour must surely have been outside, except, perhaps a hen and her chicks]: manure, 3 hens, 6 chickens 6s 2d (about 31p)"

"Chamber: 1 bed with clothes, 1 cradile huslement 10/4 (about 52p), money in his book which is owing 18/4 (about 92p)"

Roof of thatch. Landlords in the area frequently complained about the poor state of thatch on their tenants' houses

Parlour

← Ridge

Cruck blade

Windbrace

Tie beam

Chamber

William's house is shown as a 'cruck-framed' building, with each room or bay defined by a structural 'A'-frame of oak timbers. It would have been described by his neighbours as "a house of four pairs of crocks" (cruck blades). There was no upper storey, though some neighbours seem to have rested items across the tie beams of their house frames for storage. In the Dales, the cruck frames were generally encased in stone rubble walling, as shown in the sketch of the 'house' section.

The Smithy- perhaps a little lean-to structure

Purse and apparel (clothing) £1 15s 4d (about £1.77)

"In Smithy: 1 great knife, some coals, 2 little steddies (for holding workpieces?) 2 hand saws, 4 pr. tongs 4 hammers, coulter (the cutting part of a plough), halter, 67 logs, grindstone and all that belongs it, other odd things £1 16s 4d (about 63p) 1 Bible 1/6d (about 8p)"

Information about the local housing can be obtained from a variety of old documents, such as rentals and estate accounts which mention the condition of properties. Also, features of traditional vernacular architecture will survive in the old buildings of a locality. In the region of the Yorkshire Dales where William Coates lived in the 17th-century, houses were described in terms of the number of bays (normally equating to rooms) that they possessed. References are made to houses of 2, 3, 4 or more pairs of 'crocks' and of pairs of posts. It may well be that the 'houses of posts' were box-framed rather than cruck-framed. The timber-framing techniques that were available at the time allowed dwellings to be increased in length indefinitely by adding on extra bays, but they could not be increased in width because of the limit to the lengths of timber available. The rich responded to this by adding additional cross-wings to their houses, which thus gained 'T'-, 'L'- or 'E'- shaped plans. In William's case, the inventory suggests that the assessors began in his main room or 'house' and proceeded to his parlour, his chamber and then his smithie. Surprisingly, in this case they did not include his livestock, though he was plainly a farmer/small-holder. He was unusual in that there is no evidence of the paraphernalia of cheese making, commonly associated with this time/place, or of spinning yarn or weaving woollen or linen cloth, such as most of his farming neighbours did to eke out their incomes. The other farmsteads in the locality had the clutter of cottage textile making, brewing and cheese-making spilling over into every room.

Village dwellings: born of their settings

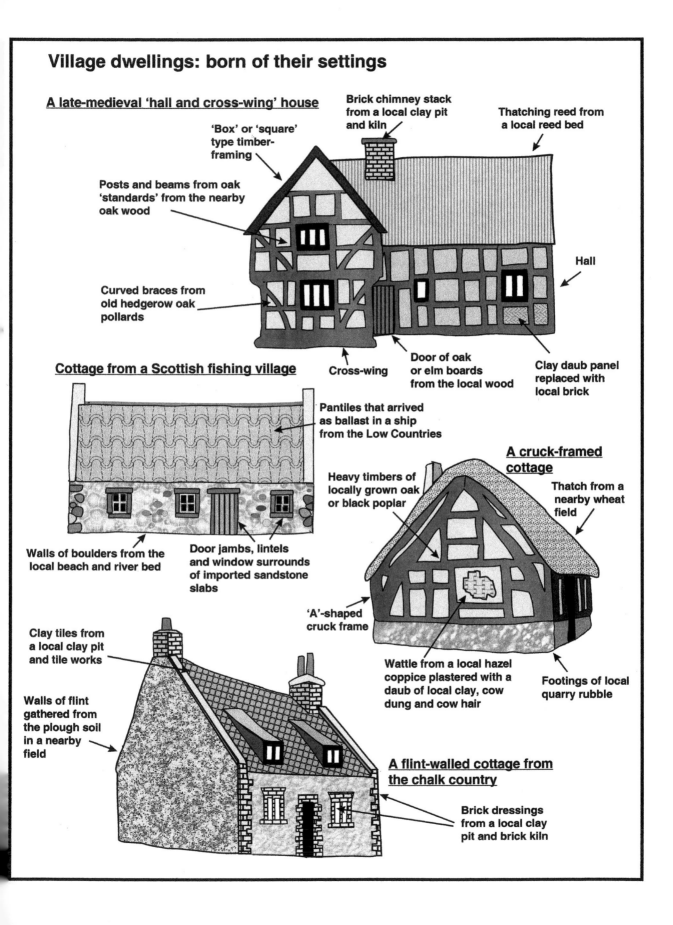

A late-medieval 'hall and cross-wing' house

Brick chimney stack from a local clay pit and kiln

Thatching reed from a local reed bed

'Box' or 'square' type timber-framing

Posts and beams from oak 'standards' from the nearby oak wood

Hall

Curved braces from old hedgerow oak pollards

Cross-wing

Door of oak or elm boards from the local wood

Clay daub panel replaced with local brick

Cottage from a Scottish fishing village

Pantiles that arrived as ballast in a ship from the Low Countries

Walls of boulders from the local beach and river bed

Door jambs, lintels and window surrounds of imported sandstone slabs

A cruck-framed cottage

Heavy timbers of locally grown oak or black poplar

Thatch from a nearby wheat field

'A'-shaped cruck frame

Wattle from a local hazel coppice plastered with a daub of local clay, cow dung and cow hair

Footings of local quarry rubble

Clay tiles from a local clay pit and tile works

Walls of flint gathered from the plough soil in a nearby field

A flint-walled cottage from the chalk country

Brick dressings from a local clay pit and brick kiln

RIGHT: Cottages at Ludham in Norfolk in different shapes and styles of the kind that develop along a route or track when the development is spontaneous rather than planned

ABOVE: *Local stone displayed in the manor house and cottages at Abbotsbury in Dorset*

but the methods differed, with the 'clay lump' of East Anglia, the 'cob' of Devon and the 'wichert' of Buckinghamshire being different formulations. Also, different techniques succeeded each other in contrasting ways. In the Midlands, timber-framing traditions yielded to brick, while in the northern Dales, stone maintained its dominance – as it still largely does, as armed with planning powers the councils can prevent the use of any other materials (except by themselves).

DOMESTIC LIFE

Village life 50 years ago was vastly different from that of today. Some 250 years ago, on the eve of the Industrial Revolution, the differences were profound. Standing in our villages are dwellings that have witnessed all the intervening changes – and those of a further 250 years back as well. All these buildings have experienced a succession of modifications that have taken them from the days of the smokehole, village pump and backyard privy to today. They look nothing like their sixteenth-, seventeenth- or eighteenth-century selves. However, it can be possible to recreate the world of a village household of centuries ago. The following box looks at the sort of things that the village sleuth might investigate.

⚒ TIP RECREATING DOMESTIC LIFE

⚒ 1. Portholes on the past may be provided by wills and by *probate inventories*, documents, demanded by the law, which itemized the possessions of a deceased person. Those concerning the village being studied may have been published and the librarian at your local reference library should be able to advise on availability.

⚒ 2. Often, the neighbours responsible for compiling the inventories proceeded through the dead person's house, room by room, recording their contents as they went. In this way, we may obtain lists of the contents of particular rooms and thus discover what each was used for. Looms and bolts of linen or woollen cloth or a spinning wheel and yarn will show that the occupant was involved in cottage textiles, though multiple occupations were very common, so there might be cheese-making gear strewn around and hams hanging up in the rafters. Most homes had home brewing equipment and a little room that served as a brewhouse, as the well water was polluted and villagers of all ages drank ale. Drinking was a crucial part of village life and estate workers were often rewarded with ale at landmarks in the village year. There were worn-out farmhands who only discovered that they were alcoholic once installed in the local workhouse, away from a supply of drink.

⚒ 3. From the ordering of rooms, and with a little understanding of the domestic architecture for the period concerned, we may be able to construct a picture of the village house and the ways in which its rooms were made to function at the date of the inventory concerned. In each case, we meet villagers whose ideas about the organization of a home were remarkably different from our own. Bathrooms, specialized bedrooms, indoor lavatories, studies – to say nothing of conservatories – simply did not exist at the village level.

⚒ 4. It is great fun to attempt to recreate scenes in the mind and to visualize how rooms and dwellings may have appeared. The historical information to be gleaned from old paintings is considerable, and the pictures have been the domain of art historians and aesthetes with different priorities. From the seventeenth century onwards there are numerous portrayals of interior backgrounds, often showing the decorations and ceramics of their day (sometimes with symbolic meanings to the content). Medieval interiors of the more prosperous villagers were often hand-decorated with floral, armorial and other motifs. There are suggestions that medieval timber-frames were sometimes brightly painted, while churches were frequently limewashed and must have stood out like icebergs from their settings.

7

EMPTY PLACES AT
THE VILLAGE FEAST

*I*N CHAPTER TWO I described the village 'Big Bang', which created thousands of new villages in countrysides that had until then been dominated by multitudes of farmsteads and hamlets. What happened to these villages and their hopeful young communities? Judging by the evidence of the Saxon and Norman documents that mention such places, most are still alive today. We cannot be precise because a few hundred or so villages must have come and gone before ever being properly recorded. Also, though a great many deserted village sites have been discovered, many more remain to be found. Substantial numbers of villages have perished and for a variety of reasons. The almost universal explanation that is offered for the death of a village by people living in its locality – the 'Black Death' – was in fact seldom able, on its own, to eradicate a settlement. Some survivors would remain or return to bring the village back to life. Other causes that are less well known were far more deadly.

WHAT KILLED VILLAGES?

*D*IFFERENT VILLAGE ASSASSINS were abroad in different places at different times. Many settlements just happened to be in the wrong place at the wrong time, but it was always the case that the weaker places with small or demoralized communities were the most vulnerable. Villages damaged in their struggle to survive one assault were more likely then to perish in the face of another. The culprits that have been identified are as follows.

LEFT: *The church at Covehithe in Norfolk, which withered away as the homes of its congregation were lost to the sea*

WAR AND GENOCIDE

On the whole, these were not the most potent causes of desertion, but settlements that had the misfortune to lie in the path of a ruthless army could be destroyed. When the army of William the Conqueror ravaged the areas inland from his landing place in 1066, English villages by the Channel coast were severely damaged. When his fury was launched against the insurgent North in 1069–70, the terrible Harrying of the North seems to have partly obliterated the settlement pattern in Yorkshire and County Durham and thousands of country folk perished. The countrysides were then recolonized, with the establishment of scores of planned Norman villages to serve the estates of the invaders. From time to time, war would return and numerous communities in northern England were relieved of tax after the Scottish raids which followed the Scottish victory at Bannockburn in 1314. In contrast, in Wales, villages populated by English and Flemish traders were planted to secure the pacification of conquered Welsh territories. The Civil War was very costly of life, but not of villages. Abbotsbury was owned by the royalist, Sir John Strangeways. In 1644, parliamentary forces attacked the garrison there and in the skirmish the powder magazine exploded, blowing up the old manor house that Sir John had built from stone pillaged from the nearby abbey ruins.

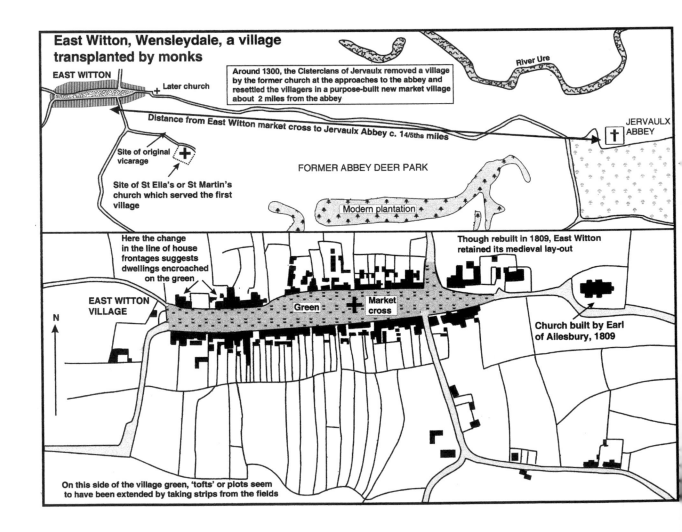

East Witton, Wensleydale, a village transplanted by monks

River Ure

EAST WITTON

+ Later church

Around 1300, the Cistercians of Jervaulx removed a village by the former church at the approaches to the abbey and resettled the villagers in a purpose-built new market village about 2 miles from the abbey

Distance from East Witton market cross to Jervaulx Abbey c. 1⅘ths miles

JERVAULX ABBEY
+

Site of original vicarage
+

FORMER ABBEY DEER PARK

Site of St Ella's or St Martin's church which served the first village

Modern plantation

Here the change in the line of house frontages suggests dwellings encroached on the green

Though rebuilt in 1809, East Witton retained its medieval lay-out

EAST WITTON VILLAGE

N

Green
+ Market cross

Church built by Earl of Ailesbury, 1809

On this side of the village green, 'tofts' or plots seem to have been extended by taking strips from the fields

ABOVE: *Wharram Percy in the Yorkshire Wolds was painstakingly excavated over several decades to provide our best understanding of lost villages.*

MONKS

Monks were no less destructive than soldiers, especially the monks of the Cistercian order, who sought isolation from the presumed evils of the world. Firstly they evicted settlements that lay too close to their new monasteries, like Herleshow village on the doorstep of Fountains Abbey, and then, as their estates expanded, they would remove households from the places where they wanted to create monastic farms or granges. A few dozen villages and hamlets perished at their hands.

COOLING OF THE CLIMATE

The first half of the era of our villages was associated with unusually warm and dry climates, so that as the population grew, people were inclined to colonize places that would later seem too marginal. Around 1300, a prolonged transition from the *Medieval Warm Period* to the *Little Ice Age* began. Skies turned grey, rain lashed down, the land would not warm up for sowing in the spring, while autumn set in before crops had ripened. Disease ravaged livestock, and villagers, who were weakened by famine, fell victim to epidemics. The most dramatic ends were those experienced by villages on low, reclaimed coastlines or soft and easily eroded cliffs. Settlements along the North Sea coast from

ABOVE: *This peaceful scene belies the devastating role played by the owners of these animals during the Tudor sheep clearances.*
RIGHT: *Many profits were made from medieval sheep ranges, including those which paid for Stokesay Castle in Shropshire and its imposing gatehouse.*

Holderness to the Wash and along the eastern shores of East Anglia were particularly badly affected. Shortage of land had also resulted in widespread coastal reclamation schemes, and in several places between Kent and the Humber estuary, sea storms, invigorated by the turbulent climate, burst through the ranks of sea walls and saturated the ground with poisonous salt. The change in the climate caused households to desert the rain-lashed uplands and abandon some villages in the vales, where the clay soil remained cold and waterlogged throughout the spring. Climatic deterioration provided the background for the greater tragedies that loomed.

THE BLACK DEATH

Arriving in 1348, the Pestilence (perhaps not bubonic plague, as was thought) was both lethal and fearfully contagious. It exterminated between a third to a half of the British population and returned again and again to claim more victims until vanishing in the seventeenth century. Despite all this, relatively few villages were killed stone dead. Communities could be terribly decimated and scarred, or driven to abandon their home for several years. Normally, however, the availability of cultivated land would draw survivors back. Anybody who had survived the Pestilence and the deaths of half their dear ones with their minds and bodies still intact faced better opportunities than had been known for generations, for the curse of over-population had been lifted.

SHEEP

These were by far the most wanton destroyers of villages. The Pestilence had transformed the economy. Where once they had been cheap and abundant, labour and tenants had become scarce and, as they discovered their scarcity value, expensive and fractious. Landlords, casting about for

other means of raising revenue from their estates could scarcely miss the example of the Cistercians and the fortune that they had made from the wool trade. In Tudor times, scarcely any villagers could feel safe as eviction and sheep clearances rolled across the countryside. Some areas in the Midlands and East Yorkshire were left with chains of emptied parishes where one could walk for miles and meet only shepherds.

PARK-MAKING

During the Middle Ages, a good few villages were removed in the creation of deer parks or hunting reserves. Later, as the castle yielded to the mansion and the medieval tradition for creating 'designed landscapes' evolved into an enthusiasm for deserted landscape parks, numerous communities were expelled from the 'emparked' areas around stately homes. Sometimes, alternative accommodation

BELOW: *The stone footings of dwellings and field walls at the deserted medieval village of Hound Tor on Dartmoor*

was provided outside the park. Quite often, an eye-catching replacement village for estate workers was built outside the park gates employing bizarre or whimsical styles of building (see Chapter Nine). In some cases, though, the villagers were left homeless.

ENGROSSMENT

This was a debilitating process that might eventually culminate in the departure of almost all the remaining tenants and leave the epitaph of an isolated church. It was a creeping form of death in which landlords consolidated leases, getting rid of the lesser lights in village life and bringing land into one ownership or a few large tenancies. It was often accompanied by the hugely resented and illegal enclosure of the commons on which small farmers depended. Several of the isolated churches in East Anglia stand at the gravesides of villages that fell to engrossment.

THE HIGHLAND CLEARANCES

Occurring in the aftermath of the defeat of Bonnie Prince Charlie and his Jacobites at Culloden in 1746, the Clearances involved a loathsome repeat of the Tudor sheep evictions in England. In order to make their estates economically competitive, chieftains and interlopers alike evicted communities from the old clan lands and replaced them with shepherds, often Borderers, and their flocks. The destruction wrought on the landscape of settlement was staggering and the open scars of tumbled dwellings still pattern the braes (slopes), straths (broad valleys) and glens, as described in Chapter Ten.

WHAT TOOLS CAN BE USED TO SEARCH FOR DESERTED VILLAGES?

*W*E ARE AT A STAGE where most of the easier discoveries have probably been made, but where hundreds of lost villages are still to be discovered. Few of these will be completely invisible in their settings; all will generate clues, and once one knows the nature of the clues, a new discovery can be established. Smaller villages – those in upland areas or those that were subordinate to larger settlements in their parishes or townships – are likely to remain undiscovered in quite large numbers. A spectrum of techniques is available and a lost settlement that may seem undetectable by one approach can easily be revealed by others. A few avenues that are available to all amateur enthusiasts now follow.

EARTHWORKS

When a community lives in a place for a while, hollows (*holloways*) will develop as feet trample the same routes. Boundary ditches (and sometimes banks) will be dug to mark property lines. Level platforms (*house platforms*) or shelves in hillslopes will be formed at the places where houses are erected. All these, and others, like grassed-over tumbledown walls, scooped out and embanked fishponds or stacked-up former garden terraces, form patterns of earthworks that may survive at the site of a deserted settlement. However, only a few seasons of ploughing can obliterate the traces, for the plough carves up land and the harrow flattens the ground.

ABOVE: *Maps are vital sources of evidence. One of the very earliest English maps, dating from the 1440s, depicted Boarstall village in Buckinghamshire. It showed the village, that was doomed to be lost, and the gatehouse, which has endured.*

MAPS

Once abandoned, villages vanish from maps (only a very small minority of lost village sites are marked on Ordnance Survey maps). Anybody interested in searching for lost villages and hamlets in a given area can ask the reference librarian or county archivist about the map coverage of the area concerned and then work through successive maps looking for settlements that vanish between two phases of mapping. Many counties were mapped at 1 inch to 1 mile in the mid-eighteenth century and county sheets can be compared with the (more accurate) maps produced at that scale in the mid-twentieth century. With just a fairly simple map it might be useful to look for parishes with double-barrelled names: the parish could be an amalgamation of an existing parish with that of a lost village neighbour. Parish shapes can be revealing, too. A big bulge in the side of a parish could be land from a similar amalgamation.

AIR PHOTOGRAPHS

Sites that seem empty or jumbled can be revealed in much greater clarity on air photographs. They may reveal *shadow marks* seen when a low sun causes slight features, like tumbled walls, ridge and furrow or house footings, to cast shadows. *Crop marks* appear, for example, when a site has been cultivated and crops growing in the rich silts of ditches stand tall and crops rooted in old roads or wall rubble are stunted and shaded. *Parch marks* are seen in hot, dry summers, when vegetation standing above stony, arid features parches and turns yellow-brown. The usefulness of an air photograph depends on the position of the aeroplane, the weather and lighting conditions and several other factors: they are not *always* brilliant tools for discoveries. Numerous commercial archives and reference collections exist, including the Luftwaffe reconnaissance archive accessible

BELOW: *Documents can provide vital clues. A will leaving money to Pudding Norton church in 1557 shows that the doomed village was still alive then.*

from the Pentagon (see in Chapter One, Reading the Ancient Settlements: air photographs). The best port of call is likely to be the local planning/heritage department, which should hold various sets of photographs, bought in, commissioned at certain times or otherwise obtained. Low-level photographs taken obliquely from a cockpit generally reveal more than 'verticals', taken downwards from higher altitude by a floor-mounted camera, which tend to flatten terrain.

DOCUMENTS

The spectrum of village documentation is immense, but to work on medieval documents in Latin, recorded in difficult calligraphic styles, will require special training. For many villages that perished in the Middle Ages, their entire documentation would fit on an A4 sheet, often just a postcard. If the site of a lost village is discovered, then a visit to the record office might be made to discover its name and anything else that might have been known about it. For the really dedicated, the medieval rolls that record taxation can chart the existence of a place that one day may vanish from its scene and the tax assessor's gaze. If the record office has the old estate papers that include the court rolls of the manor that controlled the village concerned, one can discover the realities of former village life – the humiliating and much-resented obligation to work on the demesne and the fines or 'pains' exacted for every little breach of the village disciplinary code and the taxes levelled on the village paupers.

OLD TRACKS

Lanes and tracks have destinations. If a destination vanishes, a lane may decline into a footpath, or a road become a bridleway. Maps of a locality can be scoured to see if there are any paths or bridleways that converge on a now-empty location: perhaps there was a settlement there.

POTTERY

Each period had its own distinctive pottery, which might be wheel-turned, glazed or employ a range of different 'tempering' material. A visit to the local museum may reveal the evolving styles of your own vernacular pottery tradition. Pottery is the thing most commonly used to date the times when sites were occupied. Settlements are associated with impressive concentrations of *sherds* but the find of a single fragment does not reveal a settlement, for broken pots were tossed on the midden and spread over the fields with the muck. On suspected sites, one may kick over molehills or explore the mouths of rabbit burrows: pottery, bits of old clay pipes, furnace slag, fragments of harness and all sorts of other things can be brought up.

ISOLATED CHURCHES

We have seen that these have various explanations, though the possibility that a church marks the spot of a deserted village site should always be considered. Some stood at isolated old pagan sites and some are associated with early missionaries. The Church of St Hoel at Llanhowel, St Davids is an example, with the building of about 1200 being preceded by a church of the sixth century.

ABOVE: *Isolated churches can indicate Christianized pagan sites or very early church foundations. Llanhowell, near St Davids, is a twelfth-century church that goes right back to a sixth-century foundation.*

READING LOST SETTLEMENTS

*A*S SUGGESTED, there are some techniques that an untutored enthusiast can readily adopt, like work with old maps and training the eye to pick out earthworks. There are others that require some acquired expertise and help, like reading medieval documents, recognizing pottery or the more advanced forms of air photograph interpretation. Landscape detection makes no special demands; one can go as far with it as one chooses. All localities are different and all are worth scouring for lost villages, hamlets and farmsteads. I will now introduce the different clues, challenges and techniques by drawing on work that I did at Ripley in North Yorkshire in the late 1990s. I studied one township – amounting to just a third of a parish – in great

OVERLEAF: *The isolated church at Chellington in Bedfordshire; the loss of the village that went with it may have been caused by an amalgamation of the manor with that of neighbouring Carlton.*

depth. It contained one flourishing village, but I also found two deserted villages, four deserted hamlets and various medieval farmstead sites. Each discovery had its individual package of clues and challenges and the work was done mentally and on the ground – the bureaucrats with their computer programmes had found nothing. Some, at least, of the evidence and reasoning at Ripley will apply to other localities that the reader may search. The categories of clues and techniques employed are italicized. These are the 'lost' settlements.

VILLAGES

OWLCOTES

Training the eye to pick up platforms and shelves can be rewarding. This large and elongated roadside medieval village was discovered in pasture land. The lost village was betrayed by the recognition of an unusually and unnaturally level surface when surveying in the deer park that partly contains the site. The existence of a medieval village was confirmed at once by the *pottery*, mainly of the twelfth and thirteenth centuries, that rabbits and moles had kicked up to the surface. Later, the extent of the village was confirmed by more widespread surface finds of medieval pottery. The discovery was reported to English Heritage and Owlcotes was flown in perfect winter conditions, when the grass was very short. The *air photographs* revealed details of layout and a few individual dwellings that seemed invisible from the ground. A search of *medieval documents* for the locality revealed early medieval mentions of 'Owlecotes with Ripley', though Ripley may then have been only a manor house and a few associated dwellings. The *place-name* was readily translated as 'cottages where the owls are'.

Owlcotes may have been destroyed in making the deer park in Tudor times. A stronger possibility may be that it was evacuated in order to populate the new, purpose-built manorial village of Ripley, built around 1400, when the Pestilence was rife.

BIRTHWAITE

Birthwaite was discovered when it was realized that a lane approaching an upland common was flanked by very pronounced *earthworks: house platforms* of the type left by medieval dwellings. A search of relevant *documents* for the locality showed that it survived much longer than Owlcotes. In 1607, the *manor court rolls* showed that the villagers were charged with improving the stream that ran through their little green, though in the decades that followed, the small village dwindled away. The old documents revealed the early form of the name, Birkenthwaite or 'birchwood clearing', and the search for old *place-names* showed that the village stood in an area of medieval woodland clearance with names like 'Ruddings', 'Butt Pasture', 'Buskie (i.e. bosky or wooded) Close', 'Wood Close' and 'Woodhouse Ridding' (see the map on the facing page) all telling of the removal of woodland.

Birthwaite was apparently one of the late-forming villages, born into an overcrowded countryside. It was probably founded by households from Owlcotes, which settled at the head of a track where it opened on to a partly wooded common. Small upland villages were particularly vulnerable to the environmental ills of the fourteenth century, though Birthwaite survived the medieval era but decayed during the seventeenth century. It had a 'Y'-shaped form, with a tiny green in the angle of the 'Y'.

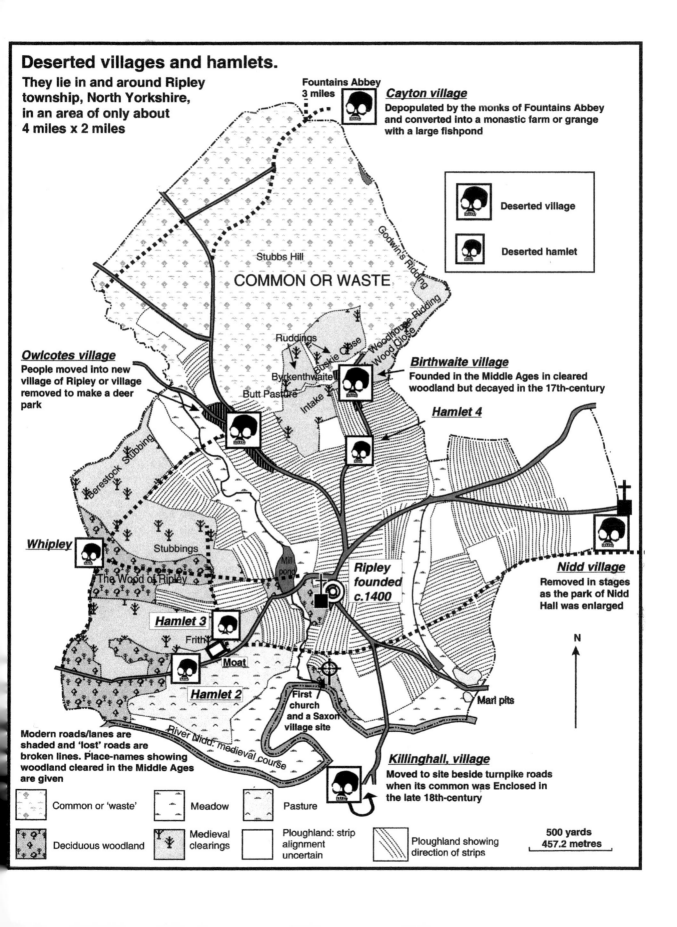

Deserted villages and hamlets.

They lie in and around Ripley township, North Yorkshire, in an area of only about 4 miles x 2 miles

Fountains Abbey 3 miles

Cayton village
Depopulated by the monks of Fountains Abbey and converted into a monastic farm or grange with a large fishpond

Deserted village

Deserted hamlet

Stubbs Hill

Godwin's Ridding

COMMON OR WASTE

Woodhouse Ridding
Wood Close

Ruddings

Buskie Close

Owlcotes village
People moved into new village of Ripley or village removed to make a deer park

Byrkenthwaite

Butt Pasture

Intake

Birthwaite village
Founded in the Middle Ages in cleared woodland but decayed in the 17th-century

Hamlet 4

Berestock Stubbing

Stubbings

Whipley

The Wood of Ripley

Mill pond

Ripley founded c.1400

Nidd village
Removed in stages as the park of Nidd Hall was enlarged

Hamlet 3

Frith

Moat

Hamlet 2

First church and a Saxon village site

N

Modern roads/lanes are shaded and 'lost' roads are broken lines. Place-names showing woodland cleared in the Middle Ages are given

River Nidd: medieval course

Marl pits

Killinghall, village
Moved to site beside turnpike roads when its common was Enclosed in the late 18th-century

Common or 'waste'

Meadow

Pasture

Deciduous woodland

Medieval clearings

Ploughland: strip alignment uncertain

Ploughland showing direction of strips

500 yards
457.2 metres

HAMLETS

WHIPLEY

The commonest form for hamlets in this area is that of a row of houses along one side of a road or of house rows facing each other across a lane. Whipley was different, for *old map* and *earthworks* evidence indicate a few houses around a green. Whipley may have existed as a settlement at the time of Domesday and it straddled the boundary between Ripley and the neighbouring township of Clint. One can trace the hamlet's road down to Ripley as a *holloway*, but the site now lies beneath a coniferous plantation and the most obvious landmark is a medieval *cross*, doubtless erected by the monks of Fountains abbey at the boundary of an estate they owned long ago. Whipley may have been weakened by the creation of the deer park across its site, though it might have already been depopulated to populate Ripley. The *place-name* is recorded in the old documents and it might mean 'clearing belonging to (someone with a name like) Wibba'.

HAMLET 2

This hamlet is known solely from the evidence of *earthworks*: a straggling string of *house platforms* of the medieval type that follow the *Roman road*. Typically, the dwellings were narrow and were arranged lengthwise along the road. Their doors would have opened directly on to the track, though as continuing traffic has worn down the road surface in places, the houses now stand above road level. Some dwelling sites are covered in brambles and other undergrowth, but where trees shade out the vegetation below, the house sites are quite clear. No name can be found. The hamlet lies on the section of Roman road in the deer park and, if it still existed, would have been removed when the Tudor park was made.

HAMLET 3

This is the most complex site. A medieval *moated house site* of some importance was discovered and a *holloway* was seen to run from it in the direction of Owlcotes. At some stage, a few families settled by this lane and slight dwelling traces and the squarish 'closes' or plots in which each house stood can be seen as *earthworks*. By Tudor times, the settlement must have been deserted, for a moated hunting tower was built in the new deer park very close by and the footings of the small tower can still be traced. Next, the deer park withdrew, land returned to agriculture and the old road seems to have come back into use, for a hedge with *hedgerow trees* (some still standing) was planted beside it, damaging the traces of the old roadside dwellings. *Annual tree ring counts* on tree stumps from the hedge suggest dates around 300 or so years ago. Then, the deer park advanced again, commandeering the site. Most of this complex story is evidenced by *earthworks* though the temporary retreat of the deer park is shown by *documents* – the late seventeenth-century leases granted by the lord of the manor to farmers who took over land in the park.

HAMLET 4

This hamlet, too, consisted of roadside dwellings – about five farmsteads on both sides of a lane running up to Birthwaite. This place can be dated by *inference*. It stands on a route that was diverted to run into the 'new' village of Ripley and so it must have come into being after 1400. The *old map evidence*

ABOVE: *A hilltop chapel overlooks the place, near Fountains Abbey, where Herleshow village lies.*

of a survey by W. Chippendale in 1752 shows that the hamlet was deserted by then. So *date brackets* of 1400–1752 can be established. The outlines of the house platforms are very plain and one house site was seen to contain masses of *pottery* of a type known as 'Cistercian ware' dating to the sixteenth century. (However, one has to be careful of the possibility of an abandoned roadside house being used as a dump and the litter in the former building also contained some blue and white Dutch ware of around 1800.) A substantial *tree* growing up through the ends of one of the dwellings confirms that it was deserted a good time ago. No name has passed on to us.

DESERTED VILLAGES IN THE IMMEDIATE AREA

Two lost villages and four lost hamlets in an area equalling just a third of a parish and around 2 × 4 miles in extent might seem a very good haul, but lying close to our township boundary we find the following villages.

NIDD

This village survived through all the threats and traumas of the Middle Ages, only to perish at the hands of park-makers when the park beside the hall was enlarged in several stages during the nineteenth century. The houses were removed and the road that had run through the village and formed its main street was greatly over-deepened so that the people in the hall would not be affronted by the sight of ordinary folk going about their business. The stages in the death and removal of Nidd can be traced through the successive *old maps* of the nineteenth century, including early *Ordnance Survey maps*, which are so detailed that one can see hedgerows being lassoed by the park, stripped of their shrubs and their individual hedgerow trees then being redeployed as ready-made landscaping materials. *Deduction* was needed to explain the great difference in level between the traces of dwellings and the deeply sunken lane.

CAYTON

The village fell victim to the monks of Fountains Abbey, built just three miles away during the 1130s. The villagers of Cayton were removed and the place became a grange with a large monastic fishpond. *Abbey documents* and the *earthworks* of the grange tell the story.

KILLINGHALL

The village is still there — but it has shifted. Formerly a straggle of farmsteads sitting on the edge of a vast common, the place would have been juddered by the Parliamentary Enclosure of common land in the valley. However, a couple of bustling turnpike roads converged in the vicinity and, their common gone, some villagers opted to move and settle beside them. The story is unfolded in the *old maps* of the eighteenth century, including the *Enclosure map* for the Forest of Knaresborough.

OVER TO YOU

*M*ANY KINDS OF expertise exist, but the greatest attribute is curiosity. It is curiosity that gets you out into the countryside; it is curiosity that sets you interrogating the scene, and it is curiosity that endows you with the persistence to see a problem through. Without the drive that is born of the love of a place combined with an insatiable curiosity about the meaning behind scenery, you will be no better than the bureaucrat with his or her computer, grinding out flawed interpretations of landscapes that do not really exist.

If curiosity is the greatest attribute, a lack of confidence is probably the greatest enemy of discovery. Experts are only experts (when they *are* experts) because they have devoted much time to developing experience and understanding. They were not experts when they romped across rugs in their nappies. People are sometimes scared to pursue an enthusiasm because they lack confidence. Lack of confidence is often a really a fear of ridicule. Yet mistakes are fine — they help you to learn.

The easiest thing to learn can often be the hardest: *to learn to ask*. In your local museum there is likely to be someone who can give you dates for the bits of pottery that you picked out of the

ABOVE: *Ickworth in Suffolk, a typical example of a lost village, lies entombed beside its church in a park.*

molehills. The county archivist should be pleased to itemize the old map coverage for your parish or give you an idea of the old documents that may assist a project and the reference librarian presides over a mass of local material and will almost certainly welcome your enquiry. All of them tend to be underpaid (though you are one of the payers). People with a little understanding of local history can sometimes become rather territorial and dismissive of 'interlopers'. Yet today every single enthusiast is needed to defend the countryside: conservational recruits must not be alienated and everyone was a beginner once. Those who know a little more should encourage these recruits – I think it was Sibelius who pointed out that there are no statues of critics. Now, more and more information is becoming available online. This is not entirely a good thing, for the incidental information that comes from a face-to-face chat with a helpful specialist can be very valuable.

8

FISHING VILLAGES

*F*OR MORE THAN 90 per cent of its life, the British village was essentially a dormitory for those subservient souls who toiled on the surrounding lands. If we could step into any period of history from Victorian times backwards, we would walk across mile upon mile of countryside without stumbling on a place that deviated from this norm. We would often encounter a village that had a few part-time craftsmen in its population – a smith, perhaps a couple of wood turners, a sawyer from a local saw pit, a collector of oak bark for the tanning industry and a few others. Even so, we would walk a long way before encountering anything resembling a real *industrial* village.

Similarly, if we went tramping along the coastline in pre-Elizabethan times we would travel a long way before we came across a true fishing village. In some sections of the coast, such places were just beginning to form, but they were small and lacked the armour of the breakwaters and piers to guard their anchorages. We might come across agricultural villages where the menfolk fished in seasons when the land was less greedy for labour and we might find a few places where the farming community had budded off a little fishing hamlet on the nearby seashore. Still, compared with the villages of ploughmen, reapers and cowherds, fishing villages were late developers. In due course and on the brink of modern times, the salty fishing port with its cottages clustered around the harbour became a national icon – this image was becoming established when Dickens' David Copperfield stayed with Peggotty's relatives in their converted boat at Great Yarmouth, the very port where Charles Dickens lived in 1848. Whiskery fishermen posing before their village homes were

LEFT: *Pittenweem, where the fishing settlement developed beside the cave occupied by an early saint*

favourite subjects for Victorian photographers, while the watercolourists of those times loved to capture the shimmering sea, racing clouds and the light glancing off the roofs of shoreline cottages. The fishing village had entered national mythology.

The allure and popularity of the fishing village increased as more artists came to visit it; coastal scenes decorated many a wall while prints of enticing harbours and cliff-poised cottages were displayed in countless railway carriages. The reason for the rise of the fishing village was the same as the reason for its popularization: accessibility. The innovations in transport that made it possible for publicists and visitors to get to the ports were *the same innovations* that allowed these places to grow by being able to export their catch to the urban markets. Refrigeration was icing to this cake. The story of the rise of the fishing village was, in large measure, the story of the increasing ability to

BELOW: *Dawn at Padstow. This place illustrates the anomalies in our understanding of towns and villages, for while most visitors would regard Padstow as a fishing village, it is a town with its own council. Having said this, on the continent of Europe there are many much larger settlements that are considered to be villages.*

distribute fish far and wide. However, the concentration of fishing in large ports, like Aberdeen and Grimsby, with fast rail connections and large fish markets, the rise of the large, sophisticated trawler and purse seine netter, and the over-fishing and depletion of stocks all played their parts in the decline of local fishing. Fortunately, when this happened, the fishing village had already acquired its attractive persona and inviting face, so that its community could forsake the perils of fishing for the profits of the tourist trade.

THE RISE OF FISHING VILLAGES

*F*ISHING HAS a very long story. It is now claimed that during the last Ice Age, more than 15,000 years ago, canoeists from southern Europe may have followed the southern margins of the Atlantic ice mass until they became established in North America. People of the Old Stone Age fished with harpoons, spears and hooks, but they did not fish commercially and they had no permanent settlements that we know of. The catch would have been eaten by the members of the hunting clan and would have been part of a nomadic life of hunting within the clan's territory. British people of the Middle Stone Age (around 10,000 to 4000 BC) gathered nuts, roots and shoots, scavenged, killed deer and wildfowl and fished. Regular visits were made to the shorelines, where enormous middens composed of discarded shells accumulated as shellfish were gathered and consumed. These huge, oval shell mounds can still be seen along rugged northern shores. However, fishing was still for local family consumption and groups remained footloose within their territories.

Even in the Middle Ages, little had happened to accelerate the development of fishing villages. Fishing must have taken place on an opportunistic basis during lulls in agricultural activity and a fishing season would have been slotted into the round of the farming year. The first steps towards commercial fishing would have occurred when villagers from coastal settlements walked inland with a basket of fish for sale. However, as the journeys lengthened the welcomes at farm and cottage doors would have rapidly become less enthusiastic as the stench of the decaying wares preceded the hawker. Without an effective way of preserving the very perishable catch, the potential for trading in fish was greatly reduced.

Some techniques were available. The Viking settlers in the Northern lands had developed methods for wind-drying split fish, while herrings could be salted and pickled in barrels. In Cornwall, pilchards were salted and squeezed to produce fish oil. Preserved fish was sometimes traded inland, and officials on land-locked manors might dispatch a trusted bondsman to buy barrels of pickled fish for feast days at the nearest sea port. However, the shortcomings of sea fishing encouraged an enthusiasm for freshwater fish, like carp and pike, rich in bones but less so in taste. Most manor houses, monasteries, palaces and castles were associated with neighbouring sets of shallow ponds where fish taken from rivers were stored. This secured a reliable supply of fish to be eaten on Fridays

OVERLEAF: *The old fishing port of St Monans in East Fife*

and on holy days and it ensured that fresh fish protein was there to complement the venison from the deer park when visiting entourages arrived.

In some cases, fishing villages were attracted to *existing* settlements of various kinds. Whitby, a medieval fishing village and later a big whaling port, grew at the estuary of the river Esk in the shadow of St Hilda's Abbey. Pittenweem in the East Neuk of Fifeshire, north of Edinburgh, was founded as a fishing village and was given Royal Burgh status in 1541. However, just above the harbour is the 'weem' or cave reputed to have been the home of the early saint, Filan. Just along the East Fife coast is St Monans, a noted North Sea fishing port, that began as a Dominican friary, founded by David II (1329–71).

The development of a mass fishing industry was held back by problems of supply rather than demand. In some parts of Britain it was possible to get a catch to market before the 'decomposition deadline'. Londoners could enjoy ready supplies of eels, lampreys and shellfish, with local oysters being common fare long before they were luxury goods.

A quay and breakwater used by fishing boats could be used by other vessels, and as fishing developed, it was usually combined with other maritime activities of varying degrees of legality. These would normally include legitimate commerce, smuggling, privateering and, sometimes, outright piracy and wrecking. After visiting Fowey in Cornwall in the 1530s, the chronicler, Leland, wrote that he found the place 'waxing rich, partly by feats of war, partly by piracy'.

Fishing quarters often developed as the seaward extensions of established settlements. Brighton ('Brighthelmstone' in the Middle Ages) seems to have developed fishing in late medieval times. The fishing section lay on the foreshore, with tracks leading inland to the rest of the settlement. In 1514, the fishing village was burned by French raiders and in the seventeenth century it was assaulted by the sea. It was finally overrun by a storm in 1705. In a few cases, like medieval Scarborough, a settlement gradually advanced seaward by building over its existing quays and creating new ones on the reclaimed shore beyond them.

THE
INDUSTRY
GROWS

WITH ITS REVOLUTIONARY acceleration in the speed of transport and its far-reaching quickening of the tempo of commerce, it was the railway that assisted the development of fishing more than any other single factor. No industry can have benefited more from the ability to get goods swiftly and surely to market. However, by the time that the railway network extended its web along the coastline other significant changes had already been at work.

As fishing expanded, part-time fishermen were encouraged to pursue full-time vocations, while ploughboys and town lads must have walked to the mushrooming fishing villages to enlist in the dangerous occupation. The early generations of professional fishermen – like the bearded men with the sou'westers and canvas shirts in the early photographs – normally owned their own boats, the boats being the family business. The difference from other enterprises was that when the business sank, half of the family would perish with it. Often, the business predated the villages, with boats

ABOVE: *Port Isaac in Cornwall, where boats are beached in a time-honoured manner*

being hauled onto an empty foreshore in a place still lacking a settlement and harbour. In a few places, like Port Isaac in Cornwall, boats are still beached on the strand.

In the middle part of the eighteenth century, a sound nucleus for a fishing industry existed on the north-eastern shores of Britain, where small boats with crews of six or seven might have been seen fishing as far as 50 miles from the land. The catch could not be got fresh to the markets in the capital or the emerging industrial towns, but cod was split and salted and dried in the sun and haddock was cured by smoking. Those who risked their lives in the small, decked boats from the English ports and in the open boats from the ports of Scotland could earn just a little more than the folk that they saw toiling in the fields as their crafts returned after up to five days at sea.

The Georgian and early Victorian eras witnessed a multiplication of fishing villages. The fishing hamlet out-ports or sea towns linked to existing villages and towns expanded, sometimes becoming fishing settlements in their own rights – and lots of new centres were established. However, the day of the thriving young fishing village and the owner–skipper was a usually a short one. Those villages that failed to secure a rail link were swiftly doomed. At first, such a place might send its catch on to a more fortunate neighbour, in the way that Aberdeen gathered up the catches from numerous villages in its region. Eventually, however, the rising cost, size and technology of fishing boats brought the end of skipper–owners and the appearance of fishing companies based in bigger ports, like Aberdeen and Yarmouth.

As electronic technology replaced intuition and experience in locating shoals, ever larger and more expensive boats worked further and further afield in search of ever-diminishing fish stocks. Fishing has become concentrated in large ports, like Peterhead on the north-eastern knuckle of Scotland. Remote-sensing devices are used to locate the dwindling shoals, while skippers switch opportunistically between white fish and prawns as they seek to finance their boats from declining resources. Meanwhile, as the more substantial parts of the industry became centralized in the most capacious all-weather harbours, less-successful villages were left to work crabbing, inshore waters, recreational fishing and tourism. Living on a pretty face is less exciting, but far more secure.

THE
LANDSCAPE
OF THE
FISHING
VILLAGE

*F*ISHING VILLAGES are not scattered in a random fashion along the coast. The fisherman and his crew did not simply require a place on land to return to sleep. Actually getting home was the main thing on their minds. The ideal requirement was to have a haven that could be reached under any weather, sea and tidal conditions, a place that was shielded from the worst weather and always accessible and beckoning no matter how violent or unhelpful the local marine environment might be. Such places were very few indeed, so that most fishermen had to settle for homes and anchorages that could be entered under most wind conditions or states of the tide.

Local topography is absolutely crucial, but it varies immensely from place to place. Along many stretches of the British coast, near-vertical cliffs present a curtain of exclusion to vessels for mile upon mile. In other places, inlets, estuaries and creeks are found at frequent intervals, with at least some of them offering shelter to navigation. As one may imagine, on any rampart-like cliff coastline, the most modest inlet is likely to be exploited, while on the lower and more indented coasts the fishing community has more choice of where to live.

On the wider scale, different marine environments offered different resources and encouraged different forms of fishing. Some Cornish ports specialized in netting pilchards and selling salt fish to Catholic southern Europe, while the nineteenth-century fishermen from North East Scotland might be found line fishing for *great fish*, the cod, haddock and ling, using locally dug mussels as bait. Some of the haddock would go to coastal places in old Kincardineshire, like Findon, where they would be smoked and emerge as *Finnan haddies*. Meanwhile the North Sea ports were heavily engaged in the pursuit of the once-vast shoals of the 'silver darlings' or herring.

Topography had a great effect upon the pattern of fishing villages. Vessels not only needed anchorages but shelter from the worst of the elements as they sought them. If one could not find a

ABOVE: *The remains of Port Quin, in Cornwall, where the men of the fishing community are said to have perished in a storm*

refuge then storms had to be ridden out at sea – always an unattractive option. The influence of the topography of a place not only controlled *whether* a settlement could exist, it could also affect the *character* of individual buildings within the fishing village. The following factors help to explain why fishing villages are where they are.

TOPOGRAPHY AND OPPORTUNITY

If an area had proximity to good fishing waters, every geographical opportunity would be exploited, no matter how small. As the fishing industry of North East Scotland took shape during the eighteenth century, an industry with about 300 boats, 9000 dependent people and some 70 fishing villages developed along 150 miles of coastline running north from Montrose and along the Moray Firth shore. Even so, the topography was often unfavourable. Sometimes a village was perched on a cliff shelf and the boats were beached or moored on the open foreshore below. Burnhaven was cursed with poor harbour facilities, and after struggling for around 60 years, its fishing community is said to have migrated to the nearby booming herring port of Peterhead in the closing years of the nineteenth century. The final ignominy came when the site of the old village was obliterated by road building in the 1970s.

LEVEL LAND

This was often at a premium. When the improving landlord, Garden of Troup, built a fishing port bearing his name beneath the towering red cliffs near the knuckle of North East Scotland, there was just a narrow shelf to place Gardenstown upon. At Whinnyfold, the cove was so confined and the encircling cliffs so steep that the village was built on the level ground atop the cliffs.

BEACHING

Along the southern and eastern coasts of England, where natural harbours were lacking, boats might be hauled up the beach and the fishing families would live in dwellings or upended boats strung along the foreshore. Hastings had no natural harbour, just a shingle beach flanked by eroding cliffs, but fisherfolk were attracted to the fish resources of nearby Rye Bay. Much of the town was destroyed by marine invasions in the fourteenth century, but at least by Elizabethan times, a fishing industry had been established. An open beach is no substitute for a storm-proof harbour and eventually the lack of a natural harbour and the failure of various schemes to build an artificial one undermined this fishing industry. Where there was no option but to drag boats onto the foreshore, a beach of shingle was generally preferred to one of sand. It was easier to haul a boat across shingle, and there was less of a tendency for the craft to bed down and become difficult to move.

IMPROVEMENTS

Many other places enjoyed success in their attempts to improve the natural topography. Pittenweem began life without an artificial harbour, with boats being grounded on sheltered beaches until a breakwater was built. One of the most picturesque of the Cornish ports is Mevagissey. Here a quay was built in medieval times, but the natural inlet forming the harbour was exposed to easterly gales. An inner harbour was built in 1774 and enjoyed the shelter of an outer harbour that was built in 1888. The work was hardly done when this was washed away in the storm associated with the Great Blizzard of 1891. At this time, the village was much smaller than today, showing that the twentieth-century prosperity has come from tourism. The village still has a small fishing fleet and further repairs to the harbour were carried out in 1998.

SPECIAL CASES

Occasionally, patrons would resort to quite unusual lengths in attempts to develop a port. At Cruden Bay, north of Aberdeen, a river was diverted to create a sheltered inlet for fishing craft, followed by the construction of a harbour in the late 1870s, where the name of the place was changed from Ward of Cruden to Port Errol.

CHANGING CIRCUMSTANCES

Some other places had excellent natural harbours and could prosper in relative safety until the lack of potential for expansion brought their slow decline. Boscastle in Cornwall had the best natural harbour on a 20-mile stretch of the north Cornish coast but it declined after just a century of prosperity when

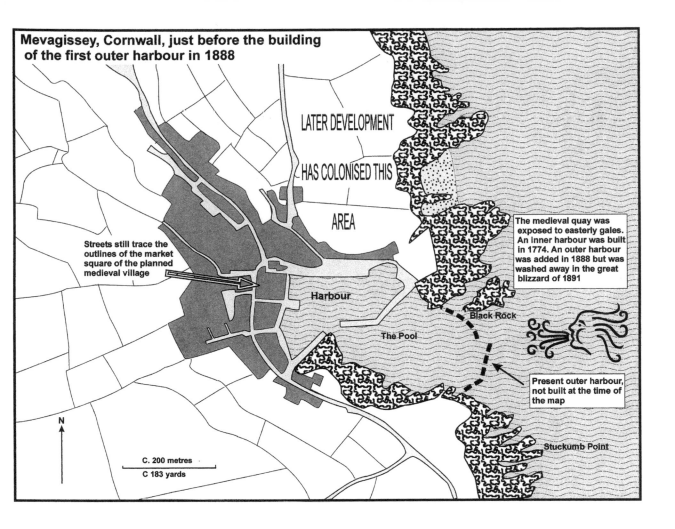

Mevagissey, Cornwall, just before the building of the first outer harbour in 1888

LATER DEVELOPMENT HAS COLONISED THIS AREA

Streets still trace the outlines of the market square of the planned medieval village

The medieval quay was exposed to easterly gales. An inner harbour was built in 1774. An outer harbour was added in 1888 but was washed away in the great blizzard of 1891

Harbour

Black Rock

The Pool

Present outer harbour, not built at the time of the map

Stuckumb Point

N

C. 200 metres
C 183 yards

it failed to gain a connection with the fast-expanding railway system. Little can its villagers have imagined that danger would come from the land, in the form of a flash flood, rather than from the sea.

MOTHER AND DAUGHTER VILLAGES

Where a fishing village has been budded off from an agricultural village one may be able to recognize the parent, standing surrounded by farmland, and the offspring at the coast. The move to the coast probably represented a shift by part of the farming community from seasonal to full-time fishing. The building sites available may not have been very inviting and the harbour not very sheltered. Occasionally, the pattern could work in reverse, for Cullen, on the Moray Firth, was a planned new settlement for evicted crofters that was built on the cliff top overlooking the older 'seatoun' of an older fishing community that straggled along a shoreline shelf.

OVERLEAF: *St Abbs in the south-east of Scotland displays a layout seen at many fishing villages, with an orderly settlement on higher, more level ground and other houses perched on shelves by the harbour.*

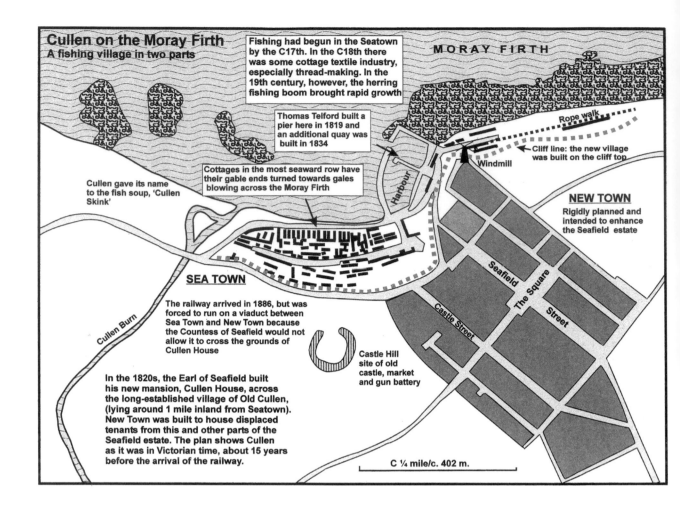

Cullen on the Moray Firth
A fishing village in two parts

MORAY FIRTH

Fishing had begun in the Seatown by the C17th. In the C18th there was some cottage textile industry, especially thread-making. In the 19th century, however, the herring fishing boom brought rapid growth

Thomas Telford built a pier here in 1819 and an additional quay was built in 1834

Rope walk

Cliff line: the new village was built on the cliff top

Windmill

Cottages in the most seaward row have their gable ends turned towards gales blowing across the Moray Firth

Cullen gave its name to the fish soup, 'Cullen Skink'

NEW TOWN
Rigidly planned and intended to enhance the Seafield estate

Harbour

Seafield Street

The Square

Castle Street

Street

SEA TOWN

Cullen Burn

The railway arrived in 1886, but was forced to run on a viaduct between Sea Town and New Town because the Countess of Seafield would not allow it to cross the grounds of Cullen House

Castle Hill site of old castle, market and gun battery

In the 1820s, the Earl of Seafield built his new mansion, Cullen House, across the long-established village of Old Cullen (lying around 1 mile inland from Seatown). New Town was built to house displaced tenants from this and other parts of the Seafield estate. The plan shows Cullen as it was in Victorian time, about 15 years before the arrival of the railway.

C ¼ mile/c. 402 m.

THE ARCHITECTURE OF FISHING

*T*HE LAYOUT AND SITING of fishing villages was greatly affected by the coastal topography, but these villages also developed their own distinctive buildings. As their communities bade farming goodbye, so the architectural requirements changed and dwellings were developed that expressed the communal ties with the sea ahead, rather than with the land behind. Existence as a fishing village could greatly affect the *housescape* of a place. We are familiar with pictures of houses stacked up the steep slopes of a cliff, exploiting every little shelf available and making for a strenuous ascent from the harbour. In northern parts of Britain, dwellings in fishing villages were often built with their *gable ends* facing towards the easterly gales that can blast, unimpeded, across the North Sea.

Fishing villages were also able to exploit a greater range of building materials than inland villages. In the East Neuk of Fife and the North Sea coast of the Borders and Northumberland, for example, the red pantiled roofs are an attractive characteristic of the dwellings. Cargo ships from Belgium and Holland used the products of their home tile-making industries as ballast – and these tiles were readily re-deployed by people living around the harbours in North Sea ports. People from these ports also copied the stepped *crow-stepped gables* that their men had seen in the Low Countries – as is evident from Scotland through to East Anglia.

In many old villages, fishermen occupied narrow dwellings that were ranged around the harbour. The ground floor was a *cellar* devoted to treating and preserving the catch, while some of the larger operators had courtyards or *fish palaces* where these operations were carried out in lean-to sheds. Domestic accommodation was in the rooms above the cellar, which must have been heavy with the smell of fish. In Scotland, the earlier fishing families tended to occupy single-storey dwellings of the *but and ben* type, with chimneys on the gable end walls and roofs of thatch. Floors were often of earth, though sometimes an old canvas sail was spread over the floor. In most fishing villages, *gentrification*, the conversion of old cottages into retirement homes, holiday cottages, restaurants and gift shops and the addition of guest houses around the margins of the old village have greatly modified buildings and completely transformed the housescape. Hardly any of the old dwellings survive in anything like their original form.

Fisher cottages and lighthouses were not the only architectural creations of the fishing industry. As the Cornish pilchard industry grew in the decades around 1800, *huers' houses* were built on cliff vantage points. From them, the sharp-eyed huers scoured the seas for signs of approaching pilchard shoals, summoning the fishermen and then directing their boats to the shoals.

LIVING
DANGEROUSLY

ISHING COMMUNITIES lived with danger and were always just a sea storm away from mass bereavement and penury. They had almost invariably originated from the neighbouring agricultural communities, but it was perhaps the danger and the fatalism that fishing bred – as well as their slightly greater affluence – that made the societies of the fishing villages different, exclusive and remote. Marriages with outsiders were very frequently strongly discouraged and the proximity of death may have explained the attraction of fundamentalist Protestant ideologies – sometimes beliefs so severe as to prohibit illustrated books or television. In the old fishing communities, death was ever on hand. Until Victorian times, men who had escaped the tempests might be seized by press gangs, caught smuggling by the militias or hung for piracy. Many met more honourable deaths as lifeboat volunteers. This threat persists today and in 1981, eight men from Mousehole died when the Penlee lifeboat capsized in hurricane-force winds. Where the fishing communities were few and well spread and the sectarian convictions intense, the taboos on intermarriage have led to the existence of some small villages where just a very few surnames are extant. The small communities are bound together by a web of interrelatedness.

The evidence of the eighteenth and nineteenth centuries shows that fishing villages tended to be founded by a small number of families from the nearby land. The pool of surnames would begin in a restricted manner, in the way that the Wests, Watts and Wisemans were the first settlers in Gardenstown. Marriages with families in fishing villages lying just along the coast could add new names to the pool, but the more exclusive the lifestyle became, the more concentrated the gene pool would be.

Life at the junction of the land and the sea also involves its own dangers. The sea may invade the land or undercut a cliff perch. Meanwhile, cliffs being steep, they are particularly prone to landslips, while the gaps in the cliff wall wrought by valleys and ravines may create useful inlets at the shore, but they can also serve as corridors for plummeting landslides. Even when the menfolk were at sea and in danger of capsizing and drowning, their families at home could be overwhelmed by a freak wave surging over the strand, caught by a flash flood thundering down a ravine or entombed by a cliff fall.

Particularly in its earlier days, fishing was a very hazardous occupation and since relatives and neighbours fished together in family-owned boats, the loss of one or two vessels from a small fishing village or hamlet could cause its virtual extinction. According to local tradition, Port Quinn, near Port Isaac in Cornwall, lost its whole fleet and all its menfolk one stormy night in the nineteenth century. The women attempted to struggle on, but eventually the settlement was abandoned.

Where the homes and workshops of the fishermen lined the foreshore at the foot of the backing cliffs, as at Crovie near Fraserburgh, life could be more convenient. There were not the perilous descents to and from the boats along steep, greasy cliff paths or rope bridges. Fish for packing and gear for mending could be brought swiftly into nearby cottages from the boats. However, such settlements were in peril at high tide whenever a storm drove waves up the beach and over the existing strand line, with the whole community being trapped against the cliffs.

The sea that provided a livelihood could also bring destruction. Brighton had supported 80 deep-water boats and perhaps 400 fishermen in Elizabethan times, but I have already mentioned the great storm of 1705 and when Daniel Defoe, the writer, diarist and spy, visited the place in 1724 he found 'a poor fishing town, old built and on the very edge of the sea'. He added:

> The sea is very unkind to this town, and has by its continual encroachments, so gained upon them,
> that in a little time more they might reasonably expect it would eat the whole town.

The North Sea has proved quite capable of overrunning whole towns as well as just villages. Ravenserodd and Ravenser are examples. The former, built on a sand spit in the Humber estuary, was inundated in 1346 and two-thirds of the doomed town were carried away, while by the end of the century it had gone entirely and bodies had been washed from its churchyard. Ravenser, its close neighbour, perished about the same time, and both now lie somewhere in the estuary just inside the great spit of Spurn Head. The relentless advance of the North Sea on the soft rocks of the coast has resulted in a succession of settlements being precipitated into the sea since Roman times. Currently, Mablethorpe in Lincolnshire is poised on the brink.

Villages on unstable cliffs and on the flanks of ravines and inlets could live dangerously. Runswick Bay, north of Whitby, is a replacement for a village that collapsed into the sea in 1682, when a landslide wrecked all the village apart from a single cottage. Two mourners at a wake recognized the danger signs and started the evacuation of the settlement. A replacement village was built on the ravine, but a smaller landslide in 1858 destroyed its iron smelter. On the south side of

ABOVE: *Safe, artificial anchorages were generally acquired in stages, as at Mevagissey.*

Whitby, Robin Hood's Bay is claimed to have been so reduced by the advancing sea that during a storm in 1893 the bowsprit of a brig burst through the window of the Bay Hotel. In 1975, a new sea wall was built.

Boscastle had flourished until the railway age and clung to the side of the Valency valley. In mid-August 1984, a coming together of sea breezes and a saturated, southerly airflow produced torrential rain, which became more intense as the bulk of Bodmin Moor forced the clouds upwards. Towering thunderclouds resulted and 12.7 cm (more than 5 inches) of rain fell in just a few hours. The ground was already saturated and flash floods on the high ground were funnelled into valleys, like the Valency. Boscastle was devastated, but fortunately this occurred in daytime and people were alert. Exactly 52 years earlier, nearby Lynmouth, just along the coast, experienced a far worse disaster when floodwater burst the banks of the East Lyn and West Lyn rivers. Waters surging to heights of 9.1 m (30 ft) tore through the fishing village and 35 people lost their lives.

ABOVE: Port Isaac in Cornwall, built on a cramped site with few level sites

The shifting of sandbanks did not produce dramatic finales, but numerous fishing villages were slowly stifled as their lifelines to the sea were choked. Silting and sandbars were a problem all the way from Sandwich in Kent, which closed to large vessels when the Stour estuary silted, to Orford in Suffolk, which was trapped behind a lengthening sandbar, and also to the lost burgh of Rattray in North East Scotland, where the consequences for the settlement were fatal. Shifting sand was also a threat on land, especially when boats and dwellings lay in a narrow zone between the strand line and a belt of sand dunes. Under conditions of storm-force winds and the over-grazing on the plants that stabilized the sands, dunes could become mobile and be driven right across a village. Kenfig, an English feudal plantation in West Glamorgan, was overwhelmed by the sands of the Severn seaboard in the fifteenth century.

Not all disasters can be blamed on Nature. In the 1890s, an invasion scare resulted in a demand for aggregate to strengthen naval dockyards in south-west England. Sir John Jackson Ltd was given a contract to dredge shingle from the beach between Hallsands and Beesands in Devon, despite protests from the local fishing community. Almost immediately, the sea began to advance on Hallsands, for there was less shingle to break the impact of the incoming waves. The village was steadily reduced, until a great storm in 1917 reduced Hallsands to just a single dwelling. The circumstances of the dredging contract are still controversial.

BUILT TO PLAN

*W*HEN WE GAZE at a 'traditional' fishing village, in reality or in a painting, the scene that we see usually seems as undisciplined and spontaneous as anything we might imagine. Cottages of differing heights and colours pack around the harbour and others, stacked on the surrounding slopes, seem to jostle to gain every shelf and perch. Actually, part of this vision is due to the way that the uneven terrain causes steps in the roof lines, and partly because different houses have experienced different conversions at different times. In fact, when we look into the old documents and study maps of the village street plan we often discover that the place concerned was a deliberate creation and was set out according to a predetermined layout. During the Middle Ages right through into Victorian times, such planned fishing villages were created.

In Cornwall, the villages of Gorran Haven, Looe and Mevagissey were deliberately created in late medieval times as the sea ports for existing villages. In the typical manner of a feudal creation, Mousehole developed when a weekly market and fair of three days at the feast of St Barnabas was granted to the Cornish manor of Alverton in 1292. Mevagissey had a market square close to its harbour which is now covered in buildings but which can be recognized in the rectangular gridwork of streets, while Gorran Haven grew at a cove used by its parent hamlet of Gorran.

In North East Scotland, the *Improvements*, which took the form of a great reorganization of country estates in the century or so following 1750, caused the eviction of thousands of impoverished tenants as the farmholdings were 'rationalized'. This was the dawning of an age of enlightenment, so rather than putting surplus tenants out on the road, the great landlords often attempted to establish mills and other sources of new employment, including fishing. Purpose-built fishing villages appeared, where the landlords might themselves build houses to let, as at Buckhaven, or offer prospective tenants incentives to build dwellings for themselves, according to careful specifications, as at St Combs. Meanwhile, in the Scottish Highlands and Islands the Clearances were more cruel and the plight of the evicted clansmen more desperate (see Chapter Ten). In 1786, an attempt to redeploy crofters in fishing villages was organized under the auspices of The British Fisheries Society. The developments were partly the brainchild of John Knox, a London bookseller, who proposed the establishment of 40 villages. This was over-ambitious, but a joint stock company was established to raise finance. Ullapool, the most expensive of the new villages, was begun in 1788 and Tobermory on Mull, Lochbay on Skye and Pultneytown near Wick also resulted. Fishing did not meet the high expectations, but the settlements found their own routes to survival and Ullapool did enjoy some success from fishing. All the settlements were precisely set out in their landscapes, with their harbours and housing provisions being preplanned, even though Pultneytown grew from a settlement of seven families to one with a population of 2000 in the course of a single generation.

LEARNING
TO READ
THE FISHING
VILLAGE

ISHING VILLAGES are different from other villages in ways both obvious and subtle. While the precise siting of a farming village seems generally to have been a somewhat arbitrary and random process, fishing villages were very carefully positioned in order to exploit the advantages of the coastal terrain. The juxtaposition of a navigable cove or inlet and a shielding headland could be crucial to success. In looking at fishing villages we should really begin by reading the coastal landscape to determine why the village was positioned here, rather than in the next bay.

Architecture can be very instructive. Generally we encounter the older dwellings around the harbour. These may preserve traces of their original uses as fish cellars and workshops with domestic rooms above and they may be built of alien materials – tiles and pantiles – that arrived as ballast. Such heavy materials were unlikely to be exported very far inland, so that the old core of the fishing village may display a vernacular architecture that is distinctly different from the old house styles apparent inland.

Gradually, a biography of a fishing village may be pieced together. It will note the initial attractions of the site and, possibly, how a population was attracted from the surrounding countryside or a single agricultural village. We should also be able to deduce how the natural anchorage was enhanced and made more secure, say by ringing the original foreshore where boats were berthed with quays and dredging the harbour and its approaches to produce a safer, deeper haven. Meanwhile, an architectural survey will identify the cottages of the old fishing community and the villas, hotels and guest houses built for those attracted by the fresh breezes and salty myths.

Evidence from the early days when a clutch of bond or crofting families began to diversify their lives by developing fishing is likely to be hard to find. Occasionally, one may be able to link the

ABOVE: *The houses at Polperro, in Cornwall, perch on every available niche above the harbour.*

fishing settlement to a *mother village* a little inland. It has been suggested that when the fishing village is itself set a little back from the sea, like Cove and Findon, north of Kincardine, this may reflect the pull of both the ancestral farmland and the new fishing grounds.

Scores of long-established fishing villages did not gain their stone quays and breakwaters until centuries after their creation. The majority originated as places where boats could be hauled ashore in a cove or inlet that offered a little shelter from the direction of the most dangerous winds. A visit to the local library or record office may actually reveal *old photographs* that record the armouring of the anchorage. It was a sad fishing village that did not attract the attention of Victorian photographers and many of the harbour constructions that are seen today were acquired in Victorian times. It is useful mentally to strip away the quays and breakwaters and see what the fundamental topographical attractions of a place may have been. As discussed, shingle beaches were normally preferred to those of sand for the beaching of ships and sand beaches tended to be more exposed. The disposition of cliffs and headlands could be important in terms of the shelter that they offered. The most favoured of the old ports were those with all-weather harbours that could be reached under any conditions. Such harbours would attract vessels from near and far in times of storm, for otherwise they would have to sit out the tempest offshore rather than gambling on gaining a harbour.

The storms that were most feared were those that threatened to drive a fleet against the shore. On 16 November, 1810, an easterly gale trapped shipping against the Lincolnshire coast. A local observer recorded:

> ... we may fairly say that from the Humber to Boston Deeps, 400 vessels have been wrecked. Dead bodies are thrown on the shore almost every tide off Mablethorpe, Theddlethorpe, Sutton, and the neighbouring parishes on the coast.

Journals and old newspapers, held in bound volumes or on microfilm, should be available in the reference library or record office serving the area under scrutiny. Disasters at sea, great and small, will be recorded and the frequency of these incidents may be surprising. The study of a long sequence of catastrophes and groundings will reveal the threat profile affecting a selected stretch of coastline.

Scores of settlements have been washed from the shores of eastern England since Roman times, but there are also fishing villages that have survived in a much reduced state after episodes of erosion or silting. The most obvious evidence of this is the presence of a misfit church – a building much too large to serve just the congregation that remains. Excellent examples of such churches can be seen at Walberswick and Covehithe on the Suffolk coast. These buildings are obviously ruined, but there are more subtle signs that a church has been reduced along with its ailing settlement. Discordant stonework can mark the blocking off of nave arcades, a scar on the side of a tower can show how a nave has been lowered or the east wall may tell of a chancel that has been shed. The former positions of settlements engulfed by an advancing sea can quite often be suggested by old roads and tracks that run towards the cliff edge. These were the routeways that served the village before it vanished; now they point to its grave. Shoreline parishes are sometimes amalgamations of an intact parish and the remains of a parish that served a lost church, and unusual parish shapes can tell a tale.

In the case of the planned fishing villages of the eighteenth and nineteenth centuries, readers interested in archive work may actually be able to trace how a place was first populated. Occupants might be attracted by advertisements placed in the press; recruitment meetings were held and handbills might be fixed to market crosses. Where estate papers have survived they might include contracts between the landlord and settlers. The accounts relating to Portgordon show that the estate spent a substantial 12s (60p) on whisky for the contract-signing ceremonies. Sometimes, the tenancy records list the occupations of the new villagers.

Few places remained *only* fishing villages, so that the settlement that one sees could be the combined product of smuggling, commercial shipping, the export of local resources, tourism and many other things. A spot of work in the local library is likely to unearth these other uses. There, one should find old *trade directories* that indicate the employments pursued by Victorian residents. Inveraray demonstrates the great swings in fortune that could be encountered. It was a modest fishing village until it was burned by the Marquis of Montrose in 1644. However, in 1743, the 3rd Duke of Argyll, chief of clan Campbell, removed the moribund settlement, built a splendid castle in its place and created a new, rigidly planned Georgian town centred on a broad main street to go with it. The imposing Classical church was built with separate sections for Gaelic- and English-speaking congregations. Fishing has lingered, but the impressive clan capital now relies heavily on tourism.

To gain an idea of the extent of the old fishing village, one can simply 'remove' all the post-Victorian architecture. The better mobility that may have helped to shift the fish catch would also attract a substantial – and far different – population of visitors and incomers. Artists, attracted to the sea skies and romance of a place, people like painters and potters, might add a new dimension to community and vocation and perhaps even endow the village with celebrity, as at St Ives or Walberswick. Stripped of its late Victorian and Edwardian villas, its craft workshops and its hotels, guest houses and souvenir shops from the first half of the twentieth century and denuded of its council housing estate and time shares, the fishing village that remains is generally seen as a rather diminutive place. Unlike the situation in most inland villages, most of the transformations have been enacted in just a century or so – so that the whole pageant can be recorded in old photographs and detailed in old newspapers.

Even if the paraphernalia of the tourist industry has become rather stifling, the fishing village still has its history. It still has its wet days too, when a foray into local landscape history could turn a gloomy spell into a day of discovery.

9

THE VILLAGE
MARCHES ON

*A*FTER THE CLOSE of the Middle Ages, the village marched on, though the ranks of new recruits were far thinner than in the centuries leading up to AD 1400, the time when retreat and decay began. The villages that have appeared between Elizabethan times and today have tended to be 'special cases', owing their existence to the whims or interventions of powerful individuals. The days of the bands of land-hungry peasant colonists largely died with the arrival of the storms, floods and gales on the eve of the Pestilence. The momentum of village formation that took place in the Anglo-Saxon centuries was never equalled. The closest approach was the establishment of dozens of new estate villages during the Improvements in the North East and lowlands of Scotland in Georgian times, as outlined in Chapter Ten, while perhaps the closest approach to concerted action involved the foundation of a few purpose-built fishing villages by the British Fisheries Society in the years around 1800, as mentioned in Chapter Eight.

It was in the eighteenth century that the village, hitherto a bucolic, shabby and grossly unsanitary place, discovered an inner beauty – or rather its romantic potential was recognized by arbiters of taste. The 'shepherd swain' – who in reality probably smelled strongly of his charges, who had a complexion provided by sunburn and dirt in fairly equal measures and who would have been infected by parasites both within and without – suddenly became a symbol of lost innocence and rustic charm. So too did his dairymaid companion and the old sage who leaned on his scythe in the

LEFT: *The Dutch Reform Church at Saltaire and the Salt factory in the distance, all accomplished in an Italianate style*

churchyard. And so too did the village. For members of cultivated and privileged society, the village could be left alone and seen (preferably from up-wind) as an engagingly ramshackle nest for rustic folk, with sagging thatch, rutted lanes, wafting smoke and geese grazing on the green. Alternatively, it could be seen as a target for progressive improvements. These would impose orderliness on the scene – but in so doing would also erect new cottages that parodied any or all of the fashionable rustic motifs. Bargeboards, dormer windows, porches, rose trellises and piecrust thatch were grist to the village-maker's mill. Reform generally involved two steps forwards and a couple more in the direction of sentimentality.

NEW
VILLAGES
FOR OLD

*M*ANY OF THE villages that appeared in Britain in the eighteenth century and up to mid-Victorian times were not strictly new but were replacements for older, often very old, villages that had in some way gained the dissatisfaction of their owners. The underlying nature of the changes was as follows.

BELOW: *Old Warden in Bedfordshire, where villagers were expected to turn out in red capes and tall hats*

Firstly, as we have seen, the castles, palaces and greater manor houses of the Middle Ages were very frequently surrounded by 'designed landscapes' with deer parks, lakes, gardens, groves, surprise views and so on. Some villages must have been removed as such medieval landscapes were created, but we do not know very much about them.

Secondly, the enthusiasm for surrounding the houses of the rich and powerful with landscape parks continued after the Middle Ages. However, while many medieval manor houses had been sited among their gardens in villages quite close to humble dwellings, it came to be considered that the great house should pose in glorious isolation. It should stand alone, with its vast park insulating it from country people and the humdrum life of working countrysides. Thus, when the old manor house was being dismantled or enlarged to become something far more fashionable and expressive of status, the old village beside it would frequently be cast down. But the third component in the eternal rural triangle – the village church – was less easy to remove. In any event, the great family needed the use of a convenient church and the village church was probably packed with the tombs of its noble dead. The church could stay, becoming ever more like a family chapel and dynastic mausoleum. This left the problem of the villagers, and there were really only two options where they were concerned. They might simply be evicted, but this would often deprive the estate of its essential workforce and rob the house of its servants. The other option was that of building a new village for them in a place where they could not pollute the pristine solitude of the park.

Thirdly, the building of the new estate villages offered interesting opportunities. They could be built in such a manner that they would advertise the benevolence of their patrons, showing them as people of progressive sensibilities who actually cared for the conditions in which their tenants lived. They might be built in an exaggeratedly rustic manner to mine the new seam of Picturesque romance associated with country life; the cottages might flaunt the arms or monogram of the estate owner, or pose as eye-catchers to trap the gaze with their fancy details. Such new villages needed to be seen by people of influence, so the preferred situation was on the roadside leading up to the park gates. There they could be admired by guests as they approached the great house. In this way, and in dozens of places, the scenic juxtaposition of the great house, the deserted village site and the park-stranded church came into being – often with a fourth element, the custom-built replacement village, lying a little apart from the trio.

SOME EXAMPLES OF REPLACEMENT VILLAGES

Although the employment of different building materials and different architectural styles can make the various estate replacement villages look quite different, their origins are remarkably similar. It often seems that the reader of village landscapes can scarcely enter a park without expecting to find a lonely church, with only the great house to keep it company, and a spread of earthworks nearby marking the old village site. The emergence, just outside the park pale, of successor villages was closely linked to their estates and the affluence, ambitions and decisions of their lords. Some were content to shuffle a community from one set of hovels into another, but some sought much more.

RIGHT: *The pioneering industrial village of Cromford in Derbyshire*

The following are some examples:

- **NUNEHAM COURTENAY**, in Oxfordshire, is the best known example because the settlement described in Goldsmith's poem 'The Deserted Village' has been identified as Newnham Courtenay. Newnham was removed by Lord Harcourt and replaced, after 1760, with a roadside settlement of rather unadorned brick cottages in 19 pairs, with a forge and an inn.
- **OLD WARDEN**, in Bedfordshire, carried the Picturesque ideal to its extreme. Lord Ongley built the highly decorative parodies of country cottages in the middle of the nineteenth century, when the villagers were obliged to adorn the scene in their scarlet capes and tall hats.
- **EDENSOR**, in Derbyshire, is a stone village of bizarre Swiss and battlemented cottages on the Chatsworth estate. Though eye-catching, it was placed out of sight from the great house. The original village was removed when Lancelot 'Capability' Brown landscaped the park after 1760.
- **MILTON ABBAS**, in Dorset, was built by Joseph Damer, MP, Lord Milton, who systematically evicted the inhabitants and bought out the leaseholders in the townlet of Milton, which he then removed. The town was replaced by a settlement of large roadside, thatched cottages, originally cramped, multiple-occupancy dwellings, which stand outside the park.
- **BLAISE HAMLET**, in Gloucestershire, was created in 1810–12 as a group of nine cottages arranged around a green to provide housing for ageing estate retainers. The Picturesque designs are as over-the-top as any that may be found.
- **NEW HOUGHTON**, in Norfolk, was built at the park gates in 1729 after the original settlement of Houghton had been emparked by Sir Robert Walpole. The church remained stranded. This demonstrates that the uprooting of a community was something that even a Prime Minister could do with impunity in the eighteenth century.
- **RIPLEY**, North Yorkshire, was not removed but the medieval village was rebuilt *in situ* by the Ingilby family in the 1820s creating stone cottages in a Swiss-influenced Tudor style and adding a French-style *hotel de ville* for good measure.
- **FOCHABERS**, in old Morayshire, was built for the 4th Duke of Gordon, who removed the old village to allow for an extension of the 'policies' or pleasure grounds around his castle in the late eighteenth century. The new settlement was rigidly planned and set out nearby around a market square.

INDUSTRIAL
VILLAGES

*I*N A SENSE, industrial villages have always existed, an example being the ruined homes of Bronze Age tin workers, whose tumbled walls litter the slopes below the summit of Rough Tor on Bodmin Moor. Although some Roman industrial areas – like complexes of pottery kilns in the East Midlands – must have produced scenes as satanic as those of the early days of the Industrial Revolution, industrial villages are a relatively modern phenomenon. In the

ABOVE: *Italianate almshouses at Saltaire, the factory village packed with humanitarian amenities created by the alpaca wool baron, Sir Titus Salt*

Middle Ages, manufacturing was often undertaken away from settlements. Water and timber were the main sources of energy, so many furnaces, forges and textile mills were in relatively remote places. Some industries, like fulling cloth, with its casks of stale urine, or hemp fibre production, with the stench from the 'retting ponds' where the foliage degraded, were distinctly unattractive near to homes, while flying sparks were a curse in any thatched settlement.

In the years around 1760, when the Revolution took shape, wool, yarn and finished cloth circulated between the markets and the farmsteads, villages and hamlets where spinning and weaving were pursued on a cottage basis. It was the creation of mills, with their higher efficiency and productivity, firstly driven by water and then by steam, that obliged the independent cottage weavers and spinners to become wage-earning millworkers. The need for the owners of mills and factories to provide accommodation for their labour forces resulted not only in the spread of urban terraced housing, but also the formation of a surprisingly large number of industrial villages.

These patrons were all individuals. Some were concerned only with profits and created the meanest of hovels, but there were a good number, many of them Quakers or other committed Nonconformists, who sought to give their workers the best housing that they could. There were some who believed that decent treatment would result in better workers – and not without grounds, for New Lanark subdued an unruly labour force by treating its workers well. Some patrons thought

ABOVE: *Not all industrial villages were blackened by 'dark satanic mills'. Gayle in Wensleydale had cottage wool carding and combing industries and was a major centre of hand-knitting in Georgian times, though few modern visitors will recognize this as an industrial village.*

that hard toil ennobled a person, while some saw that with a captive labour force, a company monopoly of retailing was too good an opportunity to be missed. The direction forward was signalled by Richard Arkwright's industrial village of Cromford, built in stages following the cotton mill built in 1771, where the unusual three-storey cottages were part of an integrated layout that, progressively, included a school and church. The old hamlet expanded to become a company town, but the dwellings were sound and solid. The mill by the canal had walls that were blank and sheer with windows only appearing at a higher level: there was no knowing that an army of bankrupted handloom weavers might not arrive and attack the place.

The table opposite shows the distinctive industrial villages of Britain.

Name	County	Function and date
Shortstown	Bedfordshire	Short Bros aircraft works, a 'garden village'; 1917
Stewartby	Bedfordshire	London Brick Co. employees; 1927
New Wolverton	Buckinghamshire	Railway village; 1838
Bromsborough Pool	Cheshire	Built for Price's Candles; c. 1850s
Port Sunlight	Cheshire	Settlement for Lever's Soap employees; 1888
Nenthead	Cumbria	Quaker London Lead Co village; 1820s
Tebay	Cumbria	Railway village; late nineteenth century
Creswell	Derbyshire	One of many colliery villages; 1890s
Cromford	Derbyshire	Richard Arkwright's mill village
Shardlow	Derbyshire	Canal village with storage, dwellings and mills; start of nineteenth century
Princeton	Devon	Created for Dartmoor prison staff; after 1811
Tuckenhay	Devon	Failed port project; c. 1805
Castle Eden	County Durham	Built for Burdon's cotton and bleach workers in late eighteenth century
Seaham	County Durham	Failed port; 1820s
Silver End	Essex	Built for Crittall's glass workers; 1920s
Warmley	Gloucestershire	Houses built for workers at (Quaker) Champion works by re-using slag from the brass foundry
Tremadoc	Gwynedd	Failed in originally intended role as an Irish Sea ferry port; c. 1800
Morriston	West Glamorgan	Housing for coal miners and copper workers associated with the Morris colliery; c. 1770
Laverstoke	Hampshire	Accommodation for papermill-workers; c. 1850
Brora	Highland	Founded as a port by the Marquess of Stafford, much demonized for his part in the clearances on the Sutherland estates; after 1810
Cronkbourne	Isle of Man	Improved housing for sailworkers; 1840s
Hersden	Kent	Colliery village; 1920s
Calder Vale	Lancashire	Quaker cotton mill village; 1830s
Fazakerley	Lancashire	Liverpool enclave for Hartley's jam workers; 1880s
Vulcan Village	Lancashire	For foundry workers; 1833
Mill Hill	Middlesex	Settlement for textile workers; 1898
Ravenscar	North Yorkshire	Declined seaside resort; c. 1912
New Earswick	North Yorkshire	Rowntree chocolate factory village in York suburbs; start of twentieth century
Blanchland	Northumberland	Village for lead miners; late eighteenth century
Street	Somerset	Quaker village for leather-workers; mid-nineteenth century
Barlaston	Staffordshire	Industrial settlement for potters; 1936
New Lanark	Strathclyde	Important mill village founded by David Dale with tenements in terraces and public buildings, including a nursery; after 1783
Eaglesham	Strathclyde	Spinning, weaving and bleaching village developed by the Earl of Eglinton; late eighteenth century
Thornliebank	Strathclyde	Village for workers at the Crum's bleachworks, printworks and dyeworks with good amenities. The Crums were friends of David Dale; after 1819
Bournville	Warwickshire	Garden village built mainly for Cadbury's chocolate factory employees; late nineteenth century
Akroyden	West Yorkshire	Model village to serve Akroyd mills; mid-nineteenth century
Harewood	West Yorkshire	Built for villagers removed from park; sited upon a turnpike and provided with a ribbon factory; c. 1760
Saltaire	West Yorkshire	Probably the most celebrated model industrial village. Built beside Salt's alpaca mill; after 1850

VILLAGES OF
CONSCIENCE
AND
THE SPIRIT

*F*OR MOST OF THE Middle Ages, only one brand of religion was available and since services leaned heavily towards liturgy and were conducted in Latin, villagers had a limited understanding of what was going on. As the period drew towards its close, philosophers like Erasmus were directing attention towards humanism and the individual, while Lutherans brought sharper, challenging views to bear on established beliefs. The debate reached out to embrace the masses and people became aware of their consciences and the demands that these consciences made. People with courage and convictions began to realize that religion came in a number of distinctly different versions, though they frequently came to believe that only one of these, their own, could be correct. Fear, intolerance and provocation culminated in the English Civil War, with its truly dreadful death toll.

If the Reformation had sought to celebrate the unity and majesty of humankind, it had spawned climates of secrecy and fear. Villagers, who may not have cared terribly about religious issues, found themselves compelled to attend the state-approved churches, hauled before tribunals to explain any failures to attend and fined heavily if found guilty. They lived in fear of expressing their innermost thoughts – for the orthodoxy demanded by one regime could overnight become heresy when that regime was toppled.

And so in Europe a certain spirit of isolationism developed. There were those who considered themselves and their friends to be blessed but believed that everybody else was wicked and dangerous. Also, there were those who sought to find their God by turning inward and who craved to be able to do so without persecution by the state and outsiders. And there were also those who thought that, given the chance, they could set an example that would show the way to a new Jerusalem. Oppression and the imposition of orthodox values do not eliminate cults and cliques. Rather, they spawn them, as the modern world demonstrates every day. A remarkable assemblage of outcast, idealistic and utopian groups established their villages in Britain even though the mass of people are unaware of their existence. Here are the main examples:

CHARTIST LAND COLONIES

These were associated with utopian ideas, which gained in strength as the harsh realities of industrialization and its consequences for society were realized (later, these would be encapsulated in the anthem 'Jerusalem'). The traditional village had already gained great symbolic importance, and its values and lifestyles were seen as wholesome alternatives to those of the town and factory. In the 1820s, the Quaker and chemist, William Allen, put current ideas about the value of rural self-sufficiency into practice and bought land in Sussex to establish a colony modelled on those of the Moravians (see below). Lindfield colony had sound cottages built by the settlers and a school and proved successful. The baton then passed to Fergus O'Connor and the Chartists. He purchased the Great Dodford estate in Gloucestershire in 1848 and Snigs End, Minster Lovell (or 'Charterville') and Lowbands settlements followed. However, MPs decided that the Land Company handling the properties was illegal and they dissolved it in 1851. The colonies proved as robust as their dwellings and resolute in their intent to survive, demonstrating that the smallholding and craftworking lifestyle could actually prove viable and be sustained.

THE MORAVIANS

The first and most important of the villages founded by dissenters were those of the *Moravians*, who established seven villages in England and Ireland in the four decades following 1744. A German Protestant sect from Moravia, now in the Czech Republic, they took refuge on an estate in Saxony, from whence colonists became established at Fulneck, within Pudsey, near Leeds. Their settlement was named after a town in Moravia. Their villages were modelled on the example of Herrnhut in Germany and at Fulneck they formed a close community of dwellings perched on a hillside shelf, with their own church and school. A communal textiles industry was developed, with proceeds being ploughed back into the village. Fairfield near Manchester and Gracehill in Ireland were among the other Moravian foundations. The Moravians exerted a powerful influence upon other utopian idealists because they showed that there were alternatives to individual enterprise that could actually work.

'OWENITE' INFLUENCES

These were very important in the foundation of model and utopian villages. David Dale founded cotton mills at New Lanark, on the river Clyde near Lanark, in 1786. His son-in-law was the reformer and industrialist, Robert Owen. When Owen obtained a share in the mills, New Lanark provided him with the opportunity to apply his philanthropic ideas and when his partners objected to the added cost of his reforms, he bought them out. The village gained an international reputation; it was unusual in that it was not organized according to any narrowly binding religious ideal and exemplified the notion that industrial employment and housing could be operated according to humane principles. New Lanark is now one of Scotland's four UNESCO World Heritage Sites. Although Owen departed to invest in an American colony, New Harmony, in 1824, he had an enormous influence on the promoters of reformed industrial villages. His disciples included J.H. Moggeridge, who believed that in a justly ordered society emigration would be unnecessary. He worked among mining communities and established improved industrial housing at Blackwood, near Monmouth, with greenery incorporated into the landscaped setting and a full range of shops and services.

THE CREATIVE SPIRIT

There are several villages that celebrate the individuality of *the creative spirit*. Some do it with aplomb and a few in ways that teeter on the edge of silliness and vanity. But there is nowhere that accomplishes the aim with such all-embracing panache as *Portmeirion*. It is a fantasy village rooted in the ethos of an Italian fishing settlement and was inspired by architect and conservationist, Clough Williams-Ellis, and built on his own peninsula on the coast of Snowdonia in the 1920s. There had been many previous exercises in the Picturesque, and romantic parodies of rustic cottages were common fare among the estate villages of England. Portmeirion is fun, though architecturally accomplished; the Italianate, colour-washed buildings, spiky skylines and Mediterranean-style

ABOVE: *Portmeirion village: tasteful fun bringing the Mediterranean to the Welsh coast*

plantings tell us how the shores of Italy might look if climate change brought thin light and watery skies to the Mediterranean. Thorpeness on the coast of Suffolk is less renowned, a resort village, never completed, that was developed for the Stuart Ogilvie family, with inns, a country club and charity cottages. Work here continued for more than two decades after its commencement in 1910.

If the arbiters of architectural taste are divided over Portmeirion and its virtues, nothing can be relied upon to unite them in rage more than a mention of the *plotlands* settlements. During the first four decades of the twentieth century, thousands of ordinary households spontaneously migrated to the Channel shores of England. It was if people had decided that they could bear the sweltering clamour of the cities no more, or as though society had decided to have one huge, irresponsible spree before it was crammed into the corset of the planning controls of 1947. Along the Channel seaboard, parts of the Thames valley and in south Essex, at places like Jaywick Sands, Pagham Beach, Peacehaven, Pitsea, Purley Park and Canvey Island, ordinary people simply took matters into their own hands and created homes out of scraps, corrugated iron, roofing felt and boards, from abandoned motor buses or from railway carriages. The homes could have the form of nibbles from the edge of a field, of shambling rows of dwellings facing each other across an unmetalled track or they could be aligned in ranks running back from a shore, or could sometimes be set out in neat gridiron patterns. In all events, a new settlement had come into being – to outcries of horror from the established opinion-makers. Lovers of unspoilt countryside quite understandably hated the plotlands, as did the bureaucracies concerned. With their unmade roads and ramshackle dwellings they contravened all the traditions of the model village. Gladdening the eye was not what they were about. At the same time, they embodied an anarchic exuberance, even an innocence: things in short supply today.

DISCOVERING
MODEL
VILLAGES

*M*ODEL VILLAGES form a very broad class. Many estate villages are replacements for predecessors that were destroyed in the making of parks, though strangely, in a few cases a decade or two could intervene between the destruction and the rebuilding. In any event, it was perfectly possible for a landowner to build a collection of 'improved' dwellings for his tenants and estate workers without any prior destruction being involved. The term 'model' itself is open to a range of interpretations. There could be no doubt that Owen's

BELOW: *The model village of Cardington in Bedfordshire, where John Howard, the prison reformer, built cottages in the 1760s*

workers in New Lanark approved of their greater space, warmth and cleanliness, but other 'model' features of dwellings seem more likely to have impressed guests at the great house nearby than their occupants. Fancy thatching work could be a nuisance and invitation to sparrows; garden trellises and paling fences had to be maintained and public lawns yielded no food but still had to be cut.

Scholars have divided villages into those that are/were *closed* or completely owned and under the control of a particular local dynasty and *open*, in which power is fragmented and no single tyrant or benefactor can rule the village roost. Closed villages are more likely to bear the exclusive imprint of the people at the hall. Dwellings in closed estate villages may sometimes display the *arms* or *cartouche* of their masters, as with some houses on the Whitbread estates in Bedfordshire. More usually, one has to hunt a little harder. *Plaques to benefactors* may be found beside public fountains and village pumps, on public clocks and schools, while in Ripley a statue of a wild boar near the market square relates to an improbable claim that a medieval Ingilby, the ancestor of the dynasty in the castle, saved his monarch from the charge of an enraged boar. Estate housing was often built all at one time to a *standardized style* employing *standardized materials*, datestones, designs and details that give the dwellings a degree of uniformity. Designs for one house could be echoed all along a terrace or row of cottages. More housing might easily be added at different times, perhaps producing short terraces of identical houses. *Details of ornamentation* that would have caused added building costs may also be detected on many estate houses, like hand-ground bricks or fancy chimneys. Where different cottages display identical wooden mouldings in their door and window surrounds, this could reveal the use of the same moulding plane in the estate joiner's workshop.

The grander of the cottage designs in the earlier schemes could derive from a *celebrated architect*, who was employed to give the great house a facelift, being invited to provide designs. Carr of York designed the new village houses at Harewood around 1760 and John Nash and George Repton worked on Blaize hamlet. Otherwise, house building could be entrusted to local rough masons and to local builders who did their own designing. As the nineteenth century progressed, the managers of estates tended increasingly to draw upon standardized published *design books*, which offered a spectrum of cottage types. In this way, identical cottages could be found at different ends of the country, while the *railway network*, with its long-distance goods capability, allowed mass-produced materials to be shipped far and wide from sources like the slate quarries of Snowdonia and Cumbria or the brick works of Bedfordshire.

Some fortunate model village dwellers gained most of their *amenities* at once. Usually, the benefits were staged. Firstly and most crucially came the provision of an unpolluted water supply to remove the threats of typhoid and cholera. The first steps might involve a safer public well, with piped supplies reaching the houses later. Until fairly modern times, villagers frequently shared a public bakehouse – one survives at Papworth St Agnes in Cambridgeshire. Coal, shifted by rail, and coke from the gasworks fuelled the cottage stove and bread ovens and made cooking more of a domestic affair. Some fortunate villagers gained a gas supply as a spin-off from nearby urban operations. The villagers of New Lanark were unusually fortunate in receiving free electricity in every home in 1898 (even though the power for the single bulb was terminated at 10 p.m., or 11 p.m. on Saturdays). They had to wait longer for

ABOVE: *Dalham in Suffolk: one of those places where the church seems to have ended up in the squire's backyard*

domestic water supplies, with cold taps being installed in 1933 and inside lavatories arriving in the same year. A very small minority of villagers today still await such a happy event.

The profound twentieth-century transformations of village life bring us into the realm of *oral history* (see Chapter Eleven) and the colourful recollections of people who can recall caps being doffed to the squire as he passed by on his hunter, the linking of the village to the national grid, the first house to sprout a TV aerial, the coalman with his horse, wagon and black sacks, the epidemics of diphtheria and poliomyelitis that made mothers live in fear and the landworkers arriving during the 1939–45 war. These wonderful people, who have seen so much, can sometimes feel neglected and sidelined. Gain their trust and they will often delight in pouring out the modern history of their village. And if you do not take it down, it may be lost forever.

During the two centuries or so when new villages, some innovative and some bizarre, were being created, the old villages marched on. They were still prone to changes and factors like the mechanization of farming and agricultural decline served as reminders that dormitories for farmworkers would not last forever. In the second half of the nineteenth century, old certainties vanished, populations bled away and the village faced a crisis of confidence. Would it survive? With rising fuel costs, landscapes often blighted by agri-business and retreating wildlife, the jury is still to decide.

10

CLACHANS AND FERMTOUNS

*I*DEAS ABOUT VILLAGES that work in England and the lowlands of Wales will not explain the rural settlements that are seen in Scotland. Having said this, Scotland is a place of great diversity: perhaps the biggest small country in the world. The traveller moving north towards Edinburgh will see plump villages and ridge and furrow in scenery that has some English characteristics. However, to move further north is to move into areas that have settlement histories and features that belong to very different traditions. The landmarks associated with English history seem to occupy different timescales in Scotland. While the Scottish Improvements corresponded in time and nature to the Agricultural Revolution in England and Wales, the Highland Clearances, which so resembled the awful Tudor sheep clearances south of the border, occurred not in late medieval times but in the eighteenth and nineteenth centuries. There are people living today who were alive when the last crofters were evicted to create *deer* (hunting) *forests* in the Highlands.

THE
COMPONENTS
OF THE SCENE

*T*HE LANDSCAPE of farming in the Highlands and North East of Scotland had a distinct system, class structure and components. Some of the internal differences were of a linguistic nature and depended on whether one was in a clan territory, where Gaelic was spoken, or an estate on the plains and plateaus to the east, where long ago power had been wielded by feudal

LEFT: *Desertion features in many views on Skye, as here at Elgol.*

ABOVE: *With houses neither tightly clustered nor dispersed, this landscape on Skye recalls the old pattern of settlement in the Highlands.*

monarchs rather than clan chiefs and where Lowland Scots was spoken. Thus, a kind of hamlet known as a *clachan* (from a Gaelic word for 'stones') in the clan lands was a *fermtoun* (i.e. a farm town or village) to the speakers of Lowland Scots. The main elements of the farming landscape were as follows.

GROUP FARMS

Land was divided and rented on the basis of *group farms* or *multiple tenancies*. The several households that made up a group farm, which might or might not have been related, lived near the centre of their lands in a hamlet – a clachan or fermtoun. As the pressure to make estates commercially viable increased after the Jacobite defeat at Culloden in 1746, so rack-renting by the chief tenants or *tacksmen* in the Highlands caused holdings to be divided and impoverishment to increase. The leases offered were usually very short, so that tenants had little incentive to improve their farms.

FERMTOUNS

In the North East, fermtouns were often designated as *milltouns*, *kirktouns* or, more rarely, *seatouns*, according to whether they were a cut above their neighbours and had a mill, a kirk or church or a position by the sea. In the uplands, part of the population might migrate with their livestock to a *buaile* (anglicized as 'booley') in the summer pastures, spending what must have been the most pleasant part of their year among the heather and thyme. The fermtouns ranged quite widely in size but were usually smaller than typical English villages. New Pitsligo, near Aberdeen, a planned creation, was Scotland's largest village in Victorian times and it occupied the space of three former fermtouns that had stood on its site.

RUNRIG

This was a system of farming adapted to the marginal farming environments of the north. As in medieval England, land was still ridged up to produce a corduroy pattern of *riggs*. Usually, this was done with an ox-plough, but on the poorest ground, manual ridging with spades was practised. Close to the clachan or fermtoun would be the *mucked land*, a single open field of ploughland that was kept constantly in production by receiving all the muck available. Livestock were folded on the field between harvests. From time to time, *breaks* were made in the adjacent land, an *out-field* or *out-by*, with pieces of ground being cropped until exhausted, and then abandoned for years to recover. Beyond the cultivated area were the common grazings of the marshes or *mosses*, *braes* or *hillslopes* and *muirs* or moors.

HARDSHIP

Although the clansmen might find excitement in skirmishing and cattle raiding, or even in driving the black cattle over the high mountain trails to markets in England, clachan and fermtoun life was generally grim. The short tenancies and rack-rents combined insecurity with poverty: scenes of maypole dancing, trysts in the churchyard and dalliance on the green were far from the realities of life in the north of Britain. The hamlets lacked the features associated with villages, being loose, undisciplined clusters of single-storey farmsteads that normally lacked any amenities. Even though some hamlets had as many dwellings as might be found in a village in England they probably had more physical similarities to the earlier Saxon villages than to the settlements of Georgian Village England. Famine that weakened their populations and disease that carried a portion away were the main landmarks of the farming calendar. Over-population combined with soil exhaustion and other environmental stresses resulted in some terrible episodes of starvation.

OVERLEAF: *Portree on Skye, where Prince Charlie shed his female disguise, bade farewell to Flora Macdonald and left Skye for Raasay*

CHANGE
BECKONS

*T*HE EIGHTEENTH CENTURY was a period fixated on progress, though in rural areas 'progress' was often interpreted as being whatever produced the largest profits for the landlords. Before Culloden, there had been a few localized experiments in rationalizing estates but the traumas of the uprising of 1745 followed by the shattering defeat of 1746 provided conditions for wholesale change.

Although many clan chieftains were well-educated, cultivated and widely travelled, clan society was a martial one and the clan was a community ever prepared for war. Chieftains measured their status according to the number of clansmen that were obliged to take up arms whenever the fiery cross was ridden through the territory. Accordingly, they encouraged over-population and members of the subservient clan struggled to survive on the smallest of holdings. After Culloden, harsh laws intended to destroy the martial culture of the Highlands were enforced, while the old clan territories were sucked into the competitive economic environment of the expanding British Empire. Disarmed clansmen, forbidden to carry weapons, wear their native dress, play the war pipes or speak their own language, had little value. Surviving hereditary chiefs and the interlopers from the Borders and England who had taken over estates realized that rack-renting starving tenants did not produce much revenue.

The answer to the dilemmas of the lairds and landlords was found in the sheep, for a long time wrongly regarded as too weak to over-winter in the Highlands. In the land rush that followed, shepherds from the Borders, their dogs and their flocks moved north, while rivers of evicted Highlanders, including families who had had their homes torched above their heads, rushed south and west. Some of the evictees settled on the shores in crofting communities, some headed for the budding industrial towns, while others took the emigrant ships to search for societies that were less profligate with their members.

Great swathes of the Highlands became deserts as the sheep plague ravaged the region for a century before culminating in shameful evictions on Skye. Liberal opinion was offended, but the Clearances continued into the twentieth century with the depopulation of deer forests to attract wealthy shooters. The Clearances remain a source of great bitterness among those who cannot understand how many of those 'down South' can be so ignorant of the terrible injustices that were imposed on communities in such relatively recent times.

On the eastern side of the Highlands, circumstances were rather different. Gaelic culture and clan traditions were less entrenched and the landlords of the North East approached estate rationalization in a different, more detached way. Surplus tenants were to be removed, leaving farmers of substance, who could pay decent rents and farm in progressive and efficient ways. Meanwhile, the landscapes of estates were changed according to fashionable notions of progress. Masses of stones and boulders being gathered from the fields and heaped in massive walls or *consumption dykes, shelter belts* and other *plantations* of conifers were established, and custom-built villages erupted like mushrooms to replace many of the old fermtouns across the plateau of Buchan, the vale of Mar and the coastal lowlands of the North Sea and Moray Firth. Sometimes, the changes involved more than just seeking viable employment for as many tenants as possible. Ambition could extend to

ABOVE: *A ruined watermill in Glengairn, doubtless part of a settlement that perished in the Clearances*

advertising and publicizing the new settlements and the opportunities that they offered with the aim of attracting outsiders of 'good character' with useful skills.

LANDSCAPES
OF
DESERTION

$\mathcal{I}$N THE AREA affected by the sheep clearances, which is to say most of the Highlands and Islands, the countrysides are strewn with the debris of abandoned homes. Most had been thatched with straw, heather or turf and many were *blackhouses* with the thatch draining into peat sandwiched between two courses of stone walling. Some were cruck-framed and supported by 'A'-shaped timber frames. Because of the shortage of timber in the region, these frames were sometimes carried away by the occupants when they departed. The blackhouses contrasted with the more modern *white houses*, with their whitened walls of rendered rubble or *harle* (pebbledash).

The deserted clachan sites look quite different from the deserted medieval villages of England. The awful events of just one or two centuries ago have left much 'fresher' traces. At worst, the house walls form spreads of rubble, but often, roofless dwellings stand right to the tops of their gables. Rambling across a deserted clachan, one realizes that the remains lack the discipline associated with deserted medieval villages and the houses have different alignments; streets or lanes may not be

ABOVE: *A traditional blackhouse on Skye, its thatch held in place by a net weighted with boulders*

apparent and greens and churches are absent. There is a haphazard feel to the arrangements, as though the cottages and their walled *kailyards* or cottage gardens had floated down, willy-nilly, from the sky. Often, there is no road connection with the world beyond to be found, though one may trace the tracks that radiated outwards to the fields.

There is a vocabulary to go with the estates and settlements, as outlined in this table.

VOCABULARY ASSOCIATED WITH ESTATES AND SETTLEMENTS

NAME PART	ORIGINAL LANGUAGE	MEANING	NAME PART	ORIGINAL LANGUAGE	MEANING
Ferm	Lowland Scots	Farm or rent	Mains	Lowland Scots	Home farm of a Scottish estate
Crof, croft	Lowland Scots	A shed or fishing hut. In the Highlands it signifies a crofter's land holding	Buaile; buaill	Gaelic	Pen, milking place, summer settlement
			Clachan	Gaelic	Hamlet, church, also stepping stones
Croftland	Lowland Scots	Good ploughland that is constantly cropped	Run-rig	Lowland Scots	Plough field where alternate ridges were worked by different tenants
Croft-rig	Lowland Scots	A plough ridge			
Policy	Lowland Scots	Pleasure grounds of a Scottish mansion	Kailyard	Lowland Scots	Cottage produce garden

THE
AFTERMATH
OF
DESTRUCTION

*I*N THE HIGHLANDS, hardly any of the places destroyed were replaced. However, in the North East the Improvements unleashed a whirlwind of new village projects – a phase of landscape transformation and settlement creation that, briefly and locally, almost compared in intensity to the Big Bang of the Saxon centuries. More than 70 new villages appeared in the North East of Scotland, mostly in the century 1750–1850, and new estate villages were created in other parts of Scotland, too. The following points help to explain the distinctive village patterns.

Firstly, the changes were executed on an estate-by-estate basis. Their organizers, the landlords and their factors or agents, were human beings and so it is not surprising that some were concerned solely to maximize the income they derived from their estates; some were genuinely motivated to create viable employment and better living conditions; most combined the pursuit of profit and social considerations, while some sought the kudos associated with 'progressive' undertakings. Thought went into the positioning of new villages within their estates. They might be sited beside lively thoroughfares, in central positions or placed to house the retainers needed to serve a mansion. Strichen was placed to lie on a proposed turnpike road between Aberdeen and Fraserburgh, exemplifying the optimism underpinning many ventures. Often, the new villages soaked up some of the surplus population of an estate, but in several cases, villagers were recruited from outside. This being the age of expanding media, newspaper advertisements were employed to attract settlers. This was the case at Tomintoul, the loftiest of British villages, which was situated at the heart of the Duke of Gordon's lands.

Secondly, the new villagers were generally seen as spearheading economic and civilizing values, like the state farms of Stalin's Russia. They would be foci for growth on their estates and would introduce mills, honest commerce, diligence and higher standards of decency and conduct. The more the settlements were gravitated towards the Gaelic Highlands rather than the Lowlands, the more urgent and patronizing the 'civilizing claims' of their lords tended to be. The founders often hoped that their villages would generate industrial growth that would bring wealth and employment to their estates. Many hopes were pinned on linen manufacture, which appeared at places like Grantown-on Spey, Archiestown and many others. Ballater was built in a virtual wilderness to function as a spa and did surprisingly well, and Burghead was one of various new anchorages. Several new coastal villages, like Buckhaven, were created to develop fishing industries.

Thirdly, for reasons both of economy and fashion, the new villages were built to geometrical layouts. At its most simple, this involved positioning dwellings to face each other across a straightened through-road, as at Lumsden. The next level in sophistication involved placing a central square either in or beside the through-road, a motif which found splendid expression at Fochabers. Despite beginning life on the drawing boards of hired draughtsmen, these villages echoed the medieval villages of England. Their houses faced directly onto the footpath and road, without any front gardens to be trampled by passing livestock, while behind, they often had long plots or kailyards with a cottage garden, space for a milk cow and workshops. In some larger examples, like Ballater, or Rhynie with its green-like square, gridiron layouts were employed. Sometimes old hostilities and prejudices were embedded in the new arrangements. For example, Glengairn, near Ballater, had been a Catholic glen and had risen for the Jacobites. After Culloden, Protestants took over many holdings, instituting a policy of sub-letting only to other Protestants.

FINDING
OUT MORE

*T*HE SCOTTISH VILLAGES make excellent subjects for the amateur enthusiast because the relevant historical phases are so recent – removing any need to struggle with medieval documents in Latin. The following sources of evidence can be drawn upon in such studies.

TIP DISCOVERING SCOTTISH VILLAGES

1. Parish-by-parish descriptions of local conditions were provided in the *Statistical Account* of the 1790s and the *New Statistical Account* of the 1840s. These can be studied in the main reference libraries.

2. More detailed archive work can reveal the newspaper advertisements, or even printed bills, which advertised for recruits to the new settlements – usually in terms that would not disgrace a modern copywriter. Thus, Strichen's entry in the *Aberdeen Journal* of 1798 told of a situation that was 'dry and healthy, moderately elevated, with an extensive tract of deep moss adjacent [peat bog – but it would have offered turf for fuel], a great command of fine spring water, and sufficiency for driving mills and machinery, lime stone, and abundance of excellent stones for building'.

3. Sometimes, landlords undertook to build houses, but often this obligation was placed on tenants, according to the landlord's guidelines concerning dimensions and materials. Sometimes, the terms of such agreements can be unearthed amongst *estate papers* in the archives.

4. The great transformations occurred in an age when mapping skills were relatively advanced. Seventeenth-century maps at a scale of ½ inch to one mile and eighteenth-century maps at twice that scale are useful, but the most valuable maps are those drawn by British military cartographers. General Roy's maps of the mid-eighteenth century are a remarkable record of the old countryside and can be found online at the Scran Trust, an educational charity. Full access to its resources can be gained by subscription. The National Library of Scotland (enquiries@nls.uk) can direct you to many old maps. To discover the situations when most of the new villages were still in their youth, First Edition Ordnance Survey maps can be accessed at old-maps.co.uk, then enter the County Gazetteer and explore the old shires of the North East.

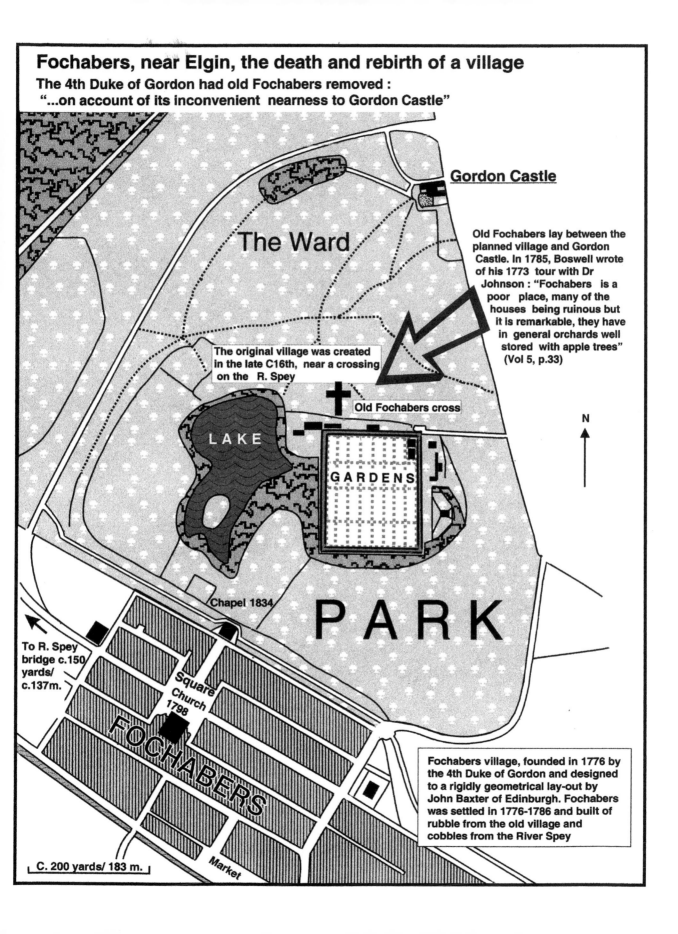

Fochabers, near Elgin, the death and rebirth of a village

The 4th Duke of Gordon had old Fochabers removed :
"...on account of its inconvenient nearness to Gordon Castle"

Gordon Castle

The Ward

Old Fochabers lay between the planned village and Gordon Castle. In 1785, Boswell wrote of his 1773 tour with Dr Johnson : "Fochabers is a poor place, many of the houses being ruinous but it is remarkable, they have in general orchards well stored with apple trees" (Vol 5, p.33)

The original village was created in the late C16th, near a crossing on the R. Spey

Old Fochabers cross

N

LAKE

GARDENS

Chapel 1834

PARK

To R. Spey bridge c.150 yards/ c.137m.

Square
Church
1798

FOCHABERS

Fochabers village, founded in 1776 by the 4th Duke of Gordon and designed to a rigidly geometrical lay-out by John Baxter of Edinburgh. Fochabers was settled in 1776-1786 and built of rubble from the old village and cobbles from the River Spey

Market

C. 200 yards/ 183 m.

11

PUTTING IT ALL TOGETHER

OW THE BATON PASSES to the reader: you are ready to take your first steps in 'reading a village'. The journey of discovery may last for but a few days – yet it could provide a lifetime of interest. Some village sleuths may want to take a narrower look at some special facet of the village, like the evolution of its layout or of its houses. The material that follows is concerned with building up the 'big picture': an all-embracing study of the village and its story. However, you can dip in or opt out at any stage. A study of villages is worthy, engaging and informative – but it should also be fun. Here I have brought together some ideas presented in previous chapters and integrated them into a framework for the orderly study of all the fascinating facets of the village. The order of investigation that is suggested is rational but it is not a straitjacket and other sequences could be tried, other trails followed and other clues run to ground.

THE NAME

E HAVE SEEN that the names of places can take us back across more than a thousand years of local history and have also seen that published translations of place-names are really informed guesses. Your village name may well be the oldest surviving aspect of the place and should never be overlooked.

LEFT: *Milestones like this one at Hadleigh in Suffolk take us back to the days of the turnpike and coach*

YOU WILL NEED

Place-name dictionaries, preferably a selection so that alternative translations can be applied. The most recommended title is Gelling, 1993 (see Selected Further Reading). Also, a map of the locality. Relatively small-scale Ordnance Survey maps should do, like the 1:50,000 or the old 1:63,000 (1 inch to 1 mile) series.

WORKPLACE

At home or in the reference library. At your computer, you can look for online dictionaries concerning languages like Welsh, Gaelic or dialects like Lowland Scots that contributed to the legacy of place-names if Old English, Old Norse or Old Danish fail to deliver. Several are available, like the Gaelic and Scots dictionaries at www.rampantscotland.com/gaelic/. Libraries should offer a selection of place-name studies concerning the county and national levels.

PROCEDURE

Write down all the suggested translations that you can find and see *which one seems best to match the local setting.* Let us take my native village, Birstwith in Nidderdale, for example. I can think of the following possible translations: 'Landing place by the fort' (i.e. *burh-staithe*); 'Barley farmstead' (*bere-stead*); and 'Birch wood' (*birk-vitr*). As the river would not have been navigable, even in Anglo-Saxon times, and the only feasible fort site is ½ mile from the river, the second and third possibilities are the most credible, and I would normally favour the third, for woodland was plentiful there. However, we should always search for the *earliest* form of a name that can be found and in Domesday Book of 1086 we find *Beristade* which takes us back to the second possibility, even though names ending in '-with' or '-wood' are common in the vicinity. It shows the importance of finding the earliest recorded form of a name. A county-by-county list of the Domesday place-names can be found in Darby and Versey, 1975. Like other useful, if expensive or out-of-print books, it is obtainable on interlibrary loan.

These enquiries lead naturally to a consideration of the village setting.

THE SETTING

*O*LD VILLAGES were in intimate contact with the settings that provided their communities with virtually all their food and resources. A century or two of divorce has masked the vital link between the village and its township, parish or manor(s), making it hard for us to appreciate just how tight the bonds between the village and its immediate surroundings really were. Barley from the surrounding fields soon found its way into all the cottage brewhouses that helped to save the people from their polluted water supplies. Rye and wheat passed from the fields to the nearby bakehouse and ovens; oats fed the horses that hauled the plough and nourished the ploughboy with broth and stews. The village was fed on, built of and warmed by the fields, pastures, meadows and woods around it. Any historic village study that ends at the limits of the built-up village area is likely to be of little value or relevance – it would be like describing a trout without mentioning the trout stream. Even if you are only studying the buildings of a village then it should be plain that the straw or reed for the thatch, the timber of the posts, beams and braces, the wattle and the daub and the stone – all were hauled in from the nearby countryside.

YOU WILL NEED

The place-name dictionaries as well as old map coverage giving as many place-names as possible.

WORKPLACE

Looking at old maps in a county record office or national library or at home with any photocopies that you have been allowed to make in those places, or looking at maps of the relevant locality online (e.g. the very useful First Edition Ordnance Survey 6 inches to 1 mile maps at www.old-maps.co.uk). Information gleaned elsewhere can be plotted at home. Where the record offices cannot supply photocopies of old maps, tracings by pencil may be required: the results can be far from ideal. When working with maps, a little light table, like those often used for making selections of photographic transparencies, is of great help for underlighting tracings.

PROCEDURE

Once you have collected your old map information, make a *base map* of the village locality by photocopying, scanning or tracing a map of a suitable scale (6 inches to 1 mile is handy). Translate all the place-names that you can find and plot them on to your base map. Some names will record places that were moist or swampy, like the holmes, mosses and carrs, while others will tell of ploughlands, like the acres, riggs and shotts, and so on. Gradually, by plotting the names – the more the better – *an image of the village setting as it was centuries ago should emerge*. In general terms, any field boundaries on your map that have slightly sinuous backwards 's' or 'c' forms are likely to mark plough strips from the old open fields, while any that are completely straight are likely to come from the carve-up of the old common fields by Parliamentary Enclosure in the period 1750–1850. To clarify the picture, you could shade the old ploughland brown, the damp, riverside meadows, where hay was made, and the pastures, where the village herds and flocks grazed, in different shades of green, the coppices and wooded pastures in darker shades of green and the commons, that contributed so much to the cottage economies, in a brownish shade of green – they tended to be over-grazed.

*I*T IS ALL ABOUT SHAPES. Reading landscapes draws on all kinds of expertise, but so many answers result from looking at the shapes things make and so recognizing familiar patterns. For example, if the property lines around a village green form a smooth line or curve until suddenly one or more plots jut out into the green, then we can be sure that we are seeing an encroachment of houses or front gardens on an older green. Similarly, a road that detaches the corner of a rectangular field must be younger than that field. It is generally easier to see the shape clues from the remote and clinical perspective of a map than it is on the ground. On the ground, attention is pulled this way and that by traffic, people, architectural details and other distractions that prevent one from seeing the basic patterns made by roads and buildings. Down in the village, strong perspective factors are at work, garden shrubs obscure the view, as do the houses and parked vehicles. The map, however, with its uncluttered bird's-eye view, may show us that the curving line of the village main street seems to be continued into the countryside by a hedgerow. Might the village road once have proceeded along this course? Similarly, the village might have its church near the riverside and then straggle up the valley side, suggesting that the village may have originally been

BELOW: *The large village pond at Nun Monkton*

ABOVE: *This landscape, from the mansion at the top down past the church and estate housing to the vicarage just below and right of the spire, was the creation of the ruling dynasty in Georgian and Victorian Birstwith in Nidderdale.*

organized along a cross-valley track that led to a ford. A map of the broad locality, say a 1:50,000 Ordnance Survey map, might show that this characteristic was echoed by other villages in the area, as in the River Cam valley near Cambridge, where several riverside villages originally grew up the slopes along cross-valley tracks.

So, maps may be *very bad* at telling us what the houses in a place look like, how they were built or whether the village concerned is a winner or a loser in the scenic stakes. However, they are *very good* at providing us with shape clues.

Perhaps the most revealing feature of a village plan is the pattern formed by its roads and lanes (also its footpaths, for some of them may have declined from being lanes, bridleways and field tracks). The roads are of interest before they reach the village that they serve. The Feckenham map of 1591 shows the importance of the several lanes (known as *straker ways* in some regions) that linked the little villages and hamlets of this area to their commons. Of course, once the commons were *enclosed* or privatized and became exclusive, these lanes would have lost their significance. One can imagine that most villages sit, like fat spiders, in the middle of a web of roads, lanes and paths. Over

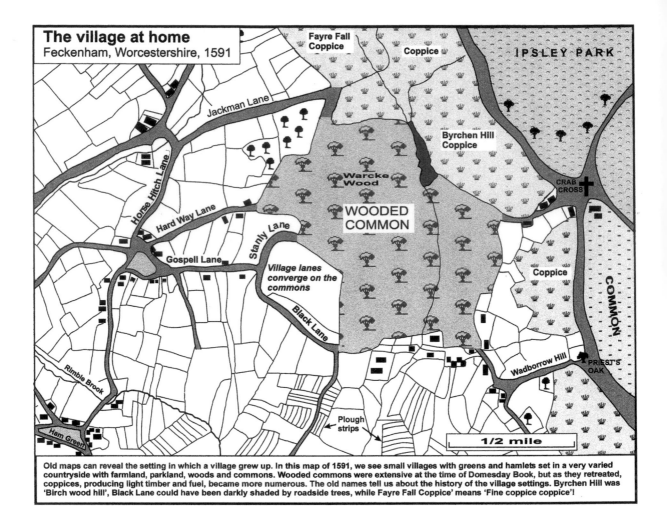

Fayre Fall Coppice

Coppice

IPSLEY PARK

Jackman Lane

Byrchen Hill Coppice

Horse Hitch Lane

Hard Way Lane

Warcke Wood

WOODED COMMON

CRAB CROSS

Stanly Lane

Gospell Lane

Village lanes converge on the commons

Coppice

COMMON

Black Lane

Rimble Brook

Wadborrow Hill

PRIEST'S OAK

Ham Green

Plough strips

1/2 mile

Old maps can reveal the setting in which a village grew up. In this map of 1591, we see small villages with greens and hamlets set in a very varied countryside with farmland, parkland, woods and commons. Wooded commons were extensive at the time of Domesday Book, but as they retreated, coppices, producing light timber and fuel, became more numerous. The old names tell us about the history of the village settings. Byrchen Hill was 'Birch wood hill', Black Lane could have been darkly shaded by roadside trees, while Fayre Fall Coppice' means 'Fine coppice coppice'!

time, some of these routes are 'promoted' like football teams moving up a division, while some will be demoted. So the classes or grades of routeways seen around a village today are unlikely to be exactly the same as those existing, say, in Elizabethan times. In looking at a village layout it is necessary to remember that what is now a nondescript farm track might once have been a highway, while that neglected trough-like holloway out in some field was ground into the landscape by the passing of countless feet, hooves and wheels before its traffic was stolen by a different route. It is also worth remembering that the more a local dynasty monopolized ownership of village property, the more control they were likely to exert over village development. In my native Birstwith, the Greenwood family owned virtually everything they surveyed from their perch in Swarcliffe Hall and the church, vicarage, school and estate housing were all of their making and placed according to their whims (see photo on p.239).

Everything that you see in your village, whether on the ground or on the map, has a reason for being there. Each kink in a road or curve in a house plot has a tale to tell. For example, if the village street swerves sharply to go around a churchyard then it could well be that the church was already in place by the time that the village came into being. Many of the clues tell a story that you can read.

A good map at a reasonably large scale – say at least 6 inches to 1 mile. Old maps, when studied in time sequence, can help to trace how a village layout has evolved. Changes during the last 150 years or so are recorded in the succession of Ordnance Survey series, though coverage of an earlier date can be governed by chance. The earlier and the more detailed a map is, the more changes it is likely to reveal.

Workplace

Reference libraries and record offices will provide the less accessible old maps, though whether maps can be photocopied may depend on factors like their fragility. More and more material is becoming available online, so before committing to a journey it is worth having a good scout around with a search engine. It can be best to work from the map to the ground. This involves a desk-based study of the maps to pick out the most interesting clues, followed by discovering how the evidence appears outdoors in the real village. The real village will display many things that are not displayed on the maps. There might be old milestones in place on the ground that show how a village back lane was once a coaching road, while the ages of dwellings seen encroaching on a green could suggest when the encroachment took place.

Procedure

The objective is to study how the layout of the village has evolved. No two villages are the same, but careful scrutiny of the shapes that make up the village plan – both on the map and on the ground – may reveal a great deal. If a village has resulted from the merging of different clusters of dwellings, this may still be detected in a 'lumpy' plan that suggests different village cores, say, around a church, two different manors, a park gate and a priory. If the church has an eccentric position it might be that the village has migrated away from it. Old maps may identify the different names that once were attached to the different village roads and lanes. Names like 'Claypits Lane', 'Turf Moor Road', 'Kiln Bank' or 'Wath (i.e. 'ford') Way' can reveal where these routes were heading.

THE FABRIC OF THE VILLAGE

THE PATTERN OF ROADS AND TRACKS is like a skeleton around which the village has developed, though the village is not normally perceived as a road network, but as a unique collection of buildings. Of modern village buildings, there is not so much to be said. They are designed by architects or taken from standard architectural designs. They have standardized fittings, like windows,

OVERLEAF: *Ramsgill in upper Nidderdale, where the small villages and hamlets all descend from monastic farms or 'granges' and where the pub is converted from a lordly hunting lodge*

the old core? Perhaps it might seem that the Great Rebuilding was confined to the homes of the more affluent yeoman and leaseholders living along the main street, while the buildings behind them remained shabby? Some place-names do identify the places where certain social classes lived, like the bonds tenants living in Bond End, the churls living in Carlton or the poor cottagers in Caldecotes ('cold cottages'). Or it might emerge that one vernacular tradition was overtaken by another – say the replacement of a tradition based on timber-framing by one based on stone – or maybe of one based on filling timber-framed panels in wattle and daub being replaced by one of filling the frame with brick *noggin* laid herringbone fashion.

It is not just the individual dwellings that are of interest, but the way in which they are distributed across the village landscape. For example, a road lined with dwellings of the same age, size and architectural character is very likely to have been developed as estate housing by the squire or some other local figure of authority. On the other hand, and more usually, the dwellings lining a village

BELOW: *Vernacular architecture comes in different strands and layers. Here at Happisburgh there is the flint tower of the church, which served as a guide to mariners, while the cottages have their own architectural tradition.*

ABOVE: *The different styles and sizes of houses and contrasting frontages show that the houses at Kersey probably developed piecemeal rather than being part of an estate programme of building.*

street might be of different ages, sizes and styles, reflecting the varying taste and affluence of former owners. Piecemeal development like this says nothing about the age of the actual street, for the original homes are likely to have been demolished or to have burned down several times over before any of the dwellings that still stand came into being.

SOME LESS FAMILIAR VILLAGE BUILDINGS

Not all the buildings in a village are houses, and some villages contain disused buildings and other structures that serve as reminders of the lives of former communities. The ones that are most likely to be encountered are identified in the following table.

STRUCTURE	LIKELY AGE	NOTES FOR RECOGNITION
Lock-up	C18–19th	Pokey little building of brick or stone where the village constable imprisoned drunks and trouble-makers. Small barred windows in walls and doors. Sometimes elaborate cylindrical or even pyramidical shapes but sometimes reminiscent of a brick privy.
Stocks	C17–19th	Were used in the Middle Ages to imprison wrong-doers and subject them to ridicule, but survivals tend to be more recent and some were still used in Georgian times. Often placed on village greens, sometimes at the base of market crosses. Sometimes the boards that held the legs survive, sometimes just the slotted stone posts that held their ends.
Market cross	Medieval–C18th	Complete medieval crosses are made of stone with a plinth that may be stepped and was slotted to hold the vertical shaft that held the lantern-shaped head. Few survive intact, so a base and broken shaft are more common. Despite the Protestant dislike of symbols, market crosses continued to be erected in villages after the Reformation.
Windmill	C17–19th	Some villages have windmills, but these mills were normally placed on elevated, windy sites. The tapering stone cylinders which were tower mills, now deprived of their caps and sails, are not uncommon. Some have now been converted into domestic dwellings.
Oast house	Usually C18–19th with some Edwardian examples	'Oast' means 'kiln' and these were kilns for drying hops and were associated with hop farms, whether inside or outside villages. Kilns of the eighteenth century had square or pyramidical chimneys, but designs introduced in Kent early in the nineteenth century had conical chimneys and the change slowly found favour in Surrey and the West Midlands. The late designs, introduced after the 1870s, again favoured a square form.
Pound or pinfold	Surviving structures are post-medieval but road names can reveal medieval pinfold locations	In the days of open, unhedged fields, the invasion of crops by roaming livestock was a common problem. Such animals would be caught and literally impounded, their owners having to pay for their release. Names relating to the pound or pinfold and the 'pinder' who operated it can often be found among village road names.
Dovecot	C15–19th	Young doves were relished in the past, but since the parent birds caused much damage to the corn, the keeping of them was confined to the lords and squires. Dovecots could be square or cylindrical stone structures, be built of weatherboarding with pointed roofs or have roofs shaped like lecterns.
Green or market house	Medieval with later alterations	These house-like buildings on or beside greens accommodated the market court and stored the stalls. The guildhalls, usually associated with church benevolent societies, looked similar. They often went through a succession of later uses, as schools, church halls or dwellings.
Tollbooth	C18–19th	These buildings combined a home for the toll collector and a booth with a sign showing the scale of charges and ticket window where travellers paid to use a stretch of improved highway. Eye-catching designs and booths projecting into the thoroughfare undermined excuses of having 'missed' the tollbooth by toll dodgers. Many were sited on village main streets.
Schools	Tudor to Victorian	The old village might contain schools of various types, those run by dames and those sponsored by charities. Some that stood on greens have vanished altogether and others have become ordinary dwellings.
Inns and taverns	All dates	Old drinking premises ranged from the grander coaching inns of the turnpike era to the shabby rooms of ale-wives. They lacked the tacky facades beloved by modern breweries. The old sign for an alehouse was simply a bush and old inns changed their names quite frequently, often adopting an aristocratic patron, a famous figure or event in their names.

Structures such as these may appear to be absent from the village chosen for study, but in quite a high proportion of villages one or more of these features will be detected, though many dovecots, guildhalls, inns, schools, tollbooths and even windmill towers have been transformed for domestic occupation.

THE OLD VILLAGE INN

MORE FAMILIAR than any of the structures mentioned above are the village inns. Inflating the age of an establishment is very good for business and claims by landlords concerning the antiquity of their hostelries should not be taken too seriously. Although many medieval villages did, indeed, have inns, these would have been small and shabby in comparison to the large roadhouses, commemorated on Christmas cards, that developed in the great coaching era of the eighteenth to early nineteenth centuries. Much remains to be learned about medieval taverns, though they were perhaps often of a rough and ready nature. In my native township of Clint in the Yorkshire Dales an inn is recorded because of a case of murder associated with it. In 1324, two Williams were drinking there and a quarrel ensued. William, son of Adam of Clint, fled and was pursued by William del Ridding (his name meant 'of the clearing'). Flushed from a temporary refuge in a village house, the former was pursued across the village, leaping over the hedges between plots as he went, but was eventually cornered in a wet ditch and shot dead with arrows. The dubious reputation of medieval inns and hostelries does seem to be verified by the high number of cases of robbery and violence heard by the courts in connection with these places.

It seems that hostelries were most likely to be encountered where travel and commerce were concentrated, as at river bridges and fords, road intersections and so on. The travelling clientele was limited, largely because villagers were not allowed to leave their manors without good cause. The manors actually controlled the brewing industry, with the ale concerned being brewed by village housewives in their cottages (home brewing was a feature of every cottage home, with the pollution of domestic water supplies providing an excellent excuse for the high consumption of ale). The quality of the ale produced on a manor was regulated by appointed ale-tasters – probably one of the few jobs about the manor that attracted a good quota of volunteers. The elevation of an ale-wife's house to the status of an inn was also regulated by the manor. Such an establishment might only be distinguished from the other village dwellings by the presence of an 'ale stake' or 'ale wisp' outside, a pole that indicated that ale could be bought within. Often, too, a bush by the door served as a sign. These primitive signs seem to have been considered important, for the proprietors of these inns and alehouses were quite often fined at manor courts for failing to display them. Towards the end of the Middle Ages it was sometimes required that the proprietors should also have a bed available for a guest. Where these rather dingy medieval places had names, they tend not to be recorded, but a survivor from the old hostelries is the surname 'Hosteler', with *osteler* being used in preference to 'innkeeper'.

Concerning old inn names, my favourite is the Ass in a Bandbox, a name satirizing Napoleon that was held by a long-defunct inn in the former village of Nidd, near Knaresborough. In any attempt

to discover the historic drinking habits of a village it is worth remembering that the venues for drinking tended to change their names quite frequently, so the names recorded in old documents or directories may not match those of any surviving establishments. I spent my childhood in a village inn that had been built by the local estate-owning dynasty and named, patriotically, the Sebastopol, after the (1854–5) siege of Sevastopol in the Crimean War. However, the distant events were soon eclipsed by momentous developments much closer to hand: the arrival of the Harrogate–Pateley Bridge branch line in 1862, so that the Sebastopol became the Station Hotel. Many inns take their names from the local estate and gentry, often the aristocrat or estate owner who was the real landlord. Names like the Devonshire Arms or the Duchy are examples. Some names come from historical events, with the Royal Oak pubs commemorating the Boscobel Oak in Shropshire, where King Charles II hid from his pursuers in 1651.

ABOVE: *The imposing manorial dovecot at Willington in Bedfordshire, erected shortly after Dissolution using materials pillaged from religious houses*
LEFT: *The windmill that served the Thaxted community*

Many names, like the Drovers, the Highland Laddie, the Scotch Bonnet and the Black/Red Bull, recall their roles as hostelries during the days of the droving trade when they were visited by Scottish and Welsh drovers. Droving could have quite an impact on the village landscape. For example, where the Welsh hill tracks converged on the main cross-country routes leading to the great urban livestock markets, and also in villages on the droving trails, like Masham in the Yorkshire Dales, there were smithies where the cattle were shod prior to their long and fateful journeys. Many hostelries catering for the droving trade had adjacent paddocks where the herds would spend a night, though these have now often been sold for housing development. Names like 'Halfpenny Patch' or 'Ha'penny Piece' attached to land beside an inn can recall the rents of ½d (0.2p) per beast paid for use of the enclosed grazing during a night. In the Welsh Marches, place-names ending in the Welsh

BELOW: *The guildhall at Long Crendon in Buckinghamshire exemplifies how some old public village buildings can almost vanish into the domestic housing pattern.*

LEFT: *A dovecote in tiles and weatherboarding to a design often seen in eastern England*

'*pwll*' mark the places with ponds where cattle could be watered as they travelled 'on the hoof'. Hostelries provided such pools and some were associated with clumps of tall trees that signalled their positions from afar.

What impresses me most about the village inn is the multitude that once existed. In many villages where there is but a single inn, opening infrequently and at unpredictable times, in the past there may have been three, four or five examples. In any village exploration, one or more dwellings may be passed that were formerly inns or the more modest parlours run by ale-wives. Apart from the tables, benches and the brewhouse (a feature of every village house) with its clutter of pails, casks and dishes and the bush or wisp outside, there was nothing to distinguish a village inn from all the other buildings around it. The Lamb, by the river bridge in Hampsthwaite in Nidderdale, became, like thousands of other such places, indistinguishable from other village dwellings. The evidence of old maps, trade directories, and, perhaps, court records may be the only way to identify a former inn. The writings of old local antiquaries can be revealing, as with Harry Speight, who wrote in 1894:

> There was formerly a well known hostelry here called the Lamb inn, which used to be frequented by the pack horse carriers passing through the village on their way between York and Skipton [now a mere bridleway]; the old pack-horse stables were done away with when the present parish stables were erected by subscription in 1866. The old inn was converted into a temperance hotel five years ago [a sure sign that the pack-horse men had gone!].

'Houses of ill repute' also had their place in the medieval landscape, being features more of the towns and main routeways than of villages. They might be recognized by place-names like 'Bordel' and from the 'lost' place-names discovered in a study of West Yorkshire medieval documents, which included Leadhouse ('Lewd house'), Gesthous ('Guest house', a euphemism) and Bismerrow (from old words meaning 'House row of shame'). Portinscale in Cumbria is thought to take its name from the sixteenth-century hut of a harlot associated with a community of German miners.

ABOVE: *The inn at Lacock in Wiltshire. Most villages contain one or more former inns that are indistinguishable from other houses.*

THE
CHURCH
AND THE
SCHOOL

*T*HE CHURCH is sure to prove a treasury of information about the parish that it serves, but most of it will be missed if it is just regarded as a building. The church will offer to the village sleuth some clues about its position within its parish, while at another level, it will be a repository for records that concern many generations of parishioners. All aspects of the placing of the church relative to its village should be considered and anything that can be gleaned about its origins will be of interest. For example, the church at Coldingham, Borders, stands directly beside the site of a former priory; the church at Bolton in Wharfedale is a surviving portion of the Augustinian priory church, while any church that has a well dedicated to saints, such as Anne or Helen, is almost sure to have taken over a pagan site.

It is important to remember that what is displayed may only be a portion of what once existed. There are books, like Pevsner's *Buildings of England* county-by-county series, that provide thumbnail sketches of the historic architecture of British churches and there are others that help one to recognize the architecture of the successive Anglo-Saxon, Norman, Transitional, Early English, Decorated, Perpendicular and (Scottish) Flamboyant styles. However, the Victorians happily imitated and combined these historic styles, particularly in their urban churches, so it is as well to consider whether or not the stone is timeworn before rushing to a conclusion. Yet even when all the masonry is properly dated and accounted for there will be much that vanished in the course of rebuilding; excavation of churches has shown them to have longer and more complex histories than was ever imagined. Still, the church remains a place of fascination. Usually, it is by far the oldest building in the village and it witnessed the births, christenings, marriages, deaths and burials of generation upon generation of villagers.

Evidence of the first generation of schools in a village will be hard to come by. Education was something of a lottery, while only a tiny proportion of people from the servile classes achieved career 'success' (the ranks of the mowers and ale-wives must have been much richer as a result). Their surnames and places of origins (often being the same) show that most monks came from the higher social orders and the best that a villager might realistically hope for would be to become a semi-educated lay brother in one of the Cistercian houses. A few village-born children did achieve very high status within the church. Children of families in bondage had to find compensation for their lord to cover absences from manorial toil incurred during education – and for the families of village paupers, this would not be easy. It was the church that provided most of such village education as might exist, with exceptionally gifted children possibly attending grammar schools or cathedral schools – though these were sited to favour urban recruits. Lucky village children might attend classes in chantry chapels associated with the village church, while the medieval records suggest that unlicensed teachers were also found in some villages. The English Reformation disrupted the main source of education that was open to villagers and was resented because of this, particularly in the North of England. Thereafter, children relied upon vicars, rectors and curates who could be almost as rustic and ill-informed as they were. Meanwhile, dissenters began to organize alternative structures for education and this was a great incentive to establishment innovations.

ABOVE: *The former smithy on the green at Thriplow in Cambridgeshire*

Then dame schools began to appear, perhaps standing to education as the ale-wives did to the hospitality industry. The dames must have varied greatly in their learning and ability and their schools were opened in a spectrum of different village niches – the upper floors of derelict moot halls, parlours or outbuildings. My native village seems to have had several – or one that migrated to different locations. For a while it perched on a tiny green just below the church and the lack of surviving physical evidence shows that it must have been both small and insubstantial. The dame schools shared the local educational landscape with charity schools, private profit-making institutions and those funded by local endowments, with the foundation of the Society for Promoting Christian Knowledge in 1699 encouraging the foundation of schools to provide a religious education for poor children. During the nineteenth century, state involvement with education increased. After 1870, School Boards were required to fill the gaps in the local educational network and the Acts of 1876 and 1880 made school attendance compulsory. Rural areas posed a particular challenge, for it had been customary for village children of all backgrounds and abilities to be absent from school to assist at crucial stages in the farming year, like hay-making and the grain, root crop and potato harvests.

Various kinds of records can be used to recreate the story of schooling in a chosen village. After 1559, all teachers had to be licensed by the appropriate bishop (though shadowy unlicensed teachers apparently practised in many places). The diocesan archives can identify the teachers concerned and also the location of their schools and the nature of the education provided. Also in these archives are 'subscription books', introduced after 1604, to ensure that teachers subscribed to the current dogma. In addition, there are the records of visitations to the parishes within a diocese, with comments on the existence of schools, the rates of attendance and the competence of the practitioners. Meanwhile, for schools established and maintained by charitable work, the records of the Charity Commissioners can be consulted. Perhaps the most evocative records are the 'log books' kept by individual village schools after about 1860. Here are recorded the high infant mortality rates

BELOW: *The tomb of Sir William Gascoigne, who died in 1463, and his wife, Margaret, in the old village church at Harewood. Many generations later, the lords ousted the village from their park.*

ABOVE: *Medieval glass in the church at Long Melford. The Cloptons were the main sponsors of the church, but Thomas and Margaret Peyton (modestly flanking St Edmund) also bought their place in the local heritage.*

that created gaps in the classroom ranks, the persistent absences of children kept back to work in the fields, the harsh punishments, the epidemics of measles, mumps, whooping cough, diphtheria and the other scourges of a Victorian childhood and, occasionally, the parents who boldly came to remonstrate after a beating had been inflicted.

A map at a scale of at least 1:25,000 or preferably larger to allow you to appreciate the position of the church within its setting and village, a notepad, guides to church architecture and a readiness to bring quite different perspectives to bear on the topic.

WORKPLACE

The churchyard and inside the church. Also the local history section of the local reference library.

PROCEDURE

Beginning in the churchyard, careful scrutiny of the fabric of the building, using binoculars where needed, may reveal the events that left their mark. These can take the form of fragments from an older church being incorporated when the church was rebuilt, the lowering of a roof because thatching was abandoned or money had to be saved, and so on. The tombstones in the churchyard will identify the names of the old village families and give information on lifespans. However, the monuments can only take you back so far and only a smallish minority of churchyards have tombstones extending back beyond the eighteenth century.

What may be found inside the church is much less predictable. Green men, monuments to the local dynasties, a brass commemorating a priest, fragments of medieval glass or even a wall painting might be there. Standing in the nave there may well be a great iron-bound parish chest, which could contain parish records, though they might be found elsewhere in the parish, in a safe, with the diocese or in the county record office, for instance. The oldest of the parish papers may be the vestry minutes and accounts, recording decisions and financial details over several centuries. Under legislation of 1538, each vestry was obliged to provide a locked chest in which records of births, baptisms, marriages and burials would be stored and after 1597 these records had to be bound in books for storage in the parish chests. The proving of wills was the responsibility of the church from medieval times until 1858, and these became vested in diocesan record offices or 'courts of peculiars'. Useful sources for church history are Taylor, 2003, and Richardson, 1975, which list the different types of historical sources.

The local history section of the reference library might well reward a visit. It was a sad region that did not attract the attentions of at least one nineteenth-century antiquarian or topographer. These people have been derided because they did not always discriminate between fact and legend, yet they had other distinct advantages not available to us. They saw a countryside that was still largely unspoiled by agri-business and building developments and they mixed with parochial communities that still lived close to the earth. Most villagers lived closer to their medieval forebears than to ourselves and folklore was still vibrant. Therefore, our late Georgian and Victorian recorders of local topography and history had access to archives of landscape and communal history that are lost to us.

ABOVE: *The ancient minster church at Wing in Buckinghamshire, with a Saxon apse and crypt – portholes across 1000 years of history*

THE
MEMORIES

IT IS TRUE THAT THINKING about shapes and understanding buildings can really help us to read a village. But let us not forget that villages were never just collections of buildings. They were also always communities. Most village communities, for most of the time, were largely or entirely illiterate. Once their members had died, their knowledge and feelings were also lost. How wonderful it would be if, say, a twelfth-century housewife, a thirteenth-century ploughboy or a Tudor innkeeper could have left us detailed records of their lives, their hardships, aspirations and beliefs. We do not have such records, for the members of the privileged minorities who could write did not consider that the day-to-day existences of the villagers that they knew deserved to be recorded. Writing was concerned with financial transactions and obligations, theological discourses or the copying of old texts; even the notion that there could be such a thing as local history scarcely existed.

Today, in these more enlightened times, a magnificent archive is lost every day. These archives are lost because nobody has bothered to record the recollections and experiences of people who lived in this world during a period of accelerated transformation. No period has witnessed such rocketing change as the twentieth century. There are people still alive in Britain who went through childhood without ever seeing or hearing an aeroplane.

Go into any village and its older residents will represent an archive of information about the place that is far larger than all that exists in the libraries and record offices. This archive is relatively easy to access and, unlike the documentary sources, you can ask to have any confusing information explained. Many academic historians were, for no good reason, 'sniffy' in their attitudes towards local history, a silly prejudice that discouraged many enquiries. For reasons that are equally unfounded, they have been doubly disparaging towards 'oral history', the form of history deriving from people's spoken recollections. This is a particularly idiotic prejudice, for oral history, which existed long before people learned to write, is our oldest form of history.

To discover the richness of oral tradition we need only read some of the books of recollections by old Suffolk farmworkers, as set down by George Ewart Evans (1909–88), like *Ask the Fellows Who Cut the Hay, Where Beards Wag All, The Farm and the Village* and *Crooked Scythe*. (I was fortunate to meet him early in my career and thought it amazing that the pioneering worker in the realm of spoken history should be badly affected by deafness.) People tend to be quite reliable guides to events that they personally experienced. However, recollections that are second- or third-hand can be very unreliable, so it is easy to see how fanciful folklore and impossible legends come into being. Within the village community there may be, say, men who remember ploughing with horses and broadcasting seed, people who remember the evacuees or the land workers arriving during the 1939–45 war, those who knew the hard realities of farming life, like the pig-killing or working in fields with only a sodden sack for shelter, but who could also remember Sunday tea, when everything on the crowded table was baked in the kitchen next door. As a young villager in the Yorkshire Dales, the old fellows taught me the names of local places, like Otter Cliff, Turpin Lair and the Long Trod, none of which ever appeared on a map. I was told about the carthorse that fell down a mine shaft and could not be got out until the next day – and in that way I realized that the 'tumulus' marked on the map was not really

You will need

A notepad or a small tape recorder, as used for dictation; an amiable and respectful manner.

Workplace

Interviewee's home, social centre or other village venue.

Procedure

Given the right approach and encouragement, people may be delighted to discover an audience for their recollections. Older people sometimes feel marginalized, sensing, rightly or wrongly, that people are not interested in their stories and memories. Through your interview, you may be seeking information about a particular problem but it could well be best to let your subject talk freely. Some of the most rewarding information is discovered by chance and an approach that is too structured might reveal less than a looser one that ranges widely. Once an interview has come to a successful conclusion you are now the possessor of an archive. What are you going to do with it?

ABOVE: *The vernacular architecture of the North Sea shores is nowhere better displayed than at St Monans in the East Neuk of Fife. Note the external staircase and the pantiles on the roof, imported as ballast in ships coming from the Low Countries.*

a prehistoric burial mound but a heap of colliery slag. A village study that does not involve villagers is (to use a Yorkshire expression) 'like Christmas cake wi'out cheese'.

A good village study deserves to be preserved. In years to come, much that seems commonplace and generally known will have been forgotten. Your study could help to preserve perishable information and it could be of great assistance to someone a generation or two down the line who also seeks to 'read' your village. Various computer programmes exist to allow a professional-style presentation (I have used CorelDRAW and Adobe Photoshop here). Desktop-publishing techniques can be used to produce a polished product, but digital techniques are evolving very quickly and who knows what will happen to our state-of-the-art techniques? It could well be safer to produce your results in old-fashioned hard copy and provide copies to the reference library and parish council, perhaps the planning department too. The village school should surely show an interest in what you have done and the standing of what my old village comrades called 'off-comers' is sure to be enhanced when it emerges that they know things about the village that the indigenous population was unaware of. If you do cultivate an interest in villages, then, when the showpiece villages are all awash with visitors, you may be found away from it all, interrogating the landscape of one of the drabber members of the village flock and discovering much more of real interest than the crowds have ever imagined.

Glossary

BAKESTONES – stones heated and used in baking

BALLISTA – Roman artillery weapon

BLACK DEATH/PESTILENCE – a medieval plague estimated to have killed between a third and a half of Europe's population; outbreaks continued in varying intensity until the 1700s

BOOLEY – temporary accommodation used by Scottish farmers in the summer months

BUTTER CROSS – cross at a market selling butter

CLACHAN – an old Scottish hamlet

CLASSICAL – conforming to the norms of Classical architecture (that of the ancient Greeks and Romans)

CLOSED VILLAGE – one under control of a local ruling family

CRANNOG – dwelling on an artificial island in a lake

CROP MARKS – marks caused by relative differences in the heights of crops

CROW-STEPPED GABLES – stair-step type of design at the top of the triangular gable end of a building

DEMESNE – the portion of a medieval estate worked directly for the lord

DENDROCHRONOLOGY – dating using the evidence of annual tree rings

DOOM PAINTING – church mural showing the Day of Judgement

DRIFT GEOLOGY – geology looking at surface deposits

FERMTOUN – an old Scottish hamlet

FIELD WALKING – walking across ploughed fields in search of pottery and other artefacts

GENTRIFICATION – a process by which low-cost housing in an area is renovated, bringing in wealthier residents

GREAT REBUILDING – movement to build superior dwellings beginning in the South East of England towards the end of the Middle Ages

GREEN HOUSE – a meeting place used on market days to decide local issues, settle disputes, etc. (SEE also *market house* and *moot hall*)

GREEN MAN – a fertility symbol seen in many cultures around the world and often featuring as carvings in churches and other buildings in Britain

HARRYING OF THE NORTH – wasting of northern England by the armies of William I

HEADROW – row of dwellings across the top of a settlement

HIGHLAND CLEARANCES – a process of agricultural change that involved the forced displacement of the population of the Scottish Highlands, leading to mass emigration

HILL FORTS – prehistoric forts, usually on hill tops

HOLLOWAYS – roads hollowed by use and then abandoned

HUT CIRCLES – traces of circular prehistoric houses

IMPROVEMENTS – agricultural reforms in Scotland corresponding in time and nature to the Agricultural Revolution in England and Wales

INVASIONISM – school of thought claiming that the native populations of Britain were driven away and replaced each time by invaders, rather than those invaders being gradually assimilated into the existing population

LAND – one of various names for a field strip

LITTLE ICE AGE – a phase of cool climate following the Medieval Warm Period

LONGHOUSE – type of simple medieval homestead

MARKET HOUSE – a meeting place used on market days to decide local issues, settle disputes, etc. (SEE also *green house* and *moot hall*)

MEDIEVAL WARM PERIOD – a period of unusually warm climate lasting from the tenth to the fourteenth centuries

MIDDEN – refuse mound

MOOT HALL – a meeting place used on market days to decide local issues, settle disputes, etc. (SEE also *green house* and *market house*)

OPEN-FIELD SYSTEM – form of farming involving huge open (i.e. unenclosed) fields

OPEN VILLAGE – one where power is fragmented and not under the control of a local ruling family

PADSTONES – stones on which posts stand; the first and last brick of an arch

PARCH MARKS – marks caused by relative differences in the degrees to which crops/grass parch out

PARLIAMENTARY ENCLOSURE – movement for the enclosure or privatization of common land

PICTURESQUE – a form of architecture/art that follows less disciplined conventions than the Classical

PINFOLD or **POUND** – enclosure for impounding stray livestock

PLOTLANDS – self-built homes erected in the early twentieth century along the Channel shores

POTLIDS – stones from which roofing 'slates' can be obtained

QUOINS – stones forming the corners of buildings

RACK-RENTING – the charging of an unreasonably high rent; a practice common in eighteenth- and nineteenth-century Ireland

RATH – an Iron Age farmstead in a circular enclosure

ROYAL VILLS – estates belonging to the king

RUNRIG – a system of farming adapted to the marginal farming environments of the North

SELION – one of various names for a field strip

SHEILA-NA-GIGS – obscene figurative carvings found on some churches, castles, and other buildings in Britain; their purpose is uncertain

SHERDS – fragments of pottery

SHOTTS – furlongs

SOLID GEOLOGY – hard rock geology

STRAKER WAYS – lanes: the name may derive from an Old English word concerning the iron rim of a wheel

STRIP – one of various names for a field strip

TACKSMEN – chief tenants of the Highlands

THREE-FIELD SYSTEM – erroneous name for the open-field system, which might involve any number of fields

TOFTS – house plots

UPCAST – earth cast up from a ditch

VERNACULAR ARCHITECTURE – a method of construction using locally available resources, the skills often being handed down through the generations

Resources and Further Information

Here is a summary of the websites, maps and other resources referred to throughout the book.

Useful websites

www.english-heritage.org.uk
English Heritage
www.nationalarchives.gov.uk
The National Archives
www.old-maps.co.uk
Old-maps.co.uk
www.rampantscotland.com
Rampant Scotland
www.rcahms.gov.uk
The Royal Commission on the Ancient and
Historical Monuments of Scotland
www.scran.ac.uk
The Scran Trust

Maps

Detailed Elizabethan estate maps
Parish maps drawn before and after the Parliamentary
    Enclosure of parishes
Seventeenth-century maps at a scale of ½ inch to 1 mile
Privately drawn eighteenth-century maps at a scale of
    1 inch to 1 mile
Eighteenth-century military and other surveys of Scotland
General Roy's maps of the mid-eighteenth century
English and Welsh 'tithe maps' of 1837–52
Large-scale Victorian maps
Ordnance Survey maps, e.g. First Edition 6 inches to 1 mile;
    1:50,000; the old 1:63,000 (1 inch to 1 mile) series
Geology maps

Other useful resources

Place-name dictionaries, e.g. Gelling, 1993; Darby and
    Versey, 1975
Regional guides to cottage and farmstead building
    traditions, e.g. Mercer, 1975
Victorian/Edwardian trade directories
A camera and a notepad
Small tape recorder/dictaphone
Desktop publishing programmes

Conversion table
for old units of measurement

Acreland: a variable unit of 8–20 acres (3.2–8.1 hectares)
Furlong, culture, shott: an immensely variable land unit composed of a parcel of strips or selions and about the size of a largish field

Hide, carucate, husbandland, ploughland: a variable land unit of about 60–180 acres (24.3–72.8 hectares)
League: a variable unit, usually about 4.8 km (3 miles)
Perch, rod, pole, perk: a variable measurement eventually standardized at 5 m (16½ feet)
Strip, selion, land: a ribbon-like portion of a tenancy varying immensely around a norm of about 1 acre (0.4 hectares)
Virgate: a very variable unit of around 30 acres (12.1 hectares)

Significant dates

Dates for the prehistoric era are approximate, with different innovations reaching different localities at different times.

10,000 BC	Melting of the ice
8500 BC	Britain becomes an island
8000 BC	End of Palaeolithic or Old Stone Age and start of Mesolithic or Middle Stone Age
4500 BC	Start of Neolithic or New Stone Age: dawn of farming
2700 BC	Start of Beaker Age of gold and copper working
2200 BC	Start of Bronze Age
650 BC	Start of Iron Age
AD 43	Roman invasion ends the prehistoric era
AD 400–500	Anglo-Saxon mercenaries settle in England
AD 410	Roman legions quit Britain
AD 410–1066	Dark Ages (though many historians dislike the term). The period when English speakers gradually gained control of England, though the latest DNA evidence shows that genes from prehistoric populations greatly predominate throughout modern Britain, incl. England
1066	Norman Conquest
1069–81	Harrying of the North
1066–1536	Middle Ages (this is a 'long' Middle Ages. Some historians include the era of the Saxon kings of England or omit the Tudor period)
1750–1850	Main period of Parliamentary Enclosures
1760	Start of the Industrial Revolution
Late C18th–early C20th	Highland Clearances
Late C19th	Village populations increasingly hit by mechanization of farming and foreign competition for agricultural products

Selected Further Reading

Addison, Sir W., *Local Styles of the English Parish Church* (Batsford, London, 1982)

Addyman, P. and Morris, R., *The Archaeological Study of Churches*, CBA research report No. 13 (1976)

Aston, M., *Interpreting the Landscape from the Air* (Tempus, Stroud, 2002)

Barker, K. and Kain, R. (eds), *Maps and History in South West England* (Exeter University Press, Exeter, 1991)

Barley, M.W., *The English Farmhouse and Cottage* (Routledge & Kegan Paul, London, 1976)

Beresford, M.W., *The Lost Villages of England* (Lutterworth, London, 1954)

Beresford, M.W. and Hurst, J.G., *Deserted Medieval Villages* (Lutterworth, London, 1971)

Beresford, M.W. and St Joseph, J.K.S., *Medieval England: An Aerial Survey*, Second Edn (Cambridge University Press, Cambridge, 1979)

Bettey, J.H., *Estates and the English Countryside* (Batsford, London, 1993)

Brown, J. and Ward, S., *The Village Shop* (David and Charles, Newton Abbott, 1990)

Brown, R.J., *English Village Architecture* (Hale, London, 2004)

Calder, N., *The English Channel* (Chatto and Windus, London, 1986)

Darby, H.C. and Versey, G.R., *Domesday Gazetteer* (Cambridge University Press, Cambridge, 1975)

Darley, G., *Villages of Vision* (Paladin, London, 1975)

Davison, A., *Six Deserted Villages in Norfolk* (East Anglian Archaeology Report, 44, Norfolk Museums Service, 1988)

Edwards, P., *Rural Life, Guide to Local Records* (Batsford, London, 1993)

Evans, G.E. *Ask the Fellows Who Cut the Hay* (Faber and Faber, London, 1956)

Evans, G.E. *The Farm and the Village* (Faber and Faber, London, 1969)

Evans, G.E. *Where Beards Wag All* (Faber and Faber, London, 1977)

Evans, G.E. *Crooked Scythe* (Faber and Faber, London, 1995)

Field, J., *Place-Names of Great Britain and Ireland* (David and Charles, Newton Abbot, 1980)

Filbee, M., *Cottage Industries* (David and Charles, Newton Abbott, 1982)

Gelling, M., *Place-Names in the Landscape* (J.M. Dent, London, 1993)

Hall, D., *Medieval Fields* (Shire, Princes Risborough, 1982)

Hardy, D. and Ward, C., *Arcadia for All* (Five Leaves, Nottingham, 2004)

Hewett, C.A., *English Historic Carpentry* (Phillimore, London, 1980)

Lewis, C., Mitchell-Fox, P. and Dyer, C., *Village, Hamlet and Field* (Manchester University Press, Manchester, 1997)

Mercer, E., *English Vernacular Houses* (Royal Commission on Historic Monuments, HMSO, London, 1975)

Millman, R.N., *The Making of the Scottish Landscape* (Batsford, London, 1975)

Muir, R., *The Lost Villages of Britain* (Michael Joseph, London, 1982)

Muir, R., *The Villages of England* (Thames & Hudson, London, 1992)

Muir, R., *The Coastlines of Britain* (Macmillan, London, 1993)

Muir, R., *Landscape Detective* (Windgather Press, Macclesfield, 2001)

Muir, R, *Ancient Trees, Living Landscapes* (Tempus, Stroud, 2005)

Penoyre, J. and J., *Houses in the Landscape* (Faber and Faber, London, 1978)

Pevsner's *Buildings of England*, county by county series (Penguin, Harmondsworth)

Platt, C., *Medieval Britain from the Air* (Guild, London, 1984)

Prebble, J., *The Highland Clearances* (Martin Secker and Warburg, London, 1963)

Richardson, J., *The Local Historian's Encyclopaedia* (Historical Publications Ltd, New Barnet, 1975)

Roberts, B.K., *The Making of the English Village* (Longman, Harlow, 1987)

Roberts, B.K., *Landscapes of Settlement* (Routledge, London, 1996)

Rodwell, W., *The Archaeology of the English Church* (Batsford, London, 1981)

Rodwell, W. and Bentley, J., *Our Christian Heritage* (George Philip, London, 1984)

Russell, R.C., *The Logic of Open Field Systems* (Society for Lincolnshire History and Archaeology, 1995)

Sill, G.G., *A Handbook of Symbols in Christian Art* (Touchstone, New York, 1996)

Smith, J.S. and Stevenson, D. (eds), *Fermfolk and Fisherfolk* (Mercat Press, Edinburgh, 1992)

Smith, R., *Land of the Lost* (John Donald, Edinburgh, 1997)

Steers, J.A., *The Coast of England and Wales in Pictures* (Cambridge University Press, Cambridge, 1960)

Summers, D.W., *Fishing off the Knuckle: The Fishing Villages of Buchan* (Centre for Scottish Studies, Aberdeen, 1988)

Taylor, C.C., *Village and Farmstead* (George Philip, London, 1983)

Taylor, R., *How to Read a Church* (Rider, London, 2003)

Wickham-Jones, C.R., *The Landscape of Scotland* (Tempus, Stroud, 2001)

INDEX

ABOVE: *An early Christian cross with interlace decoration in the churchyard at Nevern, near Newport*